Contributions to Economics

The series *Contributions to Economics* provides an outlet for innovative research in all areas of economics. Books published in the series are primarily monographs and multiple author works that present new research results on a clearly defined topic, but contributed volumes and conference proceedings are also considered. All books are published in print and ebook and disseminated and promoted globally. The series and the volumes published in it are indexed by Scopus and ISI (selected volumes).

Maria Mavri · Patricia Ikouta Mazza ·
Anastasios Karasavvoglou ·
Persefoni Polychronidou
Editors

Digital Economy and Green Growth

Opportunities and Challenges for Urban and Regional Ecosystems

Springer

Editors
Maria Mavri
University of the Aegean
Chios, Greece

Patricia Ikouta Mazza
University of the Aegean
Chios, Greece

Anastasios Karasavvoglou
International Hellenic University
Kavala, Greece

Persefoni Polychronidou
Department of Economic Sciences
International Hellenic University
Serres, Greece

ISSN 1431-1933 ISSN 2197-7178 (electronic)
Contributions to Economics
ISBN 978-3-031-66668-1 ISBN 978-3-031-66669-8 (eBook)
https://doi.org/10.1007/978-3-031-66669-8

This Springer imprint is published by the registered company Springer Nature Switzerland AG
The registered company address is: Gewerbestrasse 11, 6330 Cham, Switzerland

Preface

Over the last decade, Europe faced multiple challenges that have already caused structural changes in the way economic and regional growth strategies have been taking place. The environmental risks that come from generative causes, such as the waste of natural resources and the overconcentration of population in urban centers, the effects of the pandemic on many sectors such as those of the economy and society, as well as the direct and indirect consequences of war conflicts, make up the puzzle of contemporary challenges for the global community.

The transition to the digital era has become imperative in the last decades, with the pandemic as a key accelerator, as it made the need for digital transformation and growth of the digital economy more urgent.

Digital Transformation (DT) is a general concept that broadens horizons concerning rising forms of extended social participation and a wide range of social stakeholders. Digital technologies and ICTs provide innovative solutions to social, economic, operational, and technical challenges and make the public sector more efficient and effective. They can also enable societies to face unpredictable problems and support the development of digital solutions based on the EU's values and fundamental rights, as it happened over the last years during the pandemic. A necessary condition for the further implementation of DT is that the members and bodies of society have equal access to connectivity, to necessary technology but also to the upscaling of digital skills. According to the Council of the EU, it's crucial to seize this unique opportunity to shape the strategic direction of the DT more actively in Member States (Berlin Declaration on Digital Society and Value-Based Digital Government, 2020).

The digital transition will also contribute to the green goals, with synergies in many areas of a smart circular economy. The challenges related to the wider field of economic regional science, sustainable development, with reference to the development goals of the 2030 Agenda and Digital Transformation, are fields that attract scientific and research interest and in which we must engage to ensure a better future not only for future generations but also for today's.

This special issue includes papers on the above topics and others relating to the role that Economic and Regional Science can play in the European countries' development model and strategies that emphasize in digital transformation and highlighted the role of ICT in the economic development of countries.

The first part of the book delivers six papers, presents frameworks on the field of Digital Transformation and Digital Government concept, while the second part presents frameworks of countries' regional, sustainable, and smart growth. Four papers belong to this section.

From this perspective, this special issue of the EBEEC Conference allows us to deepen and discuss, on the one hand, the important impact that the pandemic has accelerated the digital transformation and, on the other hand, the transition to strategies that promote smart growth.

The International Conference "Economies of the Balkan and Eastern European Countries (EBEEC)" serves as an annual meeting point of policymakers of Balkan and Eastern European countries and as an important avenue of scientists and researchers from all over the world to exchange ideas, share research findings, discuss new scientific approaches, develop network for collaboration.

Over 180 scientists and students from different countries attended the conference and presented more than 120 papers in parallel sessions as well as special sessions.

The conference covered several issues such as economic growth, digital economy, and regional and sustainable development of countries, in the context digital transformation.

One of the most important reasons for a researcher to participate in a conference is the opportunity of publication that it offers to scientists. The Annual International Conference "Economies of the Balkan and Eastern European Countries" gives the opportunity to the participants to publish their work in selected journals and books. In this context, the contribution comes from Springer Editions.

This volume is the end result of papers presented to the 15th International Conference "Economies of the Balkan and Eastern European Countries" (EBEEC), which was held at the University of the Aegean in Chios, Greece, May 12–14, 2023. The book contains 10 selected papers based on their quality, originality, and innovation, which are presented at the conference and one introductory chapter. The first chapter is the Introduction, Part One on Digital Transformation and Digital Government, and Part Two on Regional, Sustainable and Smart Growth. All selected manuscripts have gone through the peer-review process and are carefully edited, certainly making a significant contribution to the broader field of economy.

Part One opens with a paper written by Vesna Lukovic, an *Independent Researcher, from Thessaloniki, Which Focuses* on social sustainability by looking at access, skills, and the ability of people to use digitalization for their own goals. The aim of the research is to look at social sustainability through the lens of digitalization in agriculture and tourism in Northern Greece.

Dimitris Papandreou, Patricia Ikouta Mazza, Maria Mavri from the *University of the Aegean* are the authors of the next paper, which presents a readiness assessment of EU countries to achieve the smart sustainable development goals through the digital transformation of local government. Specifically, the scope of this study is to assess the readiness of the different types of local governments of the member states regarding the implementation of the digital transformation of their services towards achieving the SDGs through the smart sustainable development model.

The next paper is provided by two authors from *the University of West Attica*, Eirini Manga and Nikitas Karanikolas, and one author from the Agricultural University of Athens Catherine Marinagi. They investigate the benefits and the challenges of the utilization of Machine Learning (ML) applications in public administration. The goal of the paper is to explore the benefits and challenges involved in creating smarter governments by utilizing ML applications.

A thorough review of policy and regulatory initiatives that are adopted by the EU in relation to the evolution of cloud computing as a means of innovation, economic growth, and digital sovereignty is presented by Panagiotis Kitsos from the Hellenic Open University and Paraskevi Pappa from the University of Ioannina. The aim of the paper is to serve as a bird's eye view of the current regulatory attempts in fields related to technical aspects of cloud computing in EU and shed some light on the different aspects of cloud computing design and implementation policies and regulations.

The next paper of the volume is a collaborative paper by Lambros Tsourgiannis, from the International Hellenic University and the Hellenic Open University, Stavros Valsamidis, Sotirios Papadopoulos and Polina Karagianni from the International Hellenic University. The aim of the paper is to explore the attitudes of Greek citizens towards the use of e-government applications.

The next manuscript prepared by Konstadina Kasabali, Persefoni Polychronidou, Dimitrios Kydros from the *International Hellenic University* examines the subject of Digitization and e-Government: with a systematic literature review for the European Union (EU 27) and the United Kingdom. The purpose of the research is to make a categorization of the research, to study the evolution of the number of studies in recent years, to highlight the countries that were most involved as well as the collaborations between the countries in the specific researches.

Part Two opens with a paper written by Roberta Capello and Andrea Caragliu from the Politecnico di Milano, which examines how the technological transformations affects the Global Value Chains and what strategic challenges for Europe and its territory they create. The aim of this paper is to simulate the net effects of technological transformations and global value chains, and isolate their local effects on GDP growth, thanks to a regional macro-econometric forecasting model, called Macroeconometric, Social, Sectoral, Territorial model in its fifth version (MASST5).

Chiara F. Del Bo from the Università degli Studi di Milano prepared the next paper which demystifies common misconceptions about Smart Cities. The aim of the paper is to clear some of these misconceptions, lay down what serious research allows us to say about the SC model and what we still have to explore to answer the questions above.

The next paper is delivered by Simge Dindar Tıraş and Ayça Güzel Özbek from Anadolu University, which they tried to find for both Generation Y and Generation Z, what "working" means, why they work, and what they expect from work life, workplace, leaders, and leadership, based on the assumption that the capacity of the

Z generation to access information is much higher thanks to technology. Generation Z, who started to receive education at an early age, shows faster mental development.

The last paper of this section is provided by Artemis Giourgali and Ioulia Poulaki from the University of the Aegean prepared the following paper, which provides a holistic understanding of the current crises' impact on the progress of European approach of SDGs. It offers a theoretically-oriented review that reflects the context of how the European region is affected by these challenges; and how the efforts on building more effective policies and directives may act catalytically.

With this book of selected papers, we hope to positively contribute to the area of digital economy, sustainable development, and green growth in the era of Digital Transformation of Balkan and Eastern European countries/regions. We also shed light on the role of ICT in the economic development of countries and strategies that emphasize the digital transformation. Concerning the quality of this volume, readers could be the most appropriate evaluators.

Last but not least, we would like to thank many people who made the conference a tremendous success and the researchers who submitted their work for the preparation of this book.

Chios, Greece — Maria Mavri
Chios, Greece — Patricia Ikouta Mazza
Kavala, Greece — Anastasios Karasavvoglou
Serres, Greece — Persefoni Polychronidou

Contents

Regional, Sustainable and Smart Growth

Digital Economy, Green Growth, Regional and Sustainable Development, Digital Transformation: A Brief Literature Review

Patricia Ikouta Mazza, Dimitris Papandreou, and Maria Mavri

1 Introduction

Nowadays, where globalization, digital transformation, and sustainability, are the most known and discussable concepts, Europe faces many challenges, that reform its identity, its priorities of social–economic–environmental prosperity, and its values.

What are the big challenges that Europe faced during the last decade?

Issues like Covid pandemic, Digitalization, Smart Specialization, Migration, Human Rights, Climate Change, and War between Ukraine and Russia, are the most common challenges.

The latest in relation to the pandemic wave, redefines the priorities of Europe in terms of external threats and countries' cooperation. The resilience of each country is important today and guarantees its independency and its identity too. It is true that covid bares national health systems unprepared and weak, and meanwhile, it pointed out the absence of a European strategy to treat health threats. The need to adopt a holistic health approach across Europe and the empowerment of preparation for health crises are two factors of major importance. Meanwhile, Russia's invasion of Ukraine marks a turning point for the EU. When Europe boosts its capabilities and resilience, it also has to enhance engagement with the wider world.

At the same time, the digitalized Industry gains floor every day. There is no doubt that industry in combination with technology advancement forces society to adapt and use smart technologies. This new type of information and communication

P. I. Mazza · D. Papandreou (✉) · M. Mavri
Quantitative Methods Laboratory, Department of Business Administration, University of the Aegean, 8 Michalon Street, P.S. 82100, Chios, Greece
e-mail: dpapandreou@aegean.gr

P. I. Mazza
e-mail: p.ikoutamazza@aegean.gr

M. Mavri
e-mail: m.mavri@ba.aegean.gr

M. Mavri et al. (eds.), *Digital Economy and Green Growth*, Contributions to Economics, https://doi.org/10.1007/978-3-031-66669-8_1

technology accelerates the trend of a fully automated environment, introducing in this way the concept of "Industry 4.0". Like water and steam in 1st Industrial Revolution, electricity in 2nd industrial revolution and computing in 3rd, digitalizing is the core of this latest revolution.

According to Commissioner Oettinger at Hannover Messe, *"Our challenge is to ensure that all industrial sectors make the best use of new technologies and manage their transition towards higher value digitised products and processes, commonly known as "Industry 4.0". In order to reach this goal, we have to take action in four key areas: 1) Digital innovation hubs, 2) Leadership in platforms for digital industry, 3) Closing the digital skills gap and 4) Smart regulation for smart industry."*

The integration of digital technologies by companies (technologies that affect both daily life and business such as the Internet of things, artificial intelligence, Big Data, 3D Printing, and cloud computing), in combination with sectors, which are accelerated by technology (like financial services, energy, production, and health), consists what we actually mean by the term "digital transformation".

Europe has converged in digital infrastructure, but more needs to be done to accelerate the commercial use of digital technologies. One of the main priorities of the European Union's priorities is digital transformation. EU tries to strength people's digital skills, enhance capacities and capabilities on digital technologies, highlight new opportunities for individuals and enterprises, support green growth, and ensure respect for human rights and values.

Climate change and the environmental dreadful conditions force the European Union to develop policies concerning green development. Based on the European Green Deal, Europe will be transformed into a modern and efficient economy that ensures, zero emission of greenhouse gases by 2050, economic growth decoupled from resource use, and inclusion of persons and places. During these years, Europe works transition, which protects biodiversities and ecosystems, develops a healthy food system, provides efficient safe and environmentally friendly transport, and finances sustainable investments to deliver European Green Deal.

First Vice-President of EU, **Frans Timmermans,** said: *"To build a future for our children and our planet to the benefit of everyone we are making the Sustainable Development Goals and sustainability a guiding principle in all our work. Implementing the UN 2030 Agenda is a shared commitment and needs everyone's contribution and cooperation, including Member States and civil society at large."*

But what actually the 2030 Agenda for Sustainable Development is?

It's a plan to change the word. In other words is a comprehensive plan that defines how we can diminish poverty and transform the word into a sustainable environment for all. The core of the 2030 Agenda is the 17 Sustainable Development Goals (SDGs) and associated targets, which will run to 2030.

And why sustainability is so important for our word? According to OECD, regional development is a broad term but can be seen as a general effort to enhance well-being and living standards in all region types, from cities to rural areas, and improve their contribution to national performance and more inclusive, resilient societies.

The structure of this chapter is as follows. Description of the terms of digital economy, green growth, urban and regional development, sustainable development, ESGs, Digital transformations, and Smart Life. This chapter looks like a snapshot that presents all the above concepts. It provides definitions, historical reviews, and a brief literature review of each sector.

2 Digital Economy

A common component of several attempts to define the concept of the digital economy is the reference to its transformative impact on economic activities, driven by digital technologies, data, global connectivity, and innovation. Understanding these elements is essential for policymakers, businesses, and society to navigate the opportunities and challenges of the digital era effectively.

Attempting a historical review of the evolution of the concept of the digital economy, we will find that in the late 1990s, the analysis of the digital economy was mainly concerned with Internet adoption and its economic impact, primarily focusing on activities such as *e-commerce facilitated by the internet* (Brynjolfsson & Kahin, 2002; Tapscott, 1996 at Duc et al. (2024)). As digital technologies continued to encompass broader transformations in business processes, organizational structures, and societal interactions, the term "digital economy" gradually began to gain ground against "e-economy". This transition was triggered by the mutation of economic activities themselves caused by digital technologies and digital transformation across industries, businesses, and services. More recently, the focus of the debate regarding the concept of the digital economy indeed moved. The search that is now attempted is related to the way that modern digital technologies and their general applications, the services provided, but also the development of skills exceed the limits of a narrow approach to the object of the economy. Over the past few years, *studies have focused on "digitalization" and "digital transformation," i.e., how digital products and services spill over and disrupt traditional sectors* (Ahmad & Schreyer, 2016; OECD, 2017; UNCTAD, 2017 at Duc et al. (2024)).

The digital economy has evolved into a widespread term that refers to the *promotion of economic growth through the use of new technologies and infrastructure*. The *use of ICT* is now a one-way street *for both developed and developing countries*. The digital economy now permeates all sectors of a country, from *agriculture and trade to health, education, and governance* (Oloyede et al., 2023). Modern definitions indeed attribute to the digital economy the potential to *encompass and transform all sectors of the global economy, but also aspects of social life*. In particular, the term indicates that socio-economic impacts from the use of digital technologies that including not only economic growth in general, but also jobs and service quality, in particular, can occur under conditions (Ershova et al., 2018). These include on the one hand digital technologies and on the other important "analog" parameters such as the business climate, human capital, and the regulatory framework. *This means that monitoring, evaluating, and remedial actions against the drivers of digital transformation are important elements of managing the development of the digital economy, alongside monitoring and evaluating the socio-economic impacts of the use of digital technologies* (Ershova et al., 2018).

A key parameter is the ability to *transform knowledge, experience, and socio-economic activities into standardized data, with the data element emerging as a necessary factor of production in this digital economic context* (Sun et al., 2024).

Moreover, as established from the above definitions the digital economy encompasses a broad spectrum of economic activities, interactions, and transactions facilitated by digital technologies, data, and connectivity. While definitions may vary slightly in emphasis and scope, they generally share several common elements. A fundamental element across all definitions is the centrality of digital technologies, such as the internet, mobile devices, data analytics, and information and communications technologies (ICT). These technologies serve as the foundation for enabling digital transactions, communication, and information exchange within the economy. Another common element is the importance of data and information in driving economic activities within the digital economy. Data plays a crucial role in informing decision-making, personalizing experiences, and creating value for businesses and consumers alike. The ability to collect, analyze, and leverage data is essential for unlocking insights and driving innovation. Definitions often highlight the global nature of the digital economy, emphasizing its interconnectedness and borderless nature. Digital technologies enable economic transactions and interactions to occur across geographical boundaries, facilitating trade, collaboration, and knowledge exchange on a global scale. The digital economy is characterized by the transformation of traditional business models. Digital technologies enable businesses to innovate new products, services, and delivery mechanisms, disrupting existing industries and creating new opportunities for growth and competitiveness.

Definitions often emphasize the empowerment of individuals and communities within the digital economy. Digital technologies provide individuals with greater access to information, resources, and opportunities, enabling participation in economic activities and fostering entrepreneurship and innovation. Finally, definitions recognize the challenges and opportunities presented by the digital economy. While digital technologies offer immense potential for economic growth, efficiency, and societal progress, they also pose challenges related to privacy, security, digital divide, and job displacement that need to be addressed through effective policies and regulations.

Having previously delved into the theory of the digital economy and looking for a tangible example of a concrete and contemporary application of the digital economy, the topic of Remote Work Platforms can emerge. This is a fairly typical example as due to the COVID-19 pandemic, remote work platforms like Zoom and Microsoft Teams have become essential tools for enabling remote collaboration. These platforms utilize digital technologies to facilitate a series of activities, allowing employees to work from anywhere with an internet connection. Remote work platforms have not only helped organizations maintain business continuity during the pandemic but have also transformed traditional work practices, leading to a broader acceptance of remote and flexible work arrangements. Essentially this indicative example shows how digital technologies may reshape the operation and organization of the digital economy at the level of businesses, industries, or services (Sahut & Lissillour, 2023).

3 Green Growth

Nowadays, the thinking about environment and development leads to the necessity of examining all known concepts about sustainability, green growth, and circular economy.

The concept of Green Growth is first discussed in the decade of the '90s and the core idea was to give emphasis on an environmental economic growth society with less carbon emissions and development with social characteristics.

Attempting the historical review, green growth is the end result concept of two different challenges that were expressed during the Rio Summit and were: the expansion of economic opportunities and the environmental pressures. According to the OECD, "*Green growth means fostering economic growth and development while ensuring that natural assets continue to provide the resources and environmental services on which our well-being relies.*" Two decades later, in the early of 2010, the Green Growth Strategy had been developed and announced by the OECD. This strategy has been welcomed by forty countries as a tool for expanding economic growth through the use of natural resources.

But in what terms does green growth actually refer?

What are the elements of this concept? Are they Green development, Green economy, Green trade, Green finance, or Green government? Magazzino et al. (2024) note that Green development targets the infrastructural aspects, the Green Economy involves the economic sectors, and Green Growth focuses on the economic subsectors and microeconomic scope.

Green growth policies aim to (1) enhance productivity by reducing waste, energy consumption, and by efficient use of natural recourses, (2) support governments to handle environment issues, (3) contribute to fiscal consolidation by mobilizing revenues through green taxes, (4) reduce damages and negative environmental impacts.

Green growth more specifically advocates for the proactive pursuit of complete synergy among the economy, environment, and society, aiming to secure an unceasing provision of essential services and resources from nature to sustain life on earth (Acosta et al., 2019; OECD, 2014). Sarkodie et al. (2020) note that bodies such as the OECD, African Development Bank (AfDB), and the Asian Development Bank (ADB), have all introduced programs to promote the inclusion of green growth into the national development plans of member countries (Jha et al., 2018; OECD, 2014).

Continuing with concepts that stand out the connection between development, environment and society, we introduce to our discussion "circular economy". The circular economy advocates an economic system that decouples the pressure on the environment from economic growth by replacing linear production with circular production in which waste becomes a resource (Belmonte-Urena et al., 2021). Circular economy replaces the motto "take-make-dispose" of the linear economy, with the moto "reduce, reuse, recycle". Both linear and circular economies are systems where recourses are used to make products.

At linear economy materials are collected, then products are manufactured, products are sold to consumers, and finally consumers use them and dispose of them as waste. This waste is the reason why this system is characterized as a polluting system, which also contributes to climate change. At circular economy the consumption of resources is reduced, something extremely important for Earth's sustainability. Note that material extraction and processing affects more than 55% the climate change. The utilization of components or parts of them and the recycled materials are crucial for the circular economy, as they reduce the use of materials and resources improving at the same time, Earth's sustainability. The adoption of a circular economy implies the assimilation of sustainability into industry and society in order to achieve environmental quality, economic wealth, and social inclusion (Brändström & Saidani, 2022).

Attempting circular economy through the decades we note that the roots of this system are in ecological economics and macroeconomics logistics, while the first time that scientists discussed about reuse of physical resources was in 1960.

To sum up Murray et al. (2017) and Belmonte-Urena et al. (2021) note that circular economy is "a bricolage of ideas", which suggest actions of efficient use of resources in order to reach a balance between economy, society and environment.

What is really difficult is the transition, from the linear to circular economy, as we have to choose between two different systems. If we take under consideration the globalization and technological advancements (Industry 4.0), we conclude that this transition is a multi-factorial problem.

An additional question that has to be answered is the suitability of a circular economy to industry. It is obvious that not all types of industry could follow the principals of this new type of economy. Although it is the most ambitious concept about the use of natural materials and resources, several issues emerge concerning the complexity and the suitability of the practices at industry. But we have to make clear that, the circular economy seems to be a strategy that could improve sustainability for the environment, business, and society, and could also become a pathway in order to successfully reach sustainable development goals (SDGs).

Upon concluding, we understand that the role of governments and authorities is extremely important. The reform of regulatory, financial, and production frameworks is a necessity in order to move one step further, to a sustainable and circular world.

4 Urban and Regional Development

A phenomenon that occupied the world economy in the last century was that of urbanization. The population has urbanized rapidly, and the urbanization rate is estimated to reach about 70% by 2050. The share of the population living in urban areas has been increasing continuously since 1900, when only about 16% of the world's population lived in cities. By 2000, this figure reached almost 46% and, for the first time in human history, it became greater than 50% in 2007. These trends are likely to continue in the coming decades, and according to United Nations projections, approx. 68% of the world's population will live in cities by 2050 (UN, 2018).

Urbanization contributed to the development process and had many benefits. It has been the main driver of economic growth in many countries by creating new jobs, economic diversification, improved efficiency, and better return on investment. This has resulted in the transition of the population to urban centers in search of social and economic opportunities and a better quality of life (Carling & Collins, 2018; Glaeser, 2011; Nguyen et al., 2015). At the same time, within urban centers, it is possible to accelerate research and investment in innovations by facilitating better cultural interactions, social entrepreneurship, and knowledge exchange (Angelidou & Mora, 2019).

Despite the positives, urbanization and overconcentration of population and economic activities in urban centers has led to negative externalities. These include the unequal distribution and access to urban amenities and services such as housing, increased poverty and unemployment, overpopulation and inefficient provision of infrastructure, increased energy consumption which is a key driver of climate change and increased pressure on the environment which could increase pollution and lead to the degradation of ecosystem services. These externalities are likely to worsen further in the coming decades if the population concentration in urban centers continues to increase at the same rate (Sharifi et al., 2023).

The phenomenon of urbanization and the relationship created between urban and regional areas is the subject of regional development. An urban area is a large residential area formed by non-agricultural industry and non-agricultural population. It is a complex and dynamic system. The rural area, on the other hand, is a place where workers are mainly engaged in agricultural production. Cities and villages are two systems that depend on each other, integrate with each other, and complement each other (Sharifi et al., 2023).

In recent decades, due to the phenomenon of urbanization and given the continuous expansions, increasing functionality and rapid development of urban industry and economies, cities have become important drivers of development and their surrounding peripheral areas. This process has promoted connections between cities and surrounding rural areas (Liu & Kringos, 2024), and interdependence between neighboring cities is increasing. This fact contributed to the creation of some practical problems, such as the weakening of the countryside, urban–rural differentiation, and social gaps (Li et al., 2022).

The above problems combined with the pressure for limited land use and the growing gap between urban and rural areas, made it imperative to create a regional coordination mechanism, placing regional policy at the center. Sustainable land use and long-term development have become the focus of regional coordination and interaction, which include not only rural revitalization and the promotion of integrated development of urban and rural areas but also the collective cooperative action of local governments using land resources (Li et al., 2022).

But how we moved from economic development to urban and regional development, ending up in sustainable development?

Spatial development concerning the spatial structure of an area, whether this area is a city, a village, or a large urban center has been the subject of research in recent decades. Originally for the classical liberal economists of the eighteenth and nineteenth centuries, the economic problem par excellence was to understand the causes of growth and the dynamics of economic development on a national scale in the long run. All policy changes for economic analysis for almost a century, from Smith (1776) to Mill (1848) and until the marginal revolution in the 1870s (Screpanti & Zamagni, 2001), were carried out centrally by each government. This was followed by the period of Marx's critique of political economy (Marx, 1867) and the rise of the labor movement as a powerful collective agent. With the rise of liberal economics, and certainly until the Great Depression of the 1930s, the focus in economics shifted from the dynamics of growth to market equilibrium and rational consumer behavior. However, at the end of World War II, the explanation of individual service in terms of economic rationality began to gain importance again, with the proliferation of neoclassical economic models and neo-institutional approaches to socio-economic coordination in terms of transaction cost minimization economy, sociology, and political science. Since the 1980s, neoliberalism has become the dominant ideology of market fundamentalism. In the 1960s, decolonization and the Cold War caused a renewed interest in economic "development" as a process. In the late 1950s, Hirschman (1958) made the connection between the developmental challenges of new nations and the renewed interest in regional development caused by the Scandinavian School of Institutionalism (Myrdal, 1957) and the French Growth Pole School (Perroux, 1955). The subject of discussion of the above schools was the debate on spatial polarization and regional uneven development—both within and between nations—creating new schools of thought and scientific disciplines (Martinelli et al., 2013).

"Regional science" was the result of the creation of new scientific disciplines (Isard, 1956). In the late 1960s, it emphasized the unequal power relations between "core" and "periphery" countries in the uneven spatial structure of capitalist development and the role of class structure and alliances within and across borders in its reproduction. In the 1970s, a wide variety of theories, many of them from Marxist and institutional traditions, began to address the development process by giving it its socio-spatial dimension (labor markets, production systems, and neighborhoods). In the 1980s, drawing on Marxist political economy and the German Historical School, as well as Keynesian macroeconomic policy, the regulation approach reaffirmed the interplay between capital accumulation and mode of regulation in economic development, while also providing an acknowledgment of its spatial structure. Also important in this decade was the re-emergence of institutional and evolutionary economics with a focus on innovation and growth (Freeman, 1982), which revisited Schumpeter's analysis of innovation and the dynamics of socio-economic development from a microeconomic and macroeconomic point of view. Finally, starting from the 1990s, the negative effects of population concentration in urban centers has contributed to the adoption of environmentally oriented policies and sustainable development has attracted increasing attention (Martinelli et al., 2013).

Already 30 years ago, Sachs (1980) argued that only an ecological development approach would resolve the increasingly dramatic conflict between development and the state of nature in ways other than stopping development. A similar analysis was developed by Perrin (1983), who called for an "ecological paradigm", emphasizing the dialectical relationship between the economic and ecological organization of human activity and how these dialectics could create the possibility of "autonomous territorial organization". However, despite this early link between ecological development and endogenous development, it was not until the early 2000s that sustainable development was explicitly addressed from a territorial perspective (Zuindeau, 2010). Emphasizing the dialectical relationship between the economic and ecological organization of human activity and how these dialectics could create the possibility of "autonomous territorial organization" (Martinelli et al., 2013).

Sustainable development in urban centers will be achieved through systematic inter-regional population migration to neighboring areas. Multiple cities in the same region are increasingly connected and multi-core urban areas are gradually emerging (Feng et al., 2019; Marull et al., 2013; Schoon, 2014). Broadly speaking, "polycentric urban area" refers to a form of regional organization in which many neighboring cities with different comparative advantages jointly build and share resources (Finka & Kluvánková, 2015; Su et al., 2016). An "urban agglomeration" is a typical example of a polycentric urban area. Urban cooperative development is an important part of regional integration research (Shu et al., 2018), and realizing coordinated regional development with other cities is the key to solving the contradiction of urban sustainable development.

5 Sustainable Development

Since the 70s, the world began to realize the dangers and undesirable effects of human activities, especially industrial ones, on the environment. After the Conference on the Environment in Stockholm in 1972 and the first report of the Club of Rome "Limits of Growth" ("Limits of Growth"; Meadows et al., 1972) what was really understood was that apart from the positive effects of technological progress, undesired negative effects could also occur. After this period, the environmental consciousness in the western world started to change. It was clear that regional and global environmental problems were very serious and needed to be solved. At that time, a shift occurred, which concerns the perception of things that development should be seen including among others social and environmental issues and not just economics. Sustainable Development is presented today as the only way out to deal with the current state of major environmental problems, but also the overconcentration of the population in urban centers and globalization. According to its principles, the hitherto concept of the development of the borderless economy should be replaced by a model that incorporates the basic principles of the capitalist economy, while examining the limits imposed by the natural world and seeking new business areas based on the environment. The process of defining the concept of Sustainable Development has contributed to the enrichment and expansion of the term development in the following two directions: (a) development must be seen in the widest possible way, including among others social and environmental issues and not only economic, and (b) development must be achieved in a way that does not reduce the potential of future generations while at the same time ensuring intra-generational equity. The concept of Sustainable Development is a convergence between the three pillars of economic development, social justice, and environmental protection. Sustainable development is an exemplary example of development and over the last 30 years governments, businesses, and civil society have accepted sustainable development as a guiding principle and progress has been made on sustainable development measurement models. For its consolidation, the combination of innovation, research, and new technologies is necessary, as well as the participation of private capital alongside supportive government policies. Prior to the concept of Sustainable Development was the concept of sustainability, which has its basis in classical economists. Malthus, Ricardo, Mill, Hicks, Pigou, and many others predicted that the scarcity of natural resources would lead to a slowdown and eventually a halt in economic growth (Mishra et al., 2023).

To this day, there is no commonly accepted definition of sustainable development, even though this concept is widely used in public debate. At the international level, however, many organizations active in sustainable development issues are trying to define this concept.

According to the World Bank (1992), *"Sustainable Development means development and environmental policies with a cost–benefit comparison and a careful economic analysis that will enhance environmental protection and lead to sustainable levels of social welfare"*.

According to Repetto (1986), *"the basic idea of sustainability is that current decisions should not affect the prospects for maintaining or improving living standards. This means that we should manage our economic systems so that we can live off the dividends of our resources"*. According to Redclift (1987), in an environmental approach, the term *"sustainable development indicates that the lessons of ecology can and should be applied to economic processes. It encapsulates the ideas in the Global Conservation Strategy, providing an environmental logic through which it calls for development to improve the quality of life that can be challenged and controlled"*, (Ruggerio, 2021).

According to Barbier (1987), in a social approach, *"sustainable economic development is directly related to the increase in the standard of living of the poor, which can be measured in terms of increase in food, real income, education, health care, water supply, sanitation and is only indirectly related to economic development".*

According to Pearce (1989), *"sustainable economic growth means that real GDP per capita increases over time and this increase does not threaten "feedback", either from biophysical-environmental effects (pollution, depletion of natural resources, degradation) or from social impacts".*

However, the definition with which Sustainable Development prevailed, in 1987 when the Minister of the Environment of Norway Ms. Brundtland, recommended the special Commission, to examine the issue of development and the effects it has on the environment. The Brundtland Commission issued a Report entitled "Our Common Future", in which for the first time a definition was formulated: *"for sustainable development as development that meets the needs of the present generation without limiting the ability to meet the needs of future generations".*

Despite the prevalence of the definition of the Brundtland report, attempts were also made in the 90s to define the concept of Sustainable Development. According to Lutz and Munasinghe (1991), *"sustainable development is an approach that will allow the continuous improvement of the quality of life with a lower intensity of resource use, leaving behind for future generations an undiminished or even enhanced inventory of natural resources and other assets".* According to Meadows (1998), *"Sustainable is the society that can exist for generations and generations, that can see far enough, that is flexible and wise enough, so as not to undermine either its natural or social supports systems".*

Sustainable Development was developed on the international scene by environmental non-governmental organizations and United Nations bodies and was gradually adopted by business and other international organizations beyond the United Nations while it penetrated widely and at the national level. The first major milestone in consolidating the importance of the environment on a global scale was the UN Environment Summit held in 1972 in Stockholm. This Summit, in addition to the adoption of the political Declaration and Plan of Action, led to the establishment of the UN Environment Program. Fifteen years after the Stockholm Summit, in 1987 the Brundtland Commission issued a Report entitled "Our Common Future", which linked environmental protection for the first time to the issue of economic development and social well-being and prosperity and began the consolidation of sustainable development. In 1992, twenty years after the Stockholm Summit, the UN held the World Conference on Environment and Development in Rio de Janeiro, Brazil. The main result of Rio was the drafting of a Report, known as "Agenda 21", which refers to the obligations and goals of the International Community to achieve a better life and the goals of sustainability for the twenty-first century. In 2002, the World Conference on Sustainable Development was held in Johannesburg, which is the culmination of the Stockholm conferences in 1972 and Rio in 1992. Both conferences were very important. The first highlighted the importance of the environment and the second validated the relationship between environmental protection and economic and social development. In addition, in September 2001, the United Nations presented the Millennium Development Goals (MDGs), the goals that the global community must achieve by 2015. In 2015, the United Nations General

Assembly endorsed the Sustainable Development Goals (SDGs) on its Agenda 2030 for Sustainable Development, which included 17 goals and 169 targets. Since the adoption of the 2030 Agenda, great emphasis has been placed on different levels of governance, in businesses, in financial institutions, in the public and private sectors, to achieve the objective of sustainable development (United Nations, 1973, 1983, 2015).

Today, facing the emergence of a Globalized economy does not mean that regions and countries are the same everywhere, but that their characteristics can become comparative advantages economically, socially, and environmentally. Sustainable development emphasizes the long-term compatibility of the economic, social, and environmental dimensions of human well-being while recognizing their possible competition in the short term. To achieve the parallel and balanced development of the three pillars of Sustainable Development in a country, it should be achieved in its individual structures, the regions, and by extension in the cities that make it up (Mio et al., 2020).

6 ESGs (Environmental, Social, Governance)

ESG is a new concept that deals with how to achieve the goals of the 2030 agenda of sustainable development and concerns the environment, society, and governance. However, there is still a lack of research on how to combine new business technological innovations with the new dimension of sustainability and bring competitive value to corporate value.

ESG performance assesses a company's adequacy as well as its position of responsibility in its governance, social, and environmental impact. Element "E" examines the dimension of the company's Environment. The environmental dimension includes strategies for the climate change, the natural resource utilization, the waste management, the pollution control and the energy efficiency. Similarly, the social dimension "S" relates to a company's commitment to decisions related to social aspects of employees, such as their health, safety, diversity, training, respect for human rights, social equality, quality of products, customer relations, community engagement, and philanthropic efforts. While the "G" aspect deals with corporate governance decisions and strategies, related to ensuring shareholders' rights, board composition, inclusion of independent directors, diversity within the board, executive remuneration, anti-bribery and anti-corruption measures, and forgery, among others (Fang & Hu, 2023).

Considering the interest in ESG performance, several studies have tried to identify the elements that influence organizations' ESG engagement (Abdi et al., 2022; Huang, 2021). Initially, most definitions of sustainability focused on the impact of economic activities on the nature (Delgado-Ceballos et al., 2023). Later, they expanded their definitions of sustainability to include the impacts of business activities in economic, social, and environmental aspects (Bansal, 2005). For example, Valente (2012, p. 586) pointed out that businesses had to find ways to connect social, economic, and ecological systems using *"Coordinated approaches leveraging collective cognition and operational capabilities of multiple local and of global social, ecological and economic stakeholders at work as a single network or system"*.

However, despite the volume of literature papers, we lack a universal definition of business viability, a fact that reflects the complexity of the concept and ambiguity (Meuer et al., 2020; Delgado-Ceballos et al., 2023). In general, most researchers tend to agree that sustainability has a three-dimensional structure based on economic integrity, social equity, and environmental integrity (Bansal, 2005), which is also mentioned as the 3Ps approach to business (i.e., profit, people, planet). Essentially, sustainability is seen as one intended target for businesses so that their operations do not adversely affect society or the natural environment. However, recent discussions of the strategies that businesses should adopt suggested that they positively affect socio-ecological systems by engaging in regeneration, which takes the focus away from business logic toward systems logic (Hahn & Tampe, 2021).

Although ESG evolved from the concept of sustainability, the main objective of enterprises to integrate the threefold ESG as a criterion in investment decisions is the alignment of social and environmental benefits and financial returns by identifying ESG-related risks and opportunities that are likely to affect investor and shareholder returns (Eccles et al., 2020). In other words, ESG can be characterized as the "monetization" of sustainability.

A company's ESG performance is affected by several factors, including environmental, social, and corporate governance. By evaluating companies' environmental performance, it can be determined whether they are taking effective environmental measures and how they continually improve pollution control and resource efficiency, which can help companies gain a competitive advantage. Companies need to pay attention to enhancing the management of relationships between stakeholders for the purpose of providing maximum support and assistance to all parties, thereby maximizing multiple integrated values. Several effective measures are taken to create a harmonious business environment to ensure the rights and interests of the company, where all parties involved are effectively protected. Through the implementation of measures that improve the ESG triplet, the financial position of the company has improved significantly (Jin & Lei, 2023).

Considering the environmental and climate crisis, the companies that have environmental responsibility can not only reduce the pressure of external stakeholders in their environment, but they can win the recognition and support of all parties, thereby improving the legitimacy of businesses and ultimately the achievement of their financial goals. According to the resource theory, by investing more in environmental management and environmental technologies, companies can not only gain more market share, but also effectively promote their sustainable development goals and contribute to improving their economic efficiency.

Respectively, by assuming their social responsibility companies will help to improve their social image, which will contribute to the continuous improvement of their economic situation. According to stakeholder theory, the fulfillment of social responsibility by companies can significantly improve their social capital and can effectively protect them from possible future risks, thus significantly improving their financial position. According to the theory of dissemination of information and its publicity, corporate social responsibility can help maximize transparency, reducing information asymmetry between companies and other interested parties, and will make clear to all involved the company's operating conditions and future development trends, which can reduce the risk of adverse effects and strengthen the long-term cooperation between the two parties, ultimately leading in achieving the sustainability of the company (Jin & Lei, 2023).

In today's economic environment, the implementation of the separation of powers system is necessary to strengthen corporate governance and improve the financial situation of businesses. A good corporate governance structure can significantly reduce the operating costs of a company, discourage the speculative mentality of executives, and enable greater flexibility to meet market demands, thus significantly improving the business performance. Corporate governance is a key factor in corporate sustainability helping to eliminate agency behavior and promote information sharing, thereby leading companies to achieve their long-term goals and ultimately improve their corporate value. Excellent corporate governance not only provides strong institutional support, but in the long run, protects the interests of all parties in such a way as to maximize the overall value of the company (Jin & Lei, 2023).

For a government to promote economic development, it should create a comprehensive mechanism for evaluating the implementation of strategies based on the ESG triplet, and it will provide appropriate incentives to good-performing companies. To help companies with good ESG status, the government will provide various supports such as the reduction of the tax burden, the reduction of interest rates on loans and conditions, and providing more opportunities to participate in competition. For companies with poor ESG status, the government should adopt a series of strict punitive measures to improve the investment environment of companies and the capital market with negative list establishment. This will lead to a comprehensive development path of the implementation of the ESG Regulation and companies will be a driving force in achieving its goals and sustainable and economic development (Huang, 2021).

7 Digital Transformation

The concept of "Digital Transformation" (DT) occupies the public debate, both at the academic level and at the market level. The interdisciplinary scientific approach to the term as well as its empirical treatment shows a steep increase in the last decade (Krishen et al., 2021 at Pascucci et al. (2023)). Indicative is the fact that in the Scopus database, the references to the term "DT", either in the title or in the keywords, of articles, conference papers, books, chapters, etc., reached 3,109 in the year 2021, and in the year 2000, it was only 2 (Pascucci et al., 2023).

In the first attempts to define DT, attention was focused on the role of digital technologies.

DT reflects the *use of new digital technologies (social media, mobile, analytics, or embedded devices) to enable major business improvements such as enhancing customer experience, streamlining operations, or creating new business models* (Vial (2019)).

Over the years, it has become widely accepted that the concept does not simply reflect a small or large-scale change of a technological nature (Henriette et al., 2015 at Gong and Ribiere (2021)). Beyond technology, it includes a number of parameters such as human resources, talent cultivation, leadership, culture, and others (Goran et al., 2017 at Gong and Ribiere (2021)). There are several cases where the definition of the concept is based on the results that DT can bring to an organization. It is also the argument that the main mission of DT is to improve the decision-making mechanism (Heilig et al., 2017; Roedder et al., 2016 at Gong and Ribiere (2021)). Other researchers added that it can be a significant competitive advantage (Korhonen & Halen, 2017; Schwertner, 2017 at Gong and Ribiere (2021)). Some other theories focus mainly on added value for the customer. An illustrative example is the optimization of customer needs and experiences cited by Rogers (2016) (at Gong and Ribiere (2021)) in his definitions. While some researchers insist on perceiving DT as a basically technological change, others attribute to the term more and more complex characteristics that even require the corresponding maturation (Janowski, 2015; Loebbecke & Picot, 2015; Wang et al., 2023 at Gong and Ribiere (2021)). There are even cases where the approaches are even more specialized and relate DT to areas such as business models (Berman, 2012; Bharadwaj et al., 2013; Gassmann et al., 2014; Schallmo et al., 2017 at Gong and Ribiere (2021)) or strategic planning (Bharadwaj et al., 2013; Henriette et al., 2015; Matt et al., 2015; at Gong and Ribiere (2021)). Vial (2019) *after reviewing 282 works on DT adopts an inductive approach using techniques borrowed from grounded theory* (Wolfswinkel et al., 2013 at Vial (2019)) and develop a conceptual definition of DT as *a process that aims to improve an entity by triggering significant changes to its properties through combinations of information, computing, communication, and connectivity technologies.* Bresciani et al. (2021) also describes DT as a process in which organizations leverage new technologies and the potential of connectivity to increase their effectiveness and become better positioned for innovation. This process allows them to transform many dimensions of the organization simultaneously. Reform the business model, improve the customer experience, and transform multiple business dimensions, including the business model, customer experience (which includes digitally enabled products and services), and operations (which includes processes and decision-making). It also includes in addition to the networks and the influence on the people themselves, their skills, their talents, and in general, the culture they share and influence people at the same time (Bresciani et al., 2021).

In addition to the private sector expressed through industries or businesses, governments and public administrations also play an important role in this process by setting an example and good practice. More and more in recent years public organizations choose to finance related initiatives of reengineering procedures and transforming business models (Coglianese & Lehr, 2017 at Vigoda-Gadot and Mizrahi (2024)).

In addition, the digital revolution poses new challenges to society and by extension to governments (*e.g., virtual communities, cryptocurrencies, and international knowledge networks*). This involvement in DT, among others, puts on the agenda of governments the restructuring not only of the values, but also of the regulatory framework of citizens' rights (Vigoda-Gadot & Mizrahi, 2024). In this spirit, government–citizen relations are taking new directions, moving toward smart governance (Schedler et al. at Vigoda-Gadot and Mizrahi (2024)) in order to optimize the services provided (Vigoda-Gadot & Mizrahi, 2024). Looking back some decades ago and specifically when governments decided to offer electronic services to both individuals and enterprises, the goal of that effort was the development of services fully automated (OECD, 2020 at OECD Development Co-operation Report, 2021). While streamlining procedures in individual domains, however, the overall result was often fragmented and government-centered. More recently, full-fledged digital government aims to rethink and re-engineer government processes and public services to respond to users' needs and expectations (OECD Development Co-operation Report, 2021). Experience in OECD countries shows that progress toward digital government is built on solid foundations of strategy, governance, and investment that foster collaboration between public sector entities. Thinking digitally at the outset, engaging users in the design and delivery of services, ethically governing and using public data, and nurturing digital talent and skills can then contribute to the success of digital government.

From the above definitions, we can initially draw the conclusion that DT is related, by the majority of researchers and theoreticians, to the use and exploitation of digital technologies during the routing of significant changes attempted in an organization. Changes are mostly aimed at improving its operations, reforming business models, and improving customer or citizen experiences. Despite the different wording between the definitions at a second level of analysis, common elements can also be recorded between them regarding the core of digital transformation.

One such fundamental element, which is inherent in several definitions, is the integration of digital technologies into various aspects of an organization's operations and processes. Examples include the following applications, cloud computing, artificial intelligence, data analysis, the Internet of Things (IoT), and automation, which are part of digital technologies, which sometimes have a strong element of innovation. Speaking of innovation, DT often seeks to review and reform business models by leveraging innovation to better meet the ever-changing needs and expectations of customers in the digital age. This process may involve moving from traditional product-centric models to customer- or user-centric models of services now provided using digital technologies. This project focuses on improving the customer experience through digital channels and it seeks to increase customer satisfaction by enriching personalized customer interactions and experiences across various digital platforms.

Another link between the various definitions of DT is "data", as it plays a central role in an organization. They facilitate the collection of key information and, by extension, decision-making for the purpose of continuous improvement. DT initiatives often involve collecting, analyzing, and using data to optimize processes, predict trends, and identify opportunities for innovation.

DT requires a mindset shift within Organizations to embrace innovation, flexibility, and adaptability. It highlights the importance of flexibility and adaptability to respond to rapidly changing market dynamics and technological developments. Organizations need to be able to quickly adapt their strategies, processes, and offerings to their audiences to remain competitive and compatible with the current digital landscape. To be successful, DT must be guided by a clear strategic vision, articulated by strong leadership that aligns digital initiatives with overall business goals and priorities. Leaders play a critical role in advocating for change, mobilizing resources, and fostering collaboration across the organization.

In summary, the most common elements found in definitions of digital transformation emphasize its holistic nature, including technology integration, business model innovation, customer centricity, data-driven decision-making, organizational culture and change, agility, flexibility, and strategic leadership. Understanding these elements is essential for organizations embarking on digital transformation journeys to achieve sustainable growth and competitiveness in the digital age.

8 Smart Life

The advent of digital technologies has led to the emergence of innovative concepts such as "smart cities", "smart products", and "smart services". These terms encompass the integration of digital intelligence into urban infrastructure, products, and services, with the aim of enhancing efficiency, sustainability, and quality of life.

Starting the analysis from the concept of smart cities they may be described as complex and multifaceted entities, and defining them accurately is essential for effective planning, implementation, and evaluation of related initiatives.

The term "smart city" refers to the connection of the progress of cities with the possibility of exploiting ICT, as cities are to some extent entrained by the rapid technological developments implemented in the socio-economic field in general (Alizadeh & Sharifi, 2023).

According to Caragliu et al. (2009), a city can be considered a "smart city" *when investments in human and social capital and traditional (transport) and modern (ICT) communication infrastructure fuel sustainable economic growth and a high quality of life, with a wise management of natural resources, through participatory governance* (Caragliu et al., 2009).

Projects implemented in the light of smart cities basically aim to address global challenges in general and to improve the quality of life of cities in particular (Sarifi, 2020 at Alizadeh and Sharifi (2023)).

Cities are trying *to balance the triangle of soci(et)al, environmental, and economic quality* (Fanning et al., 2022 at Dai et al. (2024)). Under these conditions, projects of a technological nature were awarded (Mondschein et al., 2021 at Dai et al. (2024)), *often termed "smart city" initiatives, to alleviate the environmental, economic, and soci(et)al pressures of the increasing city population and at the same time to increase the city quality on all these three aspects* (Hollands, 2008; Ben Letaifa, 2015; Ekman et al., 2019, Thuzar, 2011 at Dai et al. (2024)). The transition to a smart city regime (Angelidou, 2015; Letaifa, 2015; Musiolik et al., 2020a at Dai et al. (2024)) has at its core the element of *sustainable economic development* (Grossi & Trunova, 2021 at Dai et al. (2024)), which translates into an *improved and sustainable social environment for its citizens* (Ballas, 2013; Obringer & Nateghi, 2021 at Dai et al. (2024)).

As mentioned in the introduction, another concept that is part of the "Smart Life" section is that of Smart Products. According to Abramovici (2015), these goods correspond to *cyber-physical products/systems (CPS) which additionally use and integrate internet-based services* to carry out their mission. *CPS are defined as "intelligent" mechatronics products/systems capable of communicating and interacting with other CPS by using different communication channels* (Lee, 2010; Rajkumar et al., 2010 at Abramovici (2015)).

Another manifestation of the "Smart Life" concept is Smart Services. In order to deal with the rather wide possibility of interpretation of the term, Marquardt (2017) proposes *5 main characteristics*, which she considers to be helpful in trying to define services:

(1) *Connection between the physical and the digital world;*
(2) *Upgrade of value creation and economic efficiency;*
(3) *Extension of products and services at a digital level;*
(4) *Transformation of the product into a part of the service;*
(5) *Change from product centered to customer centered business models* (Steimel, 2016; euro data, 2015; Allmendinger & Lombreglia, 2005 at Marquardt (2017)).

In the effort to define the services, a parameter that plays an equally important role is the one that connects the services to the utilization of the data. The degree of dependence, the corresponding flexibility of their use, as well as their creation at an inter-company and/or cross-sector level (Kagermann et al., 2015 at Marquardt (2017)).

"Smart Services" can also be seen as services that have been customized to meet the needs of customers, utilizing relevant data, which are subject to intelligent and targeted processing (Hermann, 2016 at Marquardt (2017)). A critical parameter in both the design and provision of Smart Services is the customer-centric approach and the environment in which it operates. This is the condition that allows us to extract usable data, the processing of which is carried out through technological platforms appropriately designed for this work. These are necessary conditions when the goal is digital transformation through the change of business mentality, culture, and ultimately organization (Marquardt, 2017).

From the above definitions of the individual versions of Smart Life, it can be seen that at the heart of "smart cities", "smart products", and "smart services" is the use of "intelligence" which is largely based on data. These entities leverage various technological applications and infrastructures as well as analytics to collect, analyze, and interpret massive amounts of data in real time. Whether it's optimizing urban infrastructure, improving product functionality, or personalizing service delivery, data-driven insights drive informed decision-making and enable continuous improvement.

One element that runs through all the aforementioned concepts and even connects them is connectivity and interoperability. Smart cities, smart products, and smart services in particular thrive on connectivity and interoperability. This is because they rely on strong networks to facilitate their seamless interactions. Whether it's integrating sensors into city infrastructure, enabling devices to communicate with each other, or ensuring interoperability between service providers, a connected ecosystem is essential to unlocking the full potential of "smart solutions". In such an ecosystem, one thing they all have in common is a focus on user-centered design. Whether it's citizens in a smart city, consumers using smart products, or customers dealing with smart services, the focus is on understanding user needs, preferences, and behaviors. Design thinking principles guide the development of intelligent interfaces, seamless experiences, and personalized solutions that enhance user satisfaction and engagement.

Smart solutions, apart from focusing on the customer and his needs, must prioritize sustainability and efficiency as key goals. In smart cities, this can include optimizing energy consumption, reducing carbon emissions, and promoting environmentally friendly transport options. Smart products aim to minimize resource use, improve energy efficiency, and improve product life cycle management. Smart services focus on delivering value in a resource-efficient manner, optimizing processes, and minimizing waste. Innovation and collaboration are fundamental to the success of smart cities, smart products, and smart services. These sectors thrive in a culture of innovation, where stakeholders collaborate across sectors to co-create solutions that address complex challenges and take advantage of emerging opportunities. Whether it's public–private partnerships that drive urban innovation, interdisciplinary teams that develop cutting-edge products, or ecosystem partnerships that deliver integrated services, innovation, and collaboration drive progress and growth.

All the above aspects are compromised when the element of security and privacy protection is not present. This is certainly a common concern. In summary, smart cities, smart products, and smart services share common elements that underline their transformative potential. By leveraging data-driven intelligence, enhancing connectivity and interoperability, embracing user-centered design, prioritizing sustainability and efficiency, fostering innovation and collaboration, and ensuring security and privacy, these areas open up the way to a "smarter", "more connected", and "sustainable future".

References

Abdi, Y., Li, X., & Camara-Turull, X. (2022). Exploring the impact of sustainability (ESG) disclosure on firm value and financial performance (FP) in airline industry: The moderating role of size and age. *Environment, Development and Sustainability, 24*(4), 5052–5079. https://doi.org/10.1007/s10668-021-01649-w

Abramovici, M. (2015). Smart products. In The International Academy for Produ., L. Laperrière, & G. Reinhart (Eds.), *CIRP encyclopedia of production engineering*. Springer. https://doi.org/10.1007/978-3-642-35950-7_16785-1

Acosta, L., Maharjan, P., Peyriere, H., Galotto, L., Mamilt, R., Ho, C., & Anastasia, O. (2019). *Green growth index: Concepts, methods and applications*. Technical report, No 5. https://www.researchgate.net/publication/342690705_Green_Growth_Index_Concepts_Methods_and_Applications

Alizadeh, H., & Sharifi, A. (2023). Societal smart city: Definition and principles for post-pandemic urban policy and practice. *Cities, 134,* 104207.https://doi.org/10.1016/j.cities.2023.104207. ISSN 0264-2751.

Angelidou, M., & Mora, L. (2019). Developing synergies between social entrepreneurship and urban planning evidence from six European Cities. *disP – The Planning Review, 55*(4), 28–45.

Bansal, P. (2005). Evolving sustainably: A longitudinal study of corporate sustainable development. *Strategic Management Journal, 26*(3), 197–218.

Barbier, B. E. (1987). The concept of sustainable economic development. *Environmental Conservation, 14*(2), 101–110. Cambridge University Press.

Belmonte-Urena, L. J., Plaza-Úbeda, J. A., Vazquez-Brust, D., & Natalia Yakovleva, N. (2021). Circular economy, degrowth and green growth as pathways for research on sustainable development goals: A global analysis and future agenda. *Ecological Economics*. https://doi.org/10.1016/j.ecolecon.2021.107050

Brändström, J., & Saidani, M. (2022). Comparison between circularity metrics and LCA: A case study on circular economy strategies. *Journal of Cleaner Production, 371*, 133537. https://doi.org/10.1016/j.jclepro.2022.133537

Bresciani, S., Ferraris, F., Romano, M., & Santoro, G. (2021). *"Building a digital transformation strategy", Digital transformation management for agile organizations: A compass to sail the digital world* (pp. 5–27). Emerald Publishing Limited. https://doi.org/10.1108/978-1-80043-171-320211002

Brundtland. (1987). *Our common future: The world commission on environment and development*. Oxford University Press.

Carling, J., & Collins, F. (2018). Aspiration, desire and drivers of migration. *Journal of Ethnic and Migration Studies, 44*(6), 909–926. https://doi.org/10.1080/1369183X.2017.1384134

Caragliu, A, Del Bo, C., & Nijkamp, P. (2009). *Smart cities in Europe*. VU University Amsterdam, Faculty of Economics, Business Administration and Econometrics, Serie Research Memoranda. https://doi.org/10.1080/10630732.2011.601117

Dai, Y., Hasanefendic, S., & Bossink, B. (2024). A systematic literature review of the smart city transformation process: The role and interaction of stakeholders and technology. *Sustainable Cities and Society, 101,* 105112. https://doi.org/10.1016/j.scs.2023.105112. ISSN 2210-6707.

Delgado-Ceballos, J., Ortiz-De-Mandojana, N., Antolín-López, R., & Montiel, I. (2023). Connecting the sustainable development goals to firm-level sustainability and ESG factors: The need for double materiality. *Business Research Quarterly, 26*(1), 2–10. https://doi.org/10.1177/23409444221140919

Duc, D. T. V., Dat, T. T., Linh, D. H., & Phong, B. X. (2024). Measuring the digital economy in Vietnam. *Telecommunications Policy, 48*(3), 102683. https://doi.org/10.1016/j.telpol.2023.102683. ISSN 0308-5961.

Eccles, R. G., Lee, L. E., & Stroehle, J. C. (2020). The social origins of ESG: An analysis of Innovest and KLD. *Organization & Environment, 33*(4), 575–596.

Ershova, T., Hohlov, Y., & Shaposhnik, S. (2018). Methodology for digital economy development assessment as a tool for managing the digital transformation processes. In *2018 Eleventh International Conference "Management of large-scale system development" (MLSD)*, Moscow, Russia (pp. 1–3).https://doi.org/10.1109/MLSD.2018.8551846

Fang, X. M., & Hu, D. (2023). Corporate ESG performance and innovation: Empirical evidence from A-share listed companies. *Economic Research Journal, 58*(2), 91–106.

Feng, W., Liua, Y., & Qua, L. (2019). Effect of land-centered urbanization on rural development: A regional analysis in China. *Land Use Policy, 87*, 104072.

Finka, M., & Kluvánková, T. (2015). Managing complexity of urban systems: A polycentric approach. *Land Use Policy, 42*, 602–608.

Freeman, Ch. (1982). *The economics of industrial innovation*. Pinter Publishers.

Glaeser, E. L. (2011). *Triumph of the city: How our greatest invention makes us richer, smarter, greener, healthier, and happier*. Penguin Press.

Gong, C., & Ribiere, V. (2021). Developing a unified definition of digital transformation. *Technovation, 102,* 102217. https://doi.org/10.1016/j.technovation.2020.102217. ISSN 0166-4972.

González-Zapata, F., & Piccinin-Barbieri, M. (2021). *OECD development co-operation report making the leap from e-government to digital government*. https://www.oecd-ilibrary.org/sites/1e7a17e2-en/index.html?itemId=/content/component/1e7a17e2-en

Hahn, T., & Tampe, M. (2021). Strategies for regenerative business. *Strategic Organization, 19*(3), 456–477.

Hirschman, A. O. (1958). *The strategy of economic development*. Yale University Press.

Huang, D. Z. X. (2021). Environmental, social and governance (ESG) activity and firm performance: A review and consolidation. *Accounting and Finance, 61*(1), 335–360. https://doi.org/10.1111/acfi.12569

Isard, W. (1956). *Location and space-economy: A general theory relating to industrial location, market areas, land use, trade, and urban structure*. MIT Press.

Jha, S., Sandhu, S. C., & Wachirapunyanont, R. (2018). *Inclusive green growth index: A new benchmark for quality of growth*. Asian Development Bank.

Jin, X., & Lei, X. (2023). A study on the mechanism of ESG's impact on corporate value under the concept of sustainable development. *Sustainability, 15*, 8442. https://doi.org/10.3390/su15118442

Li, L., Ma, S., Zheng, Y., & Xiao, X. (2022). Integrated regional development: Comparison of urban agglomeration policies in China. *Land Use Policy, 114*, 105939. https://doi.org/10.1016/j.landusepol.2021.105939

Liu, Z., & Kringos, N. (2024). Transition from linear to circular economy in pavement engineering: A historical review. *Journal of Cleaner Production, 449*. https://doi.org/10.1016/j.jclepro.2024.141809

Lutz, E., & Munasinghe, M. (1991). Accounting for the environment. *Finance & Development*. https://doi.org/10.1126/science.1724-b

Ma, L., Liu, S., Fang, F., Che, X., & Chen, M. (2020). Evaluation of urban-rural difference and integration based on quality of life. *Sustainable Cities and Society, 54*, 101877. https://doi.org/10.1016/j.scs.2019.101877

Magazzino, C., Taghvaee, V., Soretz, S., Akbari, F., & Tatar, M. (2024). Defining green development and its green factors: Exploring their relationship with green economy and green growth. *Reference Module in Social Sciences*. https://doi.org/10.1016/B978-0-44-313776-1.00241-5

Marquardt, K. (2017). Smart services—Characteristics, challenges, opportunities and business models. *Proceedings of the International Conference on Business Excellence*. https://doi.org/10.1515/picbe-2017-0084

Martinelli, F., Moulaer, F., & Novy, A. (2013). Urban and regional development trajectories in contemporary capitalism. *Routledge Frontiers of Political Economy*. ISBN: 978-0-415-60894-7 (hbk). ISBN: 978-0-203-07532-6 (ebk).

Marull, J., Galletto, V., Domence, E., & Trullén, J. (2013). Emerging megaregions: A new spatial scale to explore urban sustainability. *Land Use Policy, 34*, 353–366.

Marx, K. (1986 [1867]). *Das Kapital: Kritik der politischen Ökonomie*. Dietz.

Meadows, D. (1998). Indicators and information systems for sustainable development. Sustainability Institute.

Meadows, H. D., Meadows, L. D., Randers, J., & Behrens, W. (1972). *Limits to growth*.

Meuer, J., Koelbel, J., & Hoffmann, V. H. (2020). On the nature of corporate sustainability. *Organization & Environment, 33*(3), 319–341.

Mill, S. J. (1848). *The priniciples of political economy*. John W. Parker.

Mio, C., Panfilo, S., & Blundo, B. (2020). Sustainable development goals and the strategic role of business: A systematic literature review. *Bussiness Strategy and the Environement, 29*, 3220–3245. https://doi.org/10.1002/bse.2568

Mishra, M., Desul, S., Santos, C. A. G., Mishra, S. K., Kamal, A. H. M., Goswami, S., Kalumba, A. M., Biswal, R., da Silva, R. M., dos Santos, C. A. C., & Baral, K. (2023). A bibliometric analysis of sustainable development goals (SDGs): A review of progress, challenges, and opportunities. *Environment, Development and Sustainability*, (0123456789). https://doi.org/10.1007/s10668-023-03225-w

Murray, A., Skene, K., & Haynes, K. (2017). The circular economy: An interdisciplinary exploration of the concept and application in a global context. *Journal of Business Ethics, 140*, 369–380.

Myrdal, G. (1957). *Economic theory and underdeveloped regions*. G. Duckworth.

Nguyen, L. D., Raabe, K., & Grote, U. (2015). Rural–urban migration, household vulnerability, and welfare in Vietnam. *World Development, 71*, 79–93. https://doi.org/10.1016/j.worlddev.2013.11.002

OECD. (2014). *Green growth indicators*. https://www.oecd.org/en/publications/2014/06/green-growth-indicators-2014_g1g3042b.html

OECD. (2020). *The OECD digital government policy framework: Six dimensions of a digital government*. OECD Public Governance Policy Papers, No. 02. OECD Publishing. https://doi.org/10.1787/f64fed2a-en

Oloyede, A. A., Faruk, N., Noma, N., Tebepah, E., & Nwaulune, K. A. (2023). Measuring the impact of the digital economy in developing countries: A systematic review and meta-analysis. *Heliyon, 9*(7), e17654. https://www.cell.com/action/showPdf?pii=S2405-8440%2823%2904862-4. ISSN 2405-8440.

Pascucci, F., Savelli, E., & Gistri, G. (2023). How digital technologies reshape marketing: Evidence from a qualitative investigation. *Italian Journal of Marketing, 2023*, 27–58. https://doi.org/10.1007/s43039-023-00063-6

Pearce, D. W., Markandya, A., & Barbier, E. (1989). *Blueprint for a green economy*. Earthscan.

Perrin, J. C. (1983). Economie spatiale et méso-analyse. In J. H. P. Paelinck & A. Sallez (Eds.), *Espace et localization*. Economica.

Perroux, F. (1955) 'Note sur la notion de "pôle de croissance". *Economie Appliquée, 8*, republished and trans. in McKee, D. L., Dean, R. D., & Leahy, W. H. (Eds.). (1970). *Regional economics* (pp. 93–103). The Free Press.

Redclift, M. (1987). *Sustainable development; Exploring the contradictions*. Routledge. https://doi.org/10.4324/9780203408889

Repetto, R. (1986). *World enough and time* (Vol. 8, Issue 4, 147 p.). Yale University Press. Index. ISBN: 0-300-03649-3. $5.95 paperback. https://doi.org/10.1177/027046768800800416O

Ruggerio, C. A. (2021). Sustainability and sustainable development: A review of principles and definitions. *Science of The Total Environment, 786*, 147481. https://doi.org/10.1016/j.scitotenv.2021.147481

Sachs, I. (1980). *Stratégies de l'éco-développement*. Les Éditions Ouvrières.

Sahut, J. M., & Lissillour, R. (2023). The adoption of remote work platforms after the Covid-19 lockdown: New approach, new evidence. *Journal of Business Research, 154*, 113345. https://doi.org/10.1016/j.jbusres.2022.113345. ISSN 0148-2963.

Sarkodie, A. S., Adams, S., Owusu, A. P., Leirvik, T., & Ozturk, I. (2020). Mitigating degradation and emissions in China: The role of environmental sustainability, human capital and renewable energy. *Science of the Total Environment, 719*, 137530.

Schoon. (2014). Maturing megacities. In U. Altrock & S. Schoon (Eds.), *The Pearl river delta in progressive transformation*. Springer.

Schumpeter, J. A. (1947). *Capitalism, socialism, and democracy*. Harper & Brothers Publishers.

Screpanti, E., & Zamagni, S. (2001). An outline of the history of economic thought. Clarendon Press.

Sharifi, A., Khavarian-Garmsir, A. R., Allam, Z., & Asadzadeh, A. (2023). Progress and prospects in planning: A bibliometric review of literature in urban studies and regional and urban planning, 1956–2022. *Progress in Planning, 173,* 100740. https://doi.org/10.1016/j.progress.2023.100740

Smith, A. (1776). *The wealth of nations.* W. Strahan and T. Cadell.

Su, R., Lough, M. J., & Sun, D. (2016). Variations in massive Porites growth rates at Hainan Island, northern South China. *Marine Ecology Progress Series, 546*, 47–60.

Sun, G., Fang, J., Li, J., & Wang, X. (2024). Research on the impact of the integration of digital economy and real economy on enterprise green innovation. *Technological Forecasting and Social Change, 200,* 123097. https://doi.org/10.1016/j.techfore.2023.123097. ISSN 0040-1625.

UN. (2018). *World urbanization prospects: The 2018 revision* (online ed.). In Department of Economic and Social Affairs PD. UN Department of Economic and Social Affairs (2021, 1st February 2021).

United Nations. (1973). *Report of the United Nations Conference on the Human Environment.* United Nations.

United Nations. (1983). *General assembly, "Report of the world commission on environment and development: Our common future"*. United Nations.

United Nations. (2015). *Transforming our world: The 2030 agenda for sustainable development.* Sustainable Development Knowledge Platform. https://sustainabledevelopment.un.org/post2015/transformingourworld

Valente, M. (2012). Theorizing firm adoption of sustaincentrism. *Organization Studies, 33*(4), 563–591.

Vial, G. (2019). Understanding digital transformation: A review and a research agenda. *The Journal of Strategic Information Systems, 28*(2), 118–144. https://doi.org/10.1016/j.jsis.2019.01.003. ISSN 0963-8687.

Vigoda-Gadot, E., & Mizrahi, S. (2024). The digital governance puzzle: Towards integrative theory of humans, machines, and organizations in public management. *Technology in Society, 77,* 102530. https://doi.org/10.1016/j.techsoc.2024.102530. ISSN 0160-791X.

Wang, L., Ji, Y., & Ni, Z. (2023). Spillover of stock price crash risk: Do environmental, social and governance (ESG) matter? *International Review of Financial Analysis, 89,* 102768. https://doi.org/10.1016/j.irfa.2023.102768

Wang, Z., Chu, E., & Hao, Y. (2024). Towards sustainable development: How does ESG performance promotes corporate green transformation. *International Review of Financial Analysis, 91*, 102982. https://doi.org/10.1016/j.irfa.2023.102982

World Bank. (1992). *Governance and development* (English). The World Bank. http://documents.worldbank.org/curated/en/604951468739447676/Governance-and-development

Zuindeau, B. (Ed.). (2010). *Développement durable et territoire.* Septentrion Presses Universitaires.

https://www.oecd.org/greengrowth/whatisgreengrowthandhowcanithelpdeliversustainabledevelopment.htm

https://greengrowthindex.gggi.org/wp-content/uploads/2019/10/GGGI_Green_Growth_Index_report.pdf

https://ec.europa.eu/commission/presscorner/detail/en/IP_16_3883

https://commission.europa.eu/strategy-and-policy/priorities-2019-2024/european-green-deal_en

https://www.eumonitor.eu/9353000/1/j9vvik7m1c3gyxp/vli6iyjgcqxh?ctx=vg9pj7ufwbwe

https://www.worldbank.org/en/region/eca/publication/addressing-europes-digital-dilemma

https://www.epc.eu/en/Publications/Is-the-European-Health-Union-ready-for-the-challenges-of-the-21st-cent~53947c

https://ec.europa.eu/commission/presscorner/detail/fr/SPEECH_15_4772

https://www.oecd.org/regional/regionaldevelopment.htm

Digital Transformation and Digital Government

Digitalization and Its Limits in Reducing Economic and Social Divide in Northern Greece

Vesna Lukovic

Abstract A decade-long financial crisis that started in 2008 led to economic and social instability, demographic changes and an exodus of qualified young people from Greece. The consequences of that crisis are still being felt. The aim of this paper is to explore digitalization in northern Greece from the viewpoint of bridging economic and social divides. The digital divide is analyzed by looking at access, skills, and the ability of people to use digitalization for their own goals. The focus of research is on social sustainability through the lens of digitalization in agriculture and tourism. The methodology of the research is quantitative, based on statistical analysis of data from the databases at the Eurostat, the statistical office of the European Union. Data was generated from the annual Eurostat's survey on the use of information and communication technologies in households and by individuals. The finding of this research is that the use of digital technologies in northern Greece has been growing. Greece has been trying to enhance digitalization with various projects that are co-financed by the European Union. However, there are limitations of digitalization in ensuring economic and social sustainability so as to bridge the economic and social divide.

Keywords Digitalization · Social sustainability · Agriculture · Tourism

JEL Classification O13 · Q18 · R11 · Z32

1 Introduction

In 2019 when the Zagori region of Pindos Mountains in northern Greece got broadband internet access, it was reported in the news that the region experienced a silent revolution (Euronews, 2019). When people feel that they are a part of a certain process, social sustainability may increase (Dempsey et al., 2011). It may feel as a revolution. Social sustainability is a concept of many dimensions and inclusion

---

V. Lukovic (✉)
Thessaloniki, Greece
e-mail: lukove@yahoo.com

M. Mavri et al. (eds.), *Digital Economy and Green Growth*, Contributions to Economics, https://doi.org/10.1007/978-3-031-66669-8_2

is a part of it (World Bank, 2023). Not only inclusion, but also resilience, social cohesion, and how central and local government policies are designed and implemented are important in order to strengthen and enhance social sustainability (Ballet et al., 2020). Technology can increase not only resilience but can also reduce the geographical digital divide. Greece covers an area of 132,049 km^2, of which about 63% is predominantly rural (European Commission, 2021). About 32% of people live in the rural areas where accessibility to digital technologies is at a lower level compared to urban areas. The lack of broadband and limited access to essential services and infrastructures are among those features that can contribute to a social and economic divide leading to depopulation and out-migration in rural and remote areas (Parviainen et al., 2017). It has been established that digitalization can support sustainable growth (European Parliament, 2019) considering that economies are now being influenced by technology and internet more than ever before.

This paper incorporates a general view that digital tools can help generate growth (European Central Bank, 2018) which is crucial for Greece considering its high public debt and shrinking households' disposable income since the crisis that started in 2008 (European Central Bank, 2022a, 2022b, 2022c). The Covid-19 pandemic in 2020–2021 and the conflict in Ukraine with its uncertainty brought a new dimension to the importance of technology and digitalization, particularly in rural areas. The authorities in the European Union (hereinafter: EU) have recognized the potential of digital technologies, including in the agricultural-food and tourism sector (European Commission, 2019a, 2019b, 2019c). There are many institutional reports on digitalization (European Parliament, 2019) and its benefits (European Commission, 2020), particularly with regard to access and skills in the aftermath of the Covid-19 outbreak (European Commission, 2022a). However, none of the works (to author's knowledge) has focused on northern Greece by exploring digitalization with regard to its ability to bridge the economic and social divide by looking at access, skills, and the ability of people to use digitalization for their own goals in agriculture and tourism. This paper looks at that challenge. It also briefly examines relevant data with regard to rural and urban areas in Greece vis-a-vis the average of the EU. The analysis also touches upon digitalization from the perspective of households' interaction with public authorities to receive various information and submit required forms online. The finding of the research is that there are limits to what technology can do to bridge the social and economic divide. There must be a wider strategy and collaboration to achieve social sustainability for sustainable futures in northern Greece.

The paper is structured as follows. After the introduction, Sect. 2 provides an overview of the key literature. Section 3 explains the methodology and data sources. Section 4 reviews some key stylized facts about northern Greece. That is followed by the explanation about the economic and social case for further digitalization in Sect. 5. Limitations of technology with regard to bridging the economic and social divides are discussed in Sect. 6. The findings and conclusions are outlined in the final section.

2 Literature Review

Social sustainability and its link with digitalization has been the subject of a considerable level of academic interest in recent years. Since social sustainability is a dynamic concept that includes various interdisciplinary areas, there is a diverse set of academic works in this respect. For instance, Ballet et al. (2020) argue that social sustainability implies environmental sustainability while also ensuring social cohesion. Other authors have focused on the policy dimension such as social policy and poverty (Hujo & Gaia, 2011) and on social sustainability framework in response to rapid urban growth (Cuthill, 2010).

Some authors looked at the wider perspective, finding that institutional quality of a country influences the ability of a government to achieve sustainable development goals and attain favorable results in the economic, social, and environmental dimensions of sustainability (Massuga et al., 2023). Social sustainability is closely related to peoples' welfare that goes beyond standards of living but also includes social cohesion (World Bank, 2023).

Certain authors have looked at sustainability from a sociological (Neckel, 2017) or from an environmental perspective (Gadanakis et al., 2015). Others have focused on the link between urban development and human capital (Bollman, 1999) and on the link between internet use and relative poverty in rural areas (Meng et al., 2023). Some authors (Xu et al., 2022) have emphasized that digitalization provides people with access to a large network of data which can help society and the environment. Systematic literature reviews on social sustainability in the age of digitalization (Grybauskas et al., 2022; Irajifar et al., 2023) find some contradictory conclusions in works by academics in different scientific fields.

Some recent works about the link between digitalization and sustainable development find that digitalization opens up great opportunities but also brings certain challenges (Karki & Thapa, 2021).

3 Methodology and Data

Research methodology is quantitative and based on statistical analysis. Data from the Eurostat's databases were extracted, sorted, and analyzed. They were then compared in relation to rural vs urban with a regional focus, and in some indication, comparisons have been done vis-à-vis the average of the EU. The data at the regional level in Greece was focused on northern Greece from the perspective of economic, social, and digital society sustainability.

The first-level of regions according to NUTS1 (nomenclature of the EU territorial units for statistics) in Greece are EL3-Attiki (Atica), EL4-Nisia Aigaiou, Kriti (Aegean Islands, Crete), EL5-Voreia Ellada (Northern Greece), and EL6- Kentriki Ellada (Central Greece). Since the European statistical office, the Eurostat, uses original national names for regions at NUTS nomenclatures in its databases, the original national regional names are also used in the tables and figures in this paper. For clarification purposes at this point the English names of the region of northern Greece, i.e., Voreia Ellada (EL-5) are provided in brackets as follows. The statistical region of northern Greece at the level NUTS2 comprises EL51-Anatoliki Makedonia, Thraki (Eastern Macedonia and Thrace), EL52-Kentriki Makedonia (Central Macedonia), EL 53-Dytiki Makedonia (Western Macedonia), and EL54-Ipeiros (Epirus).

In addition to data from Eurostat's databases, other data and information, including relevant institutional reports from the European Commission, International Monetary Fund (IMF), Organization for Economic Cooperation and Development (OECD) and reports from the National Bank of Greece were explored.

Data that were statistically analyzed were the Eurostat's macroeconomic regional data series (GDP by region, demographic indicators, unemployment, households' income, and other data series) and data generated from the specific Eurostat's surveys on digital society and certain information society indicators.

4 Stylized Facts About Northern Greece

After the start of the global financial crisis in 2008 and a steep increase in unemployment, many people left Greece in search of jobs elsewhere in the EU. The exodus of young and educated people affected all regions of Greece (Table 1). In nothern Greece, all subregions lost population, including in the period 2017–2021. The shrinking of population continued into 2021, despite the fact that public finances stabilized and unemployment rates fell (European Central Bank, 2022a, 2022b, 2022c).

In relation to other regions in Greece in terms of the regional composition of GDP by market prices at NUTS1 level, the contribution of northern Greece (Voreia Ellada) has been the second largest, following Attiki (Fig. 1).

4.1 Agriculture in Northern Greece

Digitalization in agriculture is typically associated with digital technologies that include services, platforms, and applications which use information and communication technologies in order to raise productivity and agricultural production (Food and Agriculture Organization of the United Nations, 2023). Digital technologies should also help improve resilience and sustainability of agricultural production.

In April 2019, a Declaration of cooperation on a smart and sustainable digital future for European agriculture and rural areas was signed by 26 EU countries (European Commission, 2019a, 2019b, 2019c). The idea was to support a successful digitalization of agriculture and rural areas.

The EU's Common Agricultural Policy after 2020 envisages that the EU member states come up with their own national strategies adjusted to their needs, which

Table 1 Population by NUTS2 regions, 2017–2021

		2017	2018	2019	2020	2021
EL	**Greece**	**10,768,193**	**10,741,165**	**10,724,599**	**10,718,565**	**10,678,632**
EL3	**Attiki**	**3,773,559**	**3,756,453**	**3,742,235**	**3,738,901**	**3,736,737**
EL4	**Nisia Aigaiou, Kriti**	**1,174,757**	**1,185,513**	**1,200,055**	**1,213,532**	**1,213,769**
EL41	Voreio Aigaio	203,700	211,137	221,098	229,516	229,155
EL42	Notio Aigaio	338,383	340,870	344,027	347,512	347,848
EL43	Kriti	632,674	633,506	634,930	636,504	636,766
EL5	**Voreia Ellada**	**3,089,659**	**3,080,730**	**3,074,204**	**3,068,650**	**3,046,697**
EL51	Anatoliki Makedonia, Thraki	602,799	601,175	599,723	598,613	594,905
EL52	Kentriki Makedonia	1,880,122	1,875,996	1,873,777	1,872,102	1,858,755
EL53	Dytiki Makedonia	271,488	269,222	267,008	264,670	262,052
EL54	Ipeiros	335,250	334,337	333,696	333,265	330,985
EL6	**Kentriki Ellada**	**2,730,218**	**2,718,469**	**2,708,105**	**2,697,482**	**2,681,429**
EL61	Thessalia	725,874	722,065	718,640	715,115	709,808
EL62	Ionia Nisia	205,431	204,562	203,869	203,149	202,371
EL63	Dytiki Ellada	663,970	659,470	655,189	651,065	646,670
EL64	Sterea Ellada	555,761	555,623	555,960	556,002	553,235

Source Eurostat (2022)

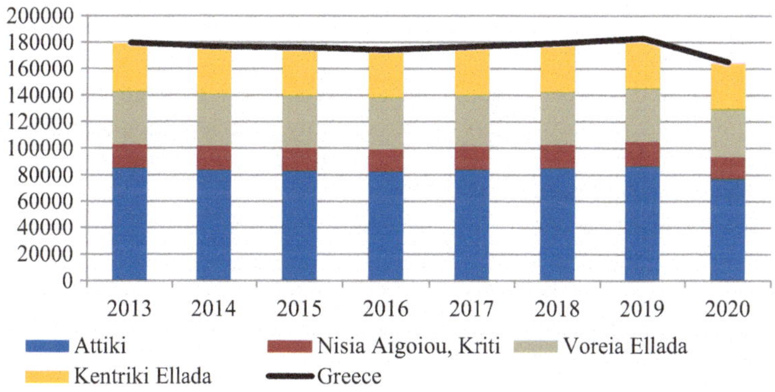

Fig. 1 Regional composition of GDP by market prices, million euros. *Source* Eurostat (2022)

includes the digitalization of farming (European Commission, 2022e). According to the Second Pillar of the Common Agricultural Policy and the Rural Development Program, EU member states manage nationally or regionally multi-annual and co-funded programs within the framework of EU funding (European Commission, 2021). The idea is that projects that link regionally dynamic sectors such as tourism, agriculture, food industries, and cultural industries can help alleviate economic and social divides.

EU structural funds are the key financing option to support public investment, not just in digitalization and bringing internet to every remote area, but also to ensure local authorities have the capacities to push for regional development and investments (European Commission, 2022f). One of the changes in the period of 2020–2027 is to reinforce support for rural areas in order to make necessary structural changes so that they can achieve the objectives of the Digital Transition Pact and the European Green Deal (European Parliament, 2022).

The "digital transformation of Greek agriculture" project aims to invest in technological infrastructure, provide services to end users, and form an integrated technological infrastructure that combines modern technologies, valid data, and scientific knowledge with a structured and adaptable system suitable to different needs of producers, agricultural consultants and businesses (European Commission, 2022g).

Agriculture is an important sector in Greece in terms of its exports (European Central Bank, 2022a, 2022b, 2022c). It employs about 450,000 people, approximately 12% of the total labor force (European Commission, 2022h). Enhancing competitiveness in agriculture by overcoming its structural issues is a key challenge. There are about 700,000 farms of around 7.7 ha on average. Farms are largely small-sized and family-owned and their number continues to decline. An important percentage of the agricultural area in Greece is facing natural or other specific constraints, being suitable for sheep and goat farming. The share of young farmers in Greece is 3.7%, one of the lowest shares in the EU where the average is 5.1% (European Commission, 2022h).

Greece has to modernize and improve low productivity industries and sectors (Ministry of Development and Investment, 2018). The country should increase its participation in global value chains as it has exported only about 50% of intermediate goods, which was below some other EU countries. Through the use of new technologies in the primary sectors of the economy, such as agriculture, the idea is to increase production, increase the variety of products, and improve the quality of production (European Commission, 2022h).

In 2020, the first year of Covid-19 pandemic, the data for northern Greece show the reduction in arable land and the reduction of permanent crops (Fig. 2).

Northern Greece contributes around 40% to the regional composition of output for agricultural industry, about 5% points less than central Greece (Kentriki Ellada), while Attiki, comprising the large Athens area, contributes only around 2.5% (Fig. 3).[1]

---

[1] As of 5 January 2023, the last available data for Greece by regions at NUTS2 level in regional economic accounts in the Eurostat's database was for the year 2018.

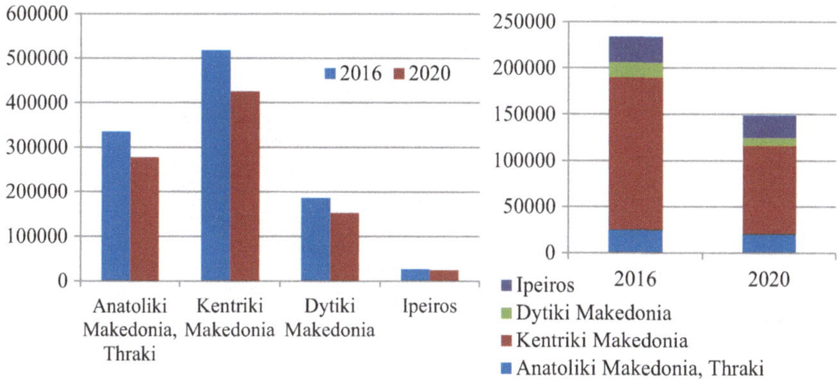

Fig. 2 Arable land (left) and permanent crops (right), hectares, in northern Greece. *Source* Eurostat (2023)

	2018
Greece	11475.72
Attiki	282.12
Nisia Aigiaou, Kriti	1424.53
Voreia Ellada	4578.96
Kentriki Ellada	5190.11

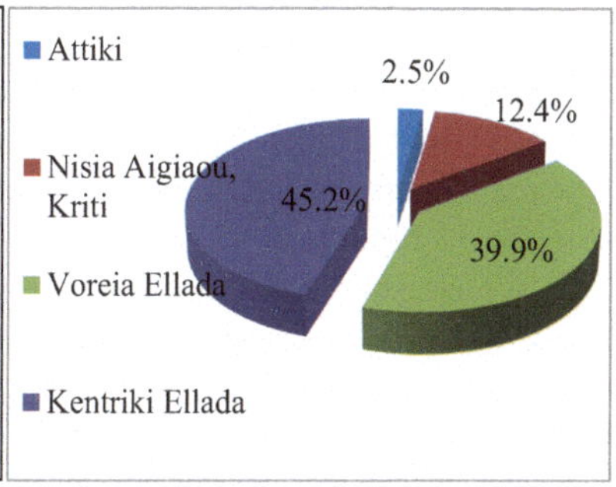

Fig. 3 Output for agricultural industry in 2018 in Greece in million euros (left) and as percentage by NUTS1 regions (right). *Source* Eurostat (2023)

Data for the subregional composition of the agricultural industry in Northern Greece shows that the highest contribution has been recorded in Kentriki Makedonia where the second largest city in Greece, Thessaloniki, is located. The region of Kentriki Makedonia contributes more than 50% of all output for agricultural industry in northern Greece (Fig. 4).

According to the 2014–2022 Rural Development Program for Greece, the digitization actions are the improvement plans for investments in smart agriculture, training, and agricultural advice to familiarize producers with new digital technologies, and broadband to rural areas (European Commission, 2021). More than 83 million euros were earmarked to empower about 10% of population with improved services/infrastructure in information and communication technologies so as to enhance social inclusion and local development (European Commission, 2022a).

Digital solutions are increasingly used across different administrative and economic sectors, fueling the demand for digital skills. According to the European Commission, in the future, these skills will be required for 9 out of 10 jobs, while 44%

	2018
Voreia Ellada	4578.96
Anatoliki Makedonia, Thraki	911.03
Kentriki Makedonia	2560.51
Dytiki Makedonia	583.23
Ipeiros	524.19

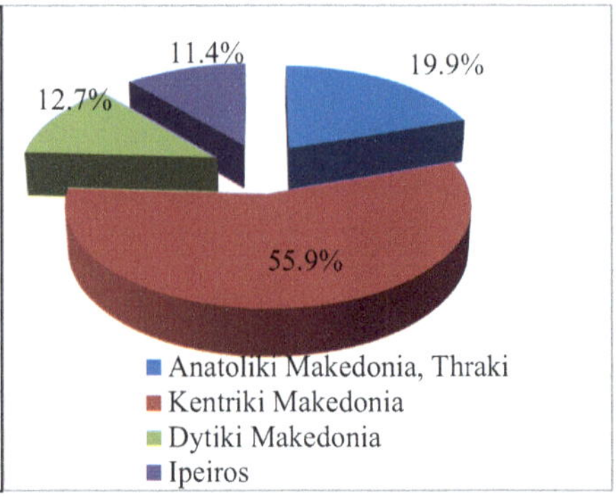

Fig. 4 Output for agricultural industry in 2018 in northern Greece, in million euros (left) and as percentage by NUTS2 regions (right). *Source* Eurostat (2023)

of the EU population do not have any basic digital skills (European Commission, 2022a).

Greece plans to use Copernicus, Europe's earth-monitoring system to maximize the potential of smart farming by gathering data from the Earth observation satellite systems of the Copernicus program and from the 6,500 earth stations that will be installed in the 13 regions of the country in three phases (European Commission, 2018). This project should cover about half of the arable land in Greece, about 15 million acres in 13 regions, and 20 of the country's most exported crops, including cotton, grain, rice, cotton, olive, vines, and citrus (European Commission, 2018). By collecting data from the earth stations such as temperature on air, water, and soil will be sorted in a data warehouse and farmers will be receiving warnings on extreme weather and personalized information on fertilization, irrigation, and plant protection.

The European Commission approved this plan as they see digitalization of agriculture and precision farming as a tool to improve the competitiveness and environmental sustainability of the European agricultural production (European Commission, 2018).

4.2 Tourism

Early works on information technology and tourism focused on many aspects of this relation, including the nature of tourism as an information business (Werthner & Klein, 1999). Never before was tourism influenced by technology and internet to the extent as it is today. Tourists and other travelers can now find accommodation online and they can compare and review options from different accommodation providers. Researchers have found that increasing mobile cellular and fixed broadband subscriptions have a significant positive effect on arrival of tourists (Lee et al., 2021).

Greece is among the most specialized countries within the accommodation subsector in the accommodation and food service sectors in the EU. A quarter of labor force in Greece is employed in tourism. In 2019, international tourist arrivals to Greece reached 34.2 million but fell to 10.1 million in 2020 due to the Covid-19 pandemic. It recovered to 18 million in 2021 as pandemic was still not finished in 2021 (Table 2). Northern Greece which was visited by more than 6 million tourists in a pre-Covid19 year 2019 recorded a fall to less than 2 million tourists but recovered in 2021 (Table 2). The numbers of tourist arrivals further improved in 2022 and 2023 and have reached pre-pandemic levels.

The European Commission has worked to boost the competitiveness of businesses in the tourism sector in the EU, create more jobs, and integrate them into global digital

Table 2 Tourist arrivals by NUTS2 regions in 2016–2021

	2016	2017	2018	2019	2020	2021
Greece	**24,996,038**	**27,211,268**	**33,585,639**	**34,202,053**	**10,104,236**	**18,015,347**
Attiki	**3,997,116**	**4,395,366**	**5,047,322**	**5,136,551**	**1,469,528**	**2,453,954**
Nisia Aigaiou, Kriti	9,900,727	10,791,142	14,108,272	14,408,935	3,808,137	7,807,653
Voreio Aigaio	431,453	486,084	535,501	557,265	133,585	251,181
Notio Aigaio	4,811,626	5,343,342	7,354,811	7,707,333	2,069,865	4,164,557
Kriti	4,657,648	4,961,716	6,217,960	6,144,337	1,604,687	3,391,915
Voreia Ellada	**5,024,491**	**5,359,904**	**6,263,922**	**6,411,711**	**1,954,515**	**3,235,148**
Anatoliki Makedonia, Thraki	809,952	871,177	936,711	958,180	312,003	474,032
Kentriki Makedonia	3,427,172	3,581,613	4,197,280	4,282,301	1,200,080	2,179,905
Dytiki Makedonia	140,477	156,471	165,213	173,584	67,048	85,021
Ipeiros	646,890	750,643	964,718	997,646	375,384	496,190
Kentriki Ellada	**6,073,704**	**6,664,856**	**8,166,123**	**8,244,856**	**2,872,056**	**4,518,592**
Thessalia	1,105,257	1,243,908	1,445,235	1,499,904	559,504	748,069
Ionia Nisia	2,095,733	2,345,186	2,951,396	2,986,597	791,583	1,704,056
Dytiki Ellada	664,512	722,951	801,929	806,706	318,665	425,408
Sterea Ellada	715,167	783,534	959,343	997,616	414,353	543,635
Peloponnisos	1,493,035	1,569,277	2,008,220	1,954,033	787,951	1,097,424

Source Eurostat (2023)

value chains (European Commission, 2022b). The idea was to empower tourism entrepreneurs and small and medium enterprises by strengthening their skill base and support the integration of tourism businesses in the digital value chains (European Commission, 2022b). In October 2022 the European Commission launched the EU Tourism Dashboard (European Commission, 2022c), a new tool to identify vulnerabilities and define strategies for improvement by both authorities and businesses. Tourism was one of the most affected sectors of the economy in regard to the Covid-19 pandemic by the measures put in place. In order to make tourism more resilient, the EU Tourism Dashboard enables tourism decision makers (on a regional or national regional level) to identify effective strategies to tackle certain vulnerabilities such as high seasonality and other dependencies.

The EU Tourism Dashboard provides visualizing statistical data in environmental impact, digitalization, socio-economic resilience, and basic tourism descriptors. Information indicators can be viewed via tourist destination at a country or regional level or subregional level and via an indicator map view. These indicators include the quality of bathing water, share of trips by train, internet speed at tourism destinations, and others (European Commission, 2022c).

Tourism in Greece is less resilient as tourist diversity is among the weakest in the EU. This is in line with the fact that high tourism seasonality makes its economic activity unbalanced and vulnerable to demand shocks. Data on tourist arrivals in 2020 and 2021 confirm this vulnerability to demand shocks (Table 2) while data on railway lines show some large reductions in total railway lines since 2009 (Table 3). With regard to northern Greece, there has been no significant improvement or addition of new railway lines since 2011 (Table 3).

Table 3 Total railway lines in Greece (kilometers)

	2011	2012	2013	2014	2015	2016	2017	2018	2019	2020
Attiki	238	183	198	198	200	200	200	200	200	200
Voreio Aigaio	:	:	:	0	0	0	0	0	0	0
Notio Aigaio	:	:	:	0	0	0	0	0	0	0
Kriti	:	:	:	0	0	0	0	0	0	0
Anatoliki Makedonia, Thraki	409	409	409	409	409	409	409	409	409	409
Kentriki Makedonia	539	539	539	539	539	539	539	539	539	539
Dytiki Makedonia	111	111	111	83	83	83	83	83	83	83
Ipeiros	0	0	0	0	0	0	0	0	0	0
Thessalia	275	269	269	270	270	270	270	270	270	270
Ionia Nisia	0	0	0	0	0	0	0	0	0	0
Dytiki Ellada	266	212	213	213	213	213	213	213	213	245
Sterea Ellada	274	274	274	274	274	274	274	327	314	314
Peloponnisos	442	251	252	252	252	252	252	252	252	285

Source Eurostat (2023)

Greek tourism destinations are digitally lagging according to the European Commission's EU Tourism Dashboard (European Commission, 2022d). Greece ranks low in the "share of trips by train" indicator that measures the relative importance of sustainable means of transportation within a tourism destination (European Commission, 2022c). In regard to train coverage of Greece, the latest data shows that since 2011 the total railways lines in Greece have fallen in most areas.

Another important element, Greece's average internet speed at tourism destinations is among the EU's lowest at 47.8 Mb/s. Not only that there is a lower level of internet access in rural areas compared to urban areas, the average internet speed is also low. Moreover, in regard to using social media to advertise tourism opportunities, only one-third of enterprises in tourism in Greece actively use it (European Commission, 2022d).

5 Economic and Social Case for Digitalization in Northern Greece

Greece is slowly emerging from a decade-long debt crisis that started in 2008. After years of contraction and stagnation, the economy grew only modestly from 2017 to 2019. GDP growth was projected to exceed 2% in 2020 (European Commission, 2019a, 2019b, 2019c) as the new government elected in July 2019 promised to follow pro-growth policies. However, the outbreak of Covid-19 and the renewed migrant crisis negatively affected growth projections for 2020 and 2021. Moreover, in 2022 the war in Ukraine, together with inflation reaching record highs and energy crisis all strained macroeconomic projections. The uncertainty continued in 2023.

Greece recorded the highest rate of unemployment in rural areas during 2013–2017, as more than one-fifth of the active population (between 15 and 64 years old) were unemployed. The percentage of unemployed has been falling since the height of the crisis, but it is still relatively high. The percentage of unemployed people in northern Greece has fallen in recent years but remained at double digits (Table 4).

The concentration of economic and social activity in a wealthier region such as Attiki can exacerbate income disparities between the populations of regions, small

Table 4 Percentage of unemployed from 15 to 74 years old, northern Greece

	2012	2013	2014	2015	2016	2017	2018	2019	2020	2021
EL5 Voreia Ellada	**25.5**	**29.3**	**27.5**	**25.8**	**24.8**	**23.0**	**20.3**	**19.1**	**18.2**	**16.8**
EL51 Anatoliki Makedonia, Thraki	22.9	26.8	24.3	23.4	22.8	19.5	16.0	16.2	17.2	18.5
EL52 Kentriki Makedonia	26.2	30.2	28.7	26.0	24.5	22.9	20.7	19.6	18.4	16.1
EL53 Dytiki Makedonia	29.7	31.6	27.6	30.8	31.3	29.1	27.0	24.6	19.7	19.8
EL54 Ipeiros	22.6	27.4	26.8	24.6	24.4	24.8	20.1	16.4	17.9	15.1

Source Eurostat (2023)

cities, and rural areas. When comparing northern Greece with Attiki, it is clear that the percentage of total population at risk of poverty and social exclusion is considerably higher in northern Greece (Table 5).

In addition to higher rates of unemployment, there is also a lower level of net income of households in northern Greece (Fig. 5).

Looking at the region of northern Greece, the largest net income of households is in Central Macedonia (Kentriki Makedonia), which is consistent with the fact that Thessaloniki, the second largest city in Greece is located in that region (Fig. 6).

Another piece of data that speaks in favor of the economic and social case for further digitalization is data on unemployment and net income of households. That data confirm the fact that the percentage of households whose housing cost burden is over 60% of their disposable income, is considerably higher in Greece compared to the average of the EU for both, cities and rural areas (Fig. 7).

Table 5 Percentage of total population at risk of poverty or social exclusion in northern Greece compared to Attiki

	2018	2019	2020	2021
EL5 Vorreia Ellada	33.5	34.0	33.5	35.3
EL51 Anatoliki Makedonia, Thraki	33.5	34.0	33.5	35.3
EL52 Kentriki Makedonia	29.3	30.6	29.5	33.7
EL 53 Dytiki Makedonia	36.5	33.6	32.8	28.9
EL 54 Ipeiros	31.1	26.8	26.2	28.0
EL3 Attiki	27.0	24.5	21.8	21.6

Source Eurostat (2023)

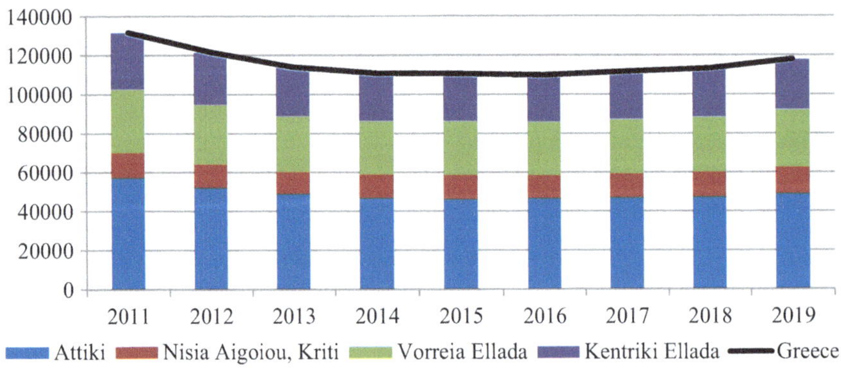

Fig. 5 Net income of households in Greece by NUTS1 regions, million euros *Source* Eurostat (2023)

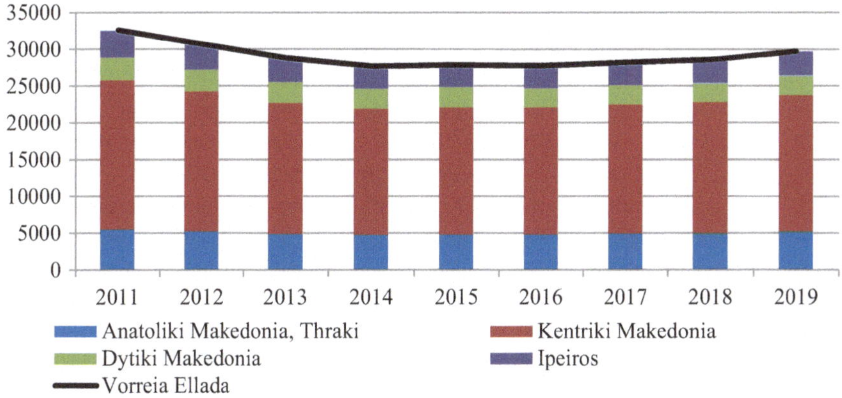

Fig. 6 Net income of households in northern Greece, million euros. *Source* Eurostat (2023)

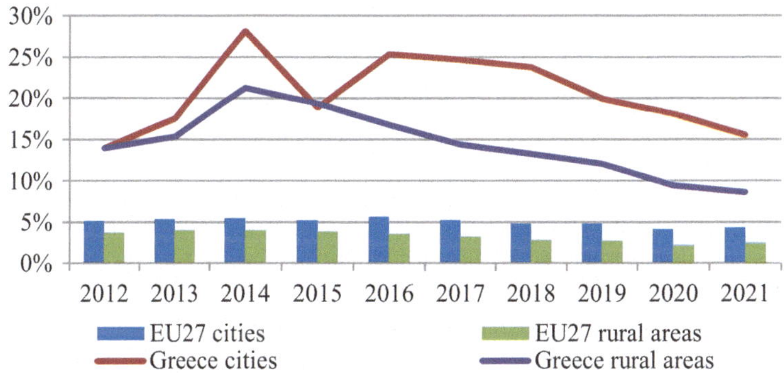

Fig. 7 Percentage of households with housing cost burden over 60% of disposable household income, cities versus rural areas. *Source* Eurostat (2023)

6 Limits of Digitalization in Reducing Economic and Social Divide

6.1 Access, Skills, and Ability of People to Use Digitalization for Their Own Objectives

The interaction between technology and people covers a wide range of areas, including social sustainability, future work, economical and societal changes, urban planning, environmental protection, and other areas in private and public sectors. In this regard, digitalization has been transforming the world not only in terms of socializing, but also in terms of working and new business models. Digitalization is typically understood as the adoption or increase in the use of digital or computer technology by an organization, industry, country, etc. and it e "encompasses a wide range of new applications of information technology in business models and products that are transforming the economy and social interactions" (EUR Lex, 2010). From the economic and social point of view in regard to bridging the economic and social divide, digitalization can increase cost-efficiency, productivity, and sustainability of economic recovery. Governments can help in this respect by providing companies, farms and citizens with services are that are more people-centered, cost-effective, and sustainable (European Commission, 2019a, 2019b, 2019c). Digital technologies can be enablers for advancement and increasing efficiencies in the existing systems as they can expand access to information and services and improve data collection and analysis.

Potential benefits of digitalization are high. One of the benefits is that by digitizing information-intensive processes, costs can be cut by up to 90% (Marcovitch & Willmot, 2014). However, people need skills to use digital tools (Paidousi & Efstratoglou, 2020). They also need access to internet. There is a significant difference between rural and urban areas in this respect. Greece lags behind the average of the EU in both indicators. Access to internet in rural areas in Greece lags behind the rural areas in the EU27 (Fig. 8). There is a difference of about 15% between access to internet in households in cities compared to households in rural areas in 2022 in Greece.

Looking at the composition of digital skills in 2021, there is a lower percentage of individuals with above basic digital skills in Greece (22%) compared to the average EU (27%). On the other hand, Greece has a higher percentage of individuals with basic overall digital skills (31%) compared to the average of the EU (Fig. 9).

The limitation of digitalization and digital technologies is that they are not the solution to all economic and social problems in Greece. The government of Greece has been trying to remedy the situation with various projects co-financed by the EU although, according to some international organizations, the projects of digital transformation in Greece face various challenges, including institutional capacities, governance, and procurement (OECD, 2022).

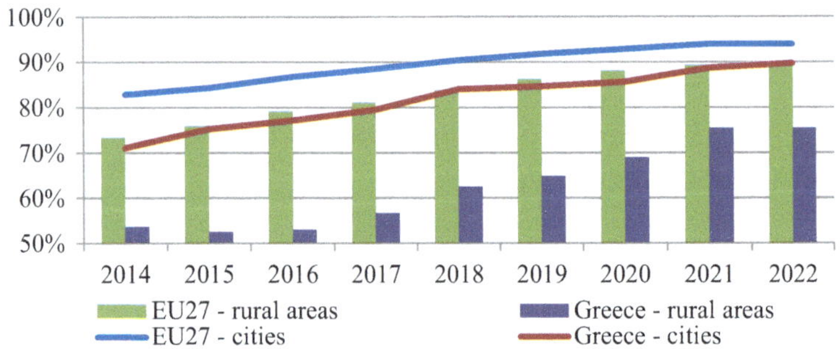

Fig. 8 Percentage of households with access to internet in cities and rural areas, Greece vis-à-vis average of the EU27. *Source* Eurostat (2023)

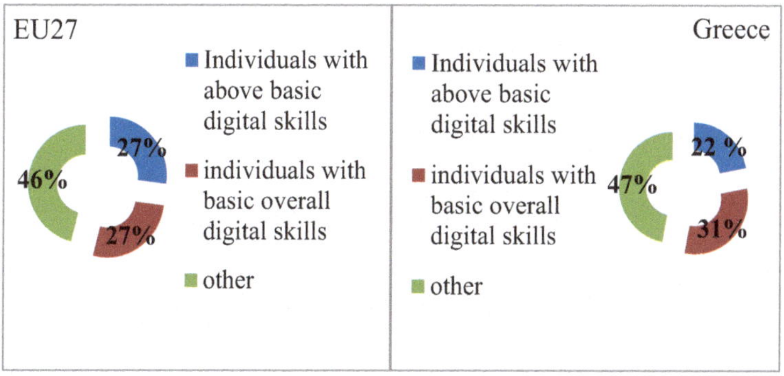

Fig. 9 Composition of digital skills in 2021, Greece vis-à-vis average of the EU27. *Source* Eurostat (2023)

The Digital Transformation Strategy for 2019–2023 (Ministry of Digital Governance, 2019) set the guide to digital transformation in the public sector of Greece in order to reduce the fragmentation of eGovernment across different areas and to modernize the public administration so as to deliver better service to citizens. The idea is to reduce the amount of physical documents and sending them to various government bodies while promoting the use of digital data between government bodies themselves and in interaction with citizens as well. The aim is to service citizens via smartphones, computers and via phone calls (for those who don't have the first two options) and finally by physical presence.

The Digital Transformation Strategy for 2020–2025 of Greece from 2022 is a strategic document that does not only set priorities for the digital transformation of the country, but to also aims to develop the digital skills at all levels and ages (European Commission, 2022b). Still, in regard to households' use of technology in their interaction with public authorities, there are reports that public authorities face certain challenges in terms of quantity and quality of staff (OECD, 2020).

There is room for improvement in some aspects of digitalization and the application of e-government. For instance, in regard to interactions with public authorities, there are large differences between rural and urban areas in Greece compared to the average of the EU. In 2021, on average 15% of individuals in cities and 18% in rural areas in the EU did not use internet for sending filled forms to public authorities although they had to submit them. That percentage was considerably higher in Greece, standing at 34% and 41%, respectively (Fig. 10).

Difficulties in developing necessary infrastructures in certain regions and the extent of the remote territories to be covered, impact on broadband coverage in rural areas across Greece (European Commission, 2021). Still, the access to internet at the level of NUTS2 regions has been steadily increasing in all regions across Greece (Fig. 11). In some regions, especially in some islands and mountainous areas, there are still internet infrastructure problems, although that has improved, especially in Nisia Aigoiou, Kriti, and Voreia Ellada. In Atikki, the wealthiest region, the share

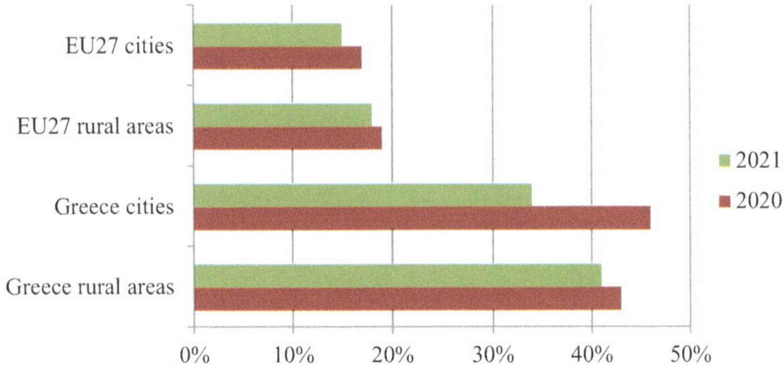

Fig. 10 Percentage of individuals not using internet for sending filled forms to public authorities although they had to submit official forms. *Source* Eurostat (2023)

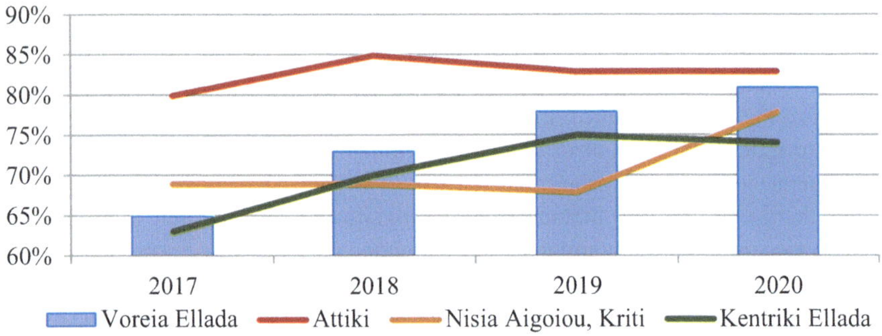

Fig. 11 Percentage of households with broadband access by region at NUTS2 level in Greece. *Source* Eurostat (2023)

of households with broadband access has been the highest, reaching 83% in 2020 (Fig. 11).

The region of northern Greece has made significant improvements in regard to information and communication technologies since 2016, as 80% of households had broadband access in 2020 (Fig. 11). Still, that didn't change the economic and social divides between the regions. For example, in 2021, in the area of Kentriki Makedonia in northern Greece, the percentage of the population at risk of poverty or social exclusion was 33.7%, while in Attiki that percentage was only 21.6% in 2021.

Technology can help regions use resources more effectively, not only in economic sectors such as agriculture and tourism, but in regard to citizens directly through the government services delivered via digital channels. However, most regions in Greece lag behind Attiki, the wealthiest region. For example, in 2021 in Northern Greece, 51% of individuals were in internet interaction with public authorities which was 17% points lower compared to Attiki (Fig. 12).

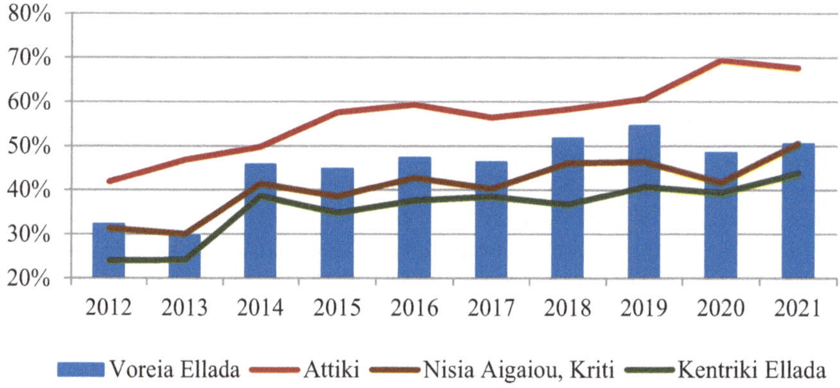

Fig. 12 Percentage of individuals in internet interaction with public authorities, by region at NUTS2 level in Greece. *Source* Eurostat (2023)

Digitalization of public services in Greece received a strong push with the Covid-19 pandemic following physical restrictions and lockdowns (Karamalis & Vasilopoulos, 2020). Still, Greece lags behind the average of the EU in this respect, although there has been an improvement in some aspects despite the heterogenity between regions. In 2021, 31.6% of individuals in Northern Greece submitted completed forms to authorities, while that share was 50.7% in Attiki (Fig. 13). The government of Greece has worked on e-governance, making it possible for people to approach various public authorities online in order to submit and exchange official documents such as certificates, various forms, and similar.

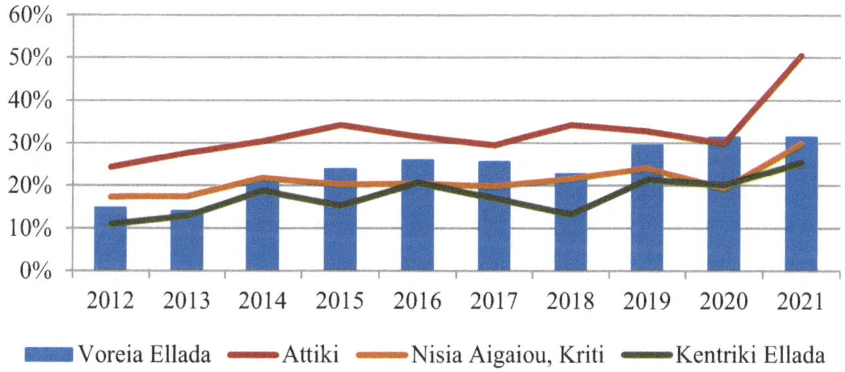

Fig. 13 Percentage of individuals who submitted completed forms to authorities online, by region at NUTS2 level in Greece. *Source* Eurostat (2023)

6.2 Agriculture

According to the Food and Agriculture Organization of the United Nations (FAO), digital technologies can have a positive impact on productivity and agricultural production, improving resilience of rural communities by integrating small producers into local, regional, and global markets and using e-commerce to reach consumers in various markets (Food and Agriculture Organization of the United Nations, 2023). In order to make the economic recovery more sustainable, Greece has to modernize low productivity industries and sectors (OECD, 2020) and increase its participation in global value chains as it currently exports only about 50% of intermediate goods, which is below some other EU countries (European Commission, 2020).

Through the use of new technologies in agriculture, the idea is to ensure production, the variety of products and improve the quality of production. According to the 2014–2022 Rural Development Program for Greece, investments are planned in smart agriculture, training, and agricultural advice about new digital technologies, and broadband to rural areas as more than half of Greece's rural population is expected to be covered by a local development strategy. About 10% of the rural population should benefit from improved services and information and communication infrastructure (European Commission, 2021). The European Commission found in 2019 that "deep institutional and structural reforms initiated in recent years to modernize the economy and the state, require many years of sustained implementation for their impact to fully unfold" (European Commission, 2019a, 2019b, 2019c).

Digitalization offers the potential in the form of access to internet and digital skills that can help agriculture and other related economic sectors. For instance, by using geospatial, ground sensor data, and other data in agricultural sector, digital technologies can improve economic and technical performance. In addition, it can improve sustainability in line with the environmental objectives of the EU (Garske et al., 2021).

However, digitalization is not a panacea for all ills. The national and regional authorities in Greece cannot turn to technology to alleviate some deeper problems such as outflow of population in rural areas, especially younger people, and their emigration to wealthier EU and other countries. The fact is that access to internet in northern Greece has been consistently increasing since 2011, but net national income has fallen in the same period (Fig. 14). There isn't a positive correlation between net national income and access to internet.

Therefore, better access to internet and better digital skills cannot fully alleviate deeper structural problems and bridge economic and social divides, including large income disparities between regions and between cities and rural areas in Greece. That disparity and other macro-economic challenges have to be tackled at the strategic and macro-economic level. In agriculture that implies support for young farmers and additional aid for small and medium farms, especially if they are in organic farming. Moreover, there is an issue of the fragmentation of agricultural land (National Bank of Greece, 2015) which leads to the question how viable the use of certain technologies in farming is, especially if there is a high cost associated with the use of technology.

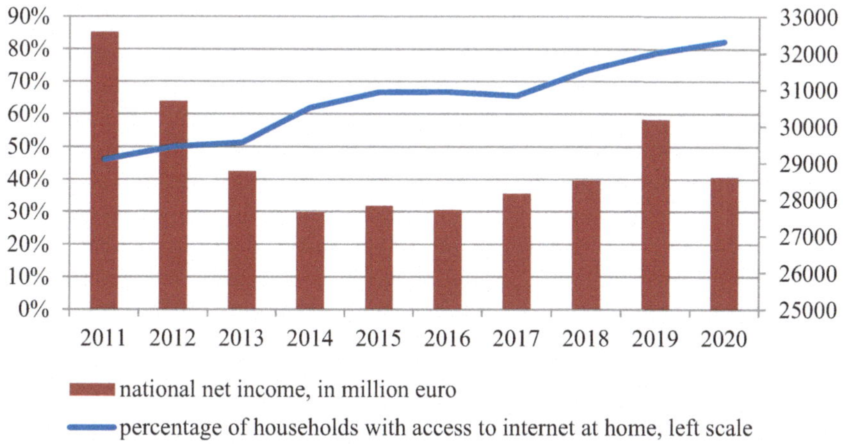

Fig. 14 Northern Greece—net national income and access to internet. *Source* Eurostat (2023)

Another issue is agri-food and its efficient promotion and branding in digital marketing. For example, Greek olive oil that is exported to Italy where, if blended with other olive oil, may be marketed as Italian branded olive oil.

Digital technologies can provide efficiency gains and resource savings, can enable more accurate measurements of emissions and environmental impacts, and that digitalization can support sustainable agriculture, but that there are limitations of what digitalization can do. In order to reduce the economic and social gap between the regions, deployment of relevant technologies should be accompanied by political, institutional, and economic factors.

In addition to the above-mentioned objective reasons about limits of technology and digitalization to bridge the economic and social divide, there are also subjective reasons. For instance, new approaches to farming by using technology might not be in line with the mentality of some Greek farmers due to the fact that most farmers are older in small family farms. They might be reluctant to use technology. Or they may have difficulties to follow technological advances; and in addition, they may prefer tradition in farming. This is in line with the fact that there is a low share of young farmers, while the majority is elderly who trust their own, proven cultivation practices. The remedy to these issues cannot be an improved access to internet and better digital skills, despite the fact that farmers may not be fully aware of advantages of the adoption of technology and smart farming.

6.3 Tourism

There are also limits to what access to internet and digital skills can do in tourism. If a distant area in a region does not have any possible particular tourist attraction or if there is no suitable accommodation facility, local access to internet and adequate skills cannot help much in this respect. Moreover, if there are some tourist attractions with the possibility of leisure, holiday, or health-related possibilities, if they are not adequately advertised on social media and/or traditional media, access to internet or digital skills can't help improve economic or social landscape of that area.

The finding is that despite the fact that access to broadband has been rising and digital skills are improving in northern Greece while e-government services are more available and user-friendly, all that did not change the economic and social divide vis-à-vis some wealthier regions in Greece. The access to internet has been consistently increasing since 2011, but economic growth didn't follow that dynamic (Fig. 15). There isn't a positive correlation between the two variables. There are some objective and subjective reasons why digitalization in tourism cannot offset some deeper structural and other problems.

Although rural areas in northern Greece can be attractive locations for leisure, tourism, work, and retirement, it remains unclear if all possible tourist attractions such ski resorts, thermal baths, lake resorts, and similar are taking the advantage of digital marketing and being promoted actively on social media and various digital platforms. Some authors have established that Greece has not fully embraced e-commerce in the tourism context (Buhalis, 2003). Access to internet is just a pre-condition for digital marketing, but it is not clear to what extent various providers of tourism-related services have prepared their development plans to set the basis for the digital transformation (Accenture & INSETE, 2021).

During the Covid-19 pandemic, the Ministry of Tourism created a digital portal to promote Greece as a tourist destination by posting videos, virtual guided tours etc. The importance of digital marketing in Greece has been extensively researched (Ziakis & Vlachopoulou, 2020), including the online presence of Thessaloniki (Papadakis & Tsakirakis, 2019). Thessaloniki is the second largest city in Greece

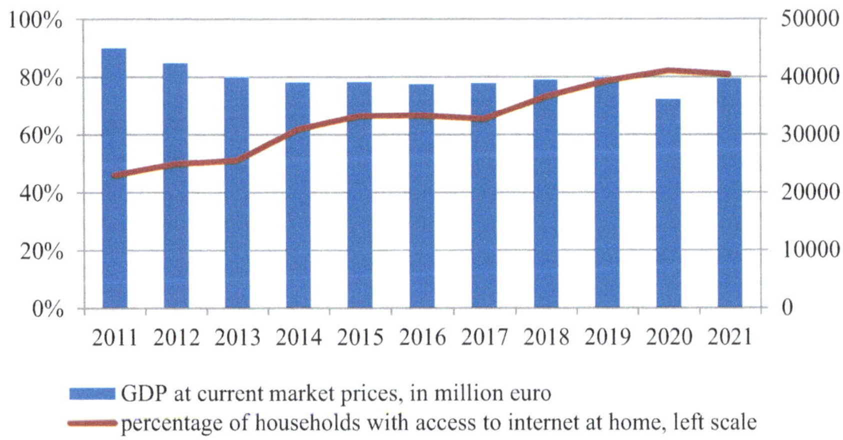

Fig. 15 Northern Greece—Gross Domestic Product (GDP) and access to internet. *Source* Eurostat (2023)

with rich history and culture. Still, for foreigners traveling outside of Thessaloniki, there is not much information about various tourist possibilities. Access to internet and digital skills cannot help in situations when there is a lack of digital or other marketing and advertising, even more so when the official authorities do not provide adequate information information online.

Although digitalization in terms of internet access and digital skills offers an opportunity to reduce economic and social divides, a broader and aggregate approach would help address investment, productivity, and sustainability challenges in areas such as northern Greece. Northern Greece needs high priority investments not only in digital infrastructures but in other infrastructures as well. For instance, from a tourist point of view, train accessibility to certain areas in northern Greece is not at a particularly high level, as confirmed by the EU Tourist Dashboard. Moreover, even in cities, there might be problems with transportation. Such an example is Thessaloniki, the second largest city in Greece where travelers have to rely on buses only because there is no metro, tram, or subway although, the subway has been in the process of being built for the last two decades (GTP Headlines, 2020).

7 Conclusions

Social sustainability, economic sustainability, and environmental sustainability are closely related. They all imply managing both positive and negative impacts of organizations, systems, processes, and activities on people and social life. Regions can capitalize on their strengths and contribute significantly to economic growth. One possibility is to utilize digital technology by having access to better, faster, and cheaper internet. However, despite the fact that access to broadband has been rising constantly and digital skills are improving in rural and remote areas, including in northern Greece, the economic and social divide between northern Greece and other regions in Greece has not been reduced over the last decade. There are objective and subjective reasons why further digitalization in agriculture and tourism cannot offset some deeper structural and other economic issues.

Improving access to internet and focusing on better digital skills is not enough. Technology and associated knowledge can transform tourism and agriculture (and agri-food systems) but a strong focus should be on people and how they can mobilize change for sustainable futures. Digitalization can bring cost efficiency in many economic aspects, including by delivering online services via public authorities. Digitalization and broadband internet access can offer new economic and social opportunities not only to businesses, hotels, schools, and other service providers in rural areas but to agriculture as well. Companies operating in agriculture could adapt their strategies in production and value chains considering technological advancements in digital areas. This is important in order to optimize resources and increase production. The government of Greece has put an additional effort into digitalization which could boost productivity and participation of small and medium farms in agricultural value chains. This could also help tourism. Still, public support should also include other initiatives, such as investing in other infrastructures, including transportation infrastructures. Northern Greece needs large investments in many areas, including in public services, particularly hospitals, schools, and similar.

The limitation of this research is that the data provided by Eurostat's surveys is limited to social information indicators about the access to technology, digital skills, and how people apply available digital options. In order to understand the attitude of people in regard to digitalization in certain sectors such as agriculture and tourism, additional and specific questions should be asked. Answers to those questions could clarify subjective reasons about people's approach to technology in those sectors. Future research could therefore benefit from focusing on behavioral questions with respect to digitalization in agriculture and tourism in northern Greece.

References

Accenture & INSETE. (2021). *Digital transformation of Greek tourism.* Retrieved May 15, 2022, from https://insete.gr/blog_news/press-release-27-05-2021-insete-digital-transformation-of-greek-tourism/?lang=en

Ballet, J., Bazin D., & Mahieu, F. R. (2020). A policy framework for social sustainability: Social cohesion, equity and safety. *Wiley, Sustainable Development, 28*(5), 1388–1394. Retrieved January 22, 2023, from https://doi.org/10.1002/sd.2092

Bollman, R. D. (1999). Human capital and rural development. What are the linkages? Statistics Canada. Agriculture Division. *AgEconSearch: Working Paper, 39,* 1–36. Retrieved February 19, 2023, from https://www150.statcan.gc.ca/n1/en/pub/21-601-m/21-601-m1999039-eng.pdf?st=Xzy5F2Ai

Buhalis, D. (2003). *eTourism developments in Greece.* Retrieved June 8, 2022, from https://www.researchgate.net/publication/228855294_eTourism_Developmentsin_Greece

Council of Europe and European Commission. (2020). *Social inclusion, digitalisation and young people.* Retrieved October 16, 2022, from https://pjp-eu.coe.int/documents/42128013/47261953/053120+Study+on+SID+Web.pdf/0057379c-2180-dd3e-7537-71c468f3cf9d

Cuthill, M. (2010). Strengthening the 'social' in sustainable development: Developing a conceptual framework for social sustainability in a rapid urban growth region in Australia. *Wiley, Sustainable Development, 18*(6), 362–373.

Dempsey, N., et al. (2011). The social dimension of sustainable development: Defining urban social sustainability. *Wiley, Sustainable Development, 19*(5), 289–300.

EUR-Lex. Access to European Union Law. (2010). *Communication from the commission to the European parliament, the council, the European economic and social committee and the committee of the regions. A digital agenda for Europe.* Retrieved May 5, 2021, from https://eur-lex.europa.eu/legal-content/en/ALL/?uri=CELEX%3A52010DC0245

Euronews. (2019). *Rural Greece enjoys the benefits as internet isolation comes to an end.* Retrieved September 15, 2022, from https://www.euronews.com/my-europe/2019/11/18/rural-greece-enjoys-the-benefits-as-internet-isolation-comes-to-an-end

European Central Bank. (2018). *Digitalisation and its impact on the economy: Insights from a survey of large companies.* Retrieved March 3, 2022, from https://www.ecb.europa.eu/pub/economic-bulletin/focus/2018/html/ecb.ebbox201807_04.en.html

European Central Bank. (2022a). *Statistical data warehouse—Quick view.* Retrieved October 9, 2022, from https://sdw.ecb.europa.eu/quickview.do?SERIES_KEY=139.AME.A.GRC.1.0.0.0.ZUTN&periodSortOrder=ASC

European Central Bank. (2022b). *Statistical data warehouse*. Retrieved November 15, 2022, from https://sdw.ecb.europa.eu/browse.do?node=bbn4628

European Central Bank. (2022c). *Statistical data warehouse—Quick view*. Retrieved October 21, 2022, from https://sdw.ecb.europa.eu/quickview.do;jsessionid=899C931AA75D72F32BC97CB407A4DB3C?SERIES_KEY=118.DD.A.GR.EXPMS.5YR.4F_N

European Commission. (2018). *Copernikus*. Retrieved November 15, 2022, from https://www.copernicus.eu/sites/default/files/2018-10/copernicus4regions.pdf

European Commission. (2019a). *Shaping Europe's digital future. EU member states join forces on digitalisation for European agriculture and rural areas*. Retrieved August 8, 2022, from https://digital-strategy.ec.europa.eu/en/news/eu-member-states-join-forces-digitalisation-european-agriculture-and-rural-areas

European Commission. (2019b). *Wik Consult. Monitoring progress in national initiatives on digitising industry. Country report. Greece*. Retrieved August 15, 2022, from https://ec.europa.eu//information_society/newsroom/image/document/2019-32/country_report_-_greece_-_final_2019_0D30BA6D-A5FB-5608-9F34E267E7515DDE_61207.pdf

European Commission. (2019c). *Digital government factsheet 2019, Greece*. Retrieved May 5, 2022, from https://joinup.ec.europa.eu/sites/default/files/inline-files/Digital_Government_Factsheets_Greece_2019.pdf

European Commission. (2020). *Shaping Europe's digital future*. Retrieved June 8, 2021, from https://ec.europa.eu/info/strategy/priorities-2019-2024/europe-fit-digital-age/shaping-europe-digital-future_en

European Commission. (2021). *Factsheet on 2014–2022 rural development programme for Greece*. Retrieved September 30, 2022, from https://agriculture.ec.europa.eu/system/files/2022-02/rdp-factsheet-greece_en_0.pdf

European Commission. (2022a). *Shaping Europe's digital future. Digital skills and jobs*. Retrieved September 5, 2022, from https://digital-strategy.ec.europa.eu/en/policies/digital-skills-and-jobs

European Commission. (2022b). *Digital skills & jobs platforms. Greece—Digital transformation strategy for 2020–2025*. Retrieved December 22, 2022 from https://digital-skills-jobs.europa.eu/en/actions/national-initiatives/national-strategies/greece-digital-transformation-strategy-2020-2025

European Commission. (2022c). *Digital transformation of EU tourism*. Retrieved July 7, 2022, from https://single-market-economy.ec.europa.eu/sectors/tourism/support-business/digital_en

European Commission. (2022d). *EU Tourism dashboard*. Retrieved December 12, 2022 from https://tourism-dashboard.ec.europa.eu/destination?lng=en&ctx=tourism&ts=TOURISM&pil=level-indicator&is=TOURISM&tl=0&tu=EL&cl=tourism&clc=environmental-impact&fvs=false

European Commission. (2022e). *Agriculture and rural development. The new common agricultural policy: 2023–27*. Retrieved December 15, 2022, from https://agriculture.ec.europa.eu/common-agricultural-policy/cap-overview/new-cap-2023-27_en

European Commission. (2022f). *Agriculture and rural development. Key policy objectives of the new CAP*. Retrieved December 15, 2022, from https://agriculture.ec.europa.eu/common-agricultural-policy/cap-overview/new-cap-2023-27/key-policy-objectives-new-cap_en

European Commission. (2022g). *CAP strategic plans*. Retrieved December 24, 2022, from https://agriculture.ec.europa.eu/cap-my-country/cap-strategic-plans_en

European Commission. (2022h). *Documents relating to the approval of the CAP strategic plans*. Retrieved December 27, 2022, from https://agriculture.ec.europa.eu/cap-my-country/cap-strategic-plans/approved-csp-0_en?f%5B0%5D=document_country_document_country%3Ahttp%3A//publications.europa.eu/resource/authority/country/GRC

European Parliament. (2019). *Contribution to growth—European digital single market, delivering improved rights for European citizens and businesses*. Retrieved July 6, 2021, from https://www.europarl.europa.eu/RegData/etudes/STUD/2019/638395/IPOL_STU(2019)638395_EN.pdf

European Parliament. (2022). *Second pillar CAP*. Retrieved December 5, 2022, from https://www.europarl.europa.eu/ftu/pdf/en/FTU_3.2.6.pdf

Eurostat (2022). Database. General and Regional Statistics. Population and social conditions. Retrieved from https://ec.europa.eu/eurostat/data/database

Eurostat (2023). Database. General and Regional Statistics. Science, technology, digital society. Retrieved from https://ec.europa.eu/eurostat/data/database

Food and Agriculture Organization of the United Nations (FAO). (2023). *Science, technology and innovation*. Retrieved April 15, 2023, from https://www.fao.org/science-technology-and-innovation/science/

Gadanakis, Y., Bennett, R., Park, J., & Areal, F. (2015). Evaluating the sustainable intensification of arable farms. *Elsevier BV, Journal of Environmental Management, 150*, 288–298.

Garske, B., Bau, A., & Ekard, F. (2021). Digitalization and AI in European agriculture: A strategy for achieving climate and biodiversity targets? *Sustainability, 13*(9), 4652. https://doi.org/10.3390/su13094652

GTP Headlines. (2020). *Thessaloniki metro set for 2023 opening*. Retrieved November 9, 2022, from https://news.gtp.gr/2020/06/05/thessaloniki-metro-set-2023-opening/

Grybauskas, A., Stefanini, A., & Ghbakhloo, M. (2022). Social sustainability in the age of digitalization: A systematic literature Review on the social implications of industry 4.0. *Elsevier BV, Technology in Society, 70*(8), 101997. https://doi.org/10.1016/j.techsoc.2022.101997

Hujo, K., & Gaia, E. (2011). Social policy and poverty: An introduction. *Wiley, International Journal of Social Welfare, 20*(3), 230–239. https://doi.org/10.1111/j.1468-2397.2011.00786.x

Irajifar, L., Chen, H., Lak, A., et al. (2023). The nexus between digitalization and sustainability: A scientometrics analysis. *ScienceDirect, Society and Politics, 9*(5), e15172. https://doi.org/10.1016/j.heliyon.2023.e15172

Karamalis, P., & Vasilopoulos, A. (2020). *The digital transformation in public sector as a response to COVID-19 pandemic: The case of Greece*. Retrieved May 15, 2022, from https://www.academia.edu/44647444/The_digital_transformation_in_public_sector_as_a_response_to_COVID_19_pandemic_The_case_of_Greece

Karki, J., & Thapa, D. (2021). Exploring the link between digitalization and sustainable development: Research agendas. In *20th Conference on e-Business, e-Services and e-Society (I3E)*, Sep 2021, Galway, Ireland (pp. 330–341). https://doi.org/10.1007/978-3-030-85447-8_29

Lee, C. C., Chen, M. P., Wu, W., & Xing, W. (2021). The impacts of ICTs on tourism development: International evidence based on a panel quantile approach. *Inf Technol Tourism, 23*, 509–547. https://doi.org/10.1007/s40558-021-00215-4

Marcovitch, S., & Willmott P. (2014). *Accelerating the digitization of business processes. Mckinsey Digital*. Retrieved May 11, 2021, from https://www.mckinsey.com/business-functions/mckinsey-digital/our-insights/accelerating-the-digitization-of-business-processes

Massuga, F., Larson, M. A., Kuhl, M. R., & Dolivera, S. L. D. (2023). The influence of global governance on the sustainable performance of countries. *Springer Nature, Environment, Development and Sustainability*. https://doi.org/10.1007/s10668-023-03827-4

Meng, Y., Lu, Y., & Liang, X. (2023). Does Internet use alleviate the relative poverty of Chinese rural residents? A case from China. *Springer Nature, Environment, Development and Sustainability*. https://doi.org/10.1007/s10668-023-03531-3

Ministry of Development and Investment. (2018). A growth strategy for the future. Retrieved May 15, 2022 from https://www.mindev.gov.gr/wp-content/uploads/2018/09/Growth-Strategy.pdf

Ministry of Digital Governance. (2019). *Digital transformation strategy 2019–2023*. Retrieved November 21, 2022, from https://digitalstrategy.gov.gr/website/static/website/assets/Digital_Transformation_Strategy_2019.pdf

National Bank of Greece. (2015). *Sectoral report. Unlocking the potential of Greek agro-food industry*. Retrieved September 6, 2022, from https://www.nbg.gr/en/group/studies-and-economic-analysis/reports/kladiki-meleti--agrodiatrofikos-tomeas--dekemvrios-2015

Neckel, S. (2017). The sustainability society: A sociological perspective. *Culture, Culture, Practice & Europeanization, 2*(2), 46–52.

OECD. (2020). *Economic surveys. Greece. Overview*. Retrieved February 7, 2022, from https://web-archive.oecd.org/2020-07-22/559318-Greece-2020-OECD-economic-survey-Overview.pdf

OECD. (2022). *Digital transformation projects in Greece's public sector. Governance, procurement and implementation.* Retrieved December 27, 2022, from https://www.oecd.org/gov/digital-transformation-projects-in-greece-s-public-sector-33792fae-en.htm

Paidousi, C., & Efstratoglou, A. (2020). *Digital inclusion and human capital in Greece. Friedrich Ebert Stiftung.* Retrieved January 15, 2023, from https://athens.fes.de/publication/digital-inclusion-and-human-capital-in-greece

Papadakis, S., & Tsakirakis K. (2019). *The digital transformation of the tourism industry. The case of Thessaloniki online presence.* Retrieved June 9, 2022, from https://repository.ihu.edu.gr/xmlui/bitstream/handle/11544/29550/s.papadakis_k.tsakirakis_htmng_11-09-2017.pdf?sequence=1

Parviainen, P., Tihinen, M., Kääriäinen, J., & Teppola, S. (2017). Tackling the digitalization chalenge: How to benefit from digitalization in practice. *International Journal of Information Systems and Project Management, 9*(5), 63–77.

Xu, J., Yu, Y., Zhang, M., & Zhang, Y. Z. (2022). Impacts of digital transformation on eco-innovation and sustainable performance: Evidence from Chinese manufacturing companies. *Elsevier, Journal of Cleaner Production, 393*, 136278. https://doi.org/10.1016/j.jclepro.2023.136278

Werthner, H., & Klein, S. (1999). *Information technology and tourism: A challenging relationship.* Springer.

World Bank. (2023). *Social sustability in development. Meeting the challenges of 21st century. New frontiers of social policy series.* International Bank for Reconstruction and Development/The World Bank.

Ziakis, C., & Vlachopoulou, M. (2020). Digital marketing in tourism: Insights from Greece. Conference paper. In *XIV Balkan Conference on Operational Research (Hybrid BALCOR 2020)* at University of Macedonia, Thessaloniki, Greece. Retrieved August 5, 2022, from https://www.researchgate.net/publication/349297284_Digital_Marketing_in_Tourism_Insights_from_Greece

Readiness Assessment of EU Countries to Achieve the Smart Sustainable Development Goals Through the Digital Transformation of Local Government

Dimitris Papandreou, Patricia Ikouta Mazza, and Maria Mavri

Abstract The transition to the digital era has become imperative in the last decades, with the pandemic as a key accelerator, as it made the need for digital transformation and growth of the digital economy more urgent. Digital transformation is a process where, in terms of sustainability in a society that must adapt to new data, it is intensified through the adoption of all those innovations that come from the 4th industrial revolution. This transformation does not only take advantage of what new technologies have to offer for the benefit of service providers and their users, but includes both new ways of shaping economic and social relationships, as well as strengthening the bond between Local Government and citizens. According to the Sustainable Developments Goals (SDGs) 2020 that were adopted in the Agenda 2030 (United Nations 2020), the Smart Sustainable Development model creates favorable conditions for development at regional level. Among other things, this model includes the use of innovation, smart management methods, integrated technological applications, as well as the direct participation of citizens. Precisely because the policies implemented at the level of local government to achieve the goals of Sustainable Development presuppose the citizens' participation, are of particular importance. Due to the fact that local authorities provide services to citizens and that their overall administrative structure shows considerable variation between E.U. members for reasons attributed to political traditions and historical, geopolitical as well as socio-economic conditions, five main types of organization can be distinguished: the Napoleonic, the Anglo-Saxon, the Scandinavian, the Federal and the East European. The scope of this study is to assess the readiness of the different types of local governments of the member states regarding the implementation of the digital transformation of their

D. Papandreou (✉) · P. I. Mazza · M. Mavri
Quantitative Methods Laboratory, Department of Business Administration, University of the Aegean, 8 Michalon Street, P.S. 82100, Chios, Greece
e-mail: dpapandreou@aegean.gr

P. I. Mazza
e-mail: p.ikoutamazza@aegean.gr

M. Mavri
e-mail: m.mavri@ba.aegean.gr

M. Mavri et al. (eds.), *Digital Economy and Green Growth*, Contributions to Economics, https://doi.org/10.1007/978-3-031-66669-8_3

services towards achieving the SDGs through the Smart Sustainable Development model. To achieve this scope, the goals of the study are

1. the presentation of the concept of digital transformation
2. the description of SDGs and the Smart Sustainable Development model
3. the recording of the administration typology of local governments of the member states and finally
4. the assessment of the readiness of member states to proceed with the digital transformation and the adoption of the Smart Sustainable Development model in correlation to their typology.

Keywords Local government · Digital transformation · Smart SDGs

JEL Classification Codes C54 · H70 · O33

1 Introduction

The pandemic of the previous years managed to significantly affect everyday life and its consequences touched various sectors, such as health, society, the economy, and the environment. Added to this condition were geopolitical developments that exacerbated the crisis, with the result that socio-economic stability was affected. To remove this imbalance, taking advantage of the assets that the new digital era can offer is a way out. It can provide solutions in the fields of work, education, and socialization. Already the digital transformation of societies has emerged after the pandemic and digital innovations are constantly emerging in all sectors. Digital transformation is a concept that concerns society that evolves in a sustainable way and can be implemented more effectively through the adoption of applications and services emerging from Industry 4.0. This change is not only related to technological progress, but also affects economic and social relations. Among them, the citizen-state relationship and in particular the local government-citizen relationship. Digital Transformation combined with the formulation and implementation of policies in terms of viability and sustainability that lead to innovative results, in addition to Smart Cities development is the path that can lead local government away from the negative consequences of COVID and the crisis of recent years.

The goal of this study is to assess the readiness of the different types of Local Governments of the E.U. members regarding the implementation of the Digital Transformation of their services and the pursuit of the SDGs using as a vehicle the Smart Sustainable Development Model. In particular, the added value of the present study is to investigate the readiness of the Local Government of European countries to adopt the innovations of digital transformation and smart city applications in relation to the management model that the Member States have chosen to organize their governance.

Regarding the methodology of this investigation, the article focuses on the quantitative data provided by modern and widespread assessment tools such as the Digital Economy and Society Index (DESI) and the E-Government Development Index (EGDI). These quantified data are grouped according to the standardization of the organization and operation of the local self-government of the member states, as reflected in the international literature. The method is based on the comparative study of statistical data and their parametric analysis.

According to the objectives of the study and the above methodology the paper is organized as follows: Sect. 2 reviews the concept of Digital Transformation. Section 3 describes the Agenda 2030 and the SDGs that were established in it and there is a discussion on how these can also promote the pillars of the Smart Cities. Section 4 presents the recording of the administration typology of Local Governments of the Member States. The assessment of the readiness of EU countries to proceed with the Digital Transformation process and the adoption of the Smart Sustainable Development Model in correlation to their typology is described in Sect. 5. Finally, conclusions are drawn in Sect. 6.

2 The Discussion of the Concept of Digital Transformation

Digital Transformation (DT) is a general concept that broadens horizons concerning rising forms of extended social participation and a wide range of social stakeholders. Digital technologies and ICTs provide innovative solutions to social, economic, operational, and technical challenges and making the public sector more efficient and effective. They can also enable societies to face unpredictable problems and support on the development of digital solutions based on the EU's values and fundamental rights, as it happened over the last years during the pandemic. A necessary condition for the further implementation of DT is that the members and bodies of society have equal access to connectivity, to necessary technology, but also to the upscaling of digital skills. According to the Council of the EU, it' s crucial to *seize this unique opportunity to shape the strategic direction of the DT more actively in Member States* (Berlin Declaration on Digital Society & Value-Based Digital Government, 2020).

In the field of economy, digitization from a technical issue has turned into a key issue of business strategies (Rogers, 2016 at Rêgo et al. (2021)). Competition in the private sector pushes companies to draw up strategies based on the possibilities provided by DT in order to optimize their final outcome (Hess et al., 2016 at Rêgo et al. (2021)).

Fitzgerald et al. (2014) at Rêgo et al. (2021) interprets DT in the business world as a great opportunity to exploit technology, such as mobile and social networks, in the direction of improving the individual functions and ultimately upgrading its overall performance and business model with the main feature being the improvement of the user experience.

At the organizational level, Vial G. approaches the term DT as a process where digital technologies synthesis parameters such as information and ICT, and digital accessibility evolve and create the adaptation of the public and private sectors. It is the competition that makes the need to integrate new technologies into the strategy of the organizations imperative, being a condition for their survival (Vial, 2019).

Herbert (2017) describes DT as a process that must be harmonized with the *culture and functions* of the Organization over time. Adaptability and flexibility are what characterize it, an element necessary for the Organization to show reflexes that will allow it to improve and develop functions that will address existing, but also future needs of both users and the Organization itself (Herbert, 2017).

When the Organizations are part of the public sector then the DT can be described as *transformational government (t-gov) accountability. It is about the evolution of e-government observed in the field of public administration for the provision of services through the utilization of technologies. Systems interface, interaction, service optimization, validity, decentralization, transparent operation and accountability are essential components* (Yildiz, 2007).

T-gov allows the DT to form part of the response to organizational, technical as well as social needs, *embracing a change in the structures, operations, and culture of government as opposed to a mere introduction of digitized procedures* (Omar et al., 2020 at Tangi et al. (2021)). On top of that T-gov can be seen as *transformation of government operations, internal and external processes and structures to enable the realization of services that meet public-sector objectives such as efficiency, transparency, accountability and citizen centricity* (Weerakkody et al., 2011 at Tangi et al. (2021)).

From the Local Government (LG) perspective Calvert (2021) in an attempt to distinguish the role of DT uses the definitions of Westerman et al.'s (2014) and Gruman's describes as the utilization of digital means to increase the efficiency and ease of access of the organization by universally changing functions, services and systems (Calvert, 2021). LGs *adopt forms of New Public Management* in order to evolve or develop services emphasizing the accountability of the public sector, when the ultimate goal remains the optimal service of the citizens. The transition from the analog to the digital world of LG is not just a technological development but indicates a radical change of the management model. Most indicative of this transformation is the shift from a central administration system, where the decision about what citizens need is made centrally by the state, to a decentralized model of administration (depending on the type of administration LGs belong to, as we will see in the 4th section) where citizens are the ones who determine the framework of service provision they will receive at both central and local level (OECD, 2016 at Calvert (2021)).

Innovation is a term that many theorists have tried to define. It relies on the definition of rising concepts, applications, and methods. Many studies have identified a large number of new technologies that lead to new forms of parches (De Vries et al., 2016 at Duygan et al. (2023)). More specifically 'services innovation' relies on changes in the administrative function including the established procedures, techniques, routines, structures, or roles while conceptual innovation stands for the development of concepts, frameworks, or good practices to support on the definition of a problem and potential way outs (Bekkers et al., 2011; De Vries et al., 2016 at

Duygan et al. (2023)). Many research projects are trying to answer about '*why*' and '*how*' innovation occurs in the private sector. In contrast to the private sector, there is not such extensive research in the public sector which is generally characterized by bureaucracy (Wang & Feeney, 2016 at Duygan et al. (2023)). Especially the opinion that prevailed is that LG is not the most representative sector when it comes to implementing innovations (Shearmur & Poirier, 2016 at Duygan et al. (2023)). But does this argument apply in practice? Since LG mandate has been mostly devolved to provide services such as *drainage, waste management, land use planning and development and construction and maintenance of basic infrastructure including roads, parks, squares,* etc. (Walker, 2014; Ringenson et al., 2018 at Duygan et al. (2023)) then innovation should play a key *role in providing services to different types of users, organizations and sectors.* Ultimately, the interaction between users, Organizations, and sectors is decisive for the effective implementation and governance of innovation in complex environments, such as LG, where the provision of quality and efficient services to citizens is the highest goal (Lee et al., 2014; Kroh, 2021 at Duygan et al. (2023)).

3 The Description of SDGs and the Smart Sustainable Development Model

Digitalization as a concept spans the individual, social, and organizational spheres simultaneously (Legner et al., 2017 in Vial (2019); Vial, 2019). We can find it in many places in our daily lives and there are many who now consider it as a necessary ingredient in a recipe aimed at development. The use of innovative technology and, at the same time, the need to protect the environment require this development to be pursued in terms of sustainability. These concepts are not new in the public debate, nor even in the economic debate, as many embraced the assessment that the lack of natural resources would lead to a slowdown and eventual cessation of economic growth (Meadows & Randers, 1992 in Mebratu (1998)). The concept of sustainability simultaneously combines development in the fields of economy and society and finds application when the conditions of sustainability and environmental protection are met.

The European Union (EU), in pursuit of the development of the economy in the context of international competition, drew up a plan known as the Lisbon Strategy. The Europe 2020 Strategy followed, where it evolved into the current Agenda 2030. The Lisbon Strategy was the first organized effort of the EU to include the protection of the environment at the heart of development. Some argue that the target setting was unrealistic, lacking coherence and being essentially a text of political positions and less a feasible action plan (Kohler, 2006; Rosenbaum, 2010). In 2010, the EU came back with a new plan called "Europe 2020: Smart, sustainable and inclusive growth". The interest is focused on the field of "Smart Development", which requires effective interventions in the educational sector, technologies, and the utilization of knowledge capital. It is about prioritizing smart and sustainable, non-discriminatory growth aimed at the EU's sustainable social market economy, while taking into account the conditions of international recognition and production (Development, Transforming our world: The Sustainable Agenda, A/RES/70/1 2015, 2015):

- Smart development: Economic development with pillars of knowledge and innovation.
- Sustainable development: Strengthening a competitive and at the same time green economy with a rational distribution of resources.
- Inclusive development: Promoting an economy that ensures high employability and cohesion at territorial and social level.

In order to achieve the above objectives, EU policies focus on 5 central axes: Employment, Research & Development, Climate Change and Energy, Education, Poverty and Social Exclusion.

Following the "EU 2020 Strategy", at the 70th General Assembly of the United Nations, in 2015, the 2030 Agenda was approved under the title: "Transforming our world: The 2030 Agenda for Sustainable Development" and 17 Sustainable Development Goals (SDGs) and 169 goals (Development, Transforming our world: The Agenda for Sustainable, A/RES/70/1 2015, 2015).

The 2030 Agenda can be characterized as one of the most daring international agreements that the UN has achieved in its history. This is because it simultaneously includes all three dimensions of sustainable development—social, environmental, and economic—in policy making. Additionally, it strengthens the connection and harmonization of the relevant institutional frameworks in the SDGs. It is an international plan for prosperity and peace that involves the participation of all parties involved. Central to the "Agenda 2030" are the thematic goals ("5 Ps") which aim to eradicate poverty and bring development in sustainable terms, internationally by 2030. These goals focus on ensuring dignity, international stability, the protection of the planet, the creation of fair and resilient societies, but also prosperous households. The goals bind all countries, regardless of their development so far, and during their parameterization at the national level, the individual national realities, growth rate, policies, and priorities are taken into account (European Commission, 2015).

Goal 1: No poverty: "*End poverty in all its forms everywhere*" (U.N.D.P., 2020).

Goal 2: Zero hunger (No hunger): "*End hunger, achieve food security and improved nutrition, and promote sustainable agriculture*".

Goal 3: Good health and well-being: "*Ensure healthy lives and promote well-being for all at all ages*".

Goal 4: Quality education: "*Ensure inclusive and equitable quality education and promote lifelong learning opportunities for all*".

Goal 5: Gender equality: "*Achieve gender equality and empower all women and girls*".

Goal 6: Clean water and sanitation: "*Ensure availability and sustainable management of water and sanitation for all*".

Goal 7: Affordable and clean energy: "*Ensure access to affordable, reliable, sustainable and modern energy for all*".

Goal 8: Decent work and economic growth: *"Promote sustained, inclusive and sustainable economic growth, full and productive employment and decent work for all"*.

Goal 9: Industry, Innovation, and Infrastructure: *"Build resilient infrastructure, promote inclusive and sustainable industrialization, and foster innovation"*.

Goal 10: Reduced inequality: *"Reduce income inequality within and among countries"*.

Goal 11: Sustainable cities and communities: *"Make cities and human settlements inclusive, safe, resilient, and sustainable"*.

Goal 12: Responsible consumption and production: *"Ensure sustainable consumption and production patterns"*.

Goal 13: Climate action: *"Take urgent action to combat climate change and its impacts by regulating emissions and promoting developments in renewable energy"*.

Goal 14: Life below water: *"Conserve and sustainably use the oceans, seas and marine resources for sustainable development"*.

Goal 15: Life on land: *"Protect, restore and promote sustainable use of terrestrial ecosystems, sustainably manage forests, combat desertification, and halt and reverse land degradation and halt biodiversity loss"*.

Goal 16: Peace, justice, and strong institutions: *"Promote peaceful and inclusive societies for sustainable development, provide access to justice for all and build effective, accountable and inclusive institutions at all levels"*.

Goal 17: Partnership for the goals: *"Strengthen the means of implementation and revitalize the global partnership for sustainable development"*.

The "EU 2030 Agenda" puts human at the center of the discussion and how he can live in a sustainable regime. Sustainability was a cornerstone of the "EU 2020 strategy", which defined the following development pillars:

I. Smart growth, strengthening education, and focusing on innovation.
II. Sustainable development, pursuit of low carbon emissions to manage the issue of climate change and environmental protection.
III. Development without discrimination, through the creation of employment opportunities and the eradication of poverty. In recent years, the concept of Smart development has emerged, which we have seen applied mainly through the shift of cities to the use of new technologies and their evolution into "Smart Cities".

Innovation is at the core of smart cities that aim to create conditions that favor both efficiency and sustainability. Their mission is also based on the concept of Sustainable Development. A society that upgrades its knowledge and strengthens its innovation can be characterized as a Smart City. It utilizes technology in order to provide quality services to its members. The Center for Regional Science at the Vienna University of Technology conducted a study in which six main parameters are defined according to which it is possible to categorize 70 medium-sized European cities. These parameters are *smart economy, smart mobility, smart environment, smart people, smart living and finally, smart governance.*

It is concluded that a city can be called "smart" if it invests in people, society, knowledge, in classic transport, but also modern (ICT) infrastructure. These investments must be aimed at sustainable economic development and a quality standard of living, with a rational use of natural resources, while ensuring participatory governance and the involvement of citizens.

In the Vienna project, the SDGs have been integrated into the Vienna Smart Cities Strategy. Recognizing that the Smart City goals and the SDGs are closely linked, the strategy includes targeting and actions that can serve them. For example, upgrading digital tools for shared mobility and expanding smart charging infrastructure for electric vehicles serves the goal of halving per capita CO_2 emissions in the field of transport by 2030, while increasing accessibility and air quality (Giffinger et al., 2007, 2023).

How can Smart City applications help accelerate progress towards the SDGs?

A recent study among 167 cities concluded that cities moving faster towards the SDGs were faster in adopting technological applications, data, and collaborative networks (Blasi et al., 2022).

The contribution of Smart Sustainable Cities was also highlighted in the 2030 Agenda, as it was part of the 17 goals to achieve Sustainable Development.

The goal referred to in Sustainable cities and communities worldwide is SDG-11. It guides countries to shape inclusive, safe, resilient and sustainable cities and human settlements. The population of the planet is increasing and in order to be sustainable, modern, sustainable cities must be built. There is a need for intelligent planning of the urban environment through which the security and resilience of cities are sought, which should be both affordable and "green". This specific goal is in line with the six pillars of the Smart City concept.

Finally, it is noted that all the parameters that make up the concept of a Smart City are at the same time structural elements of the three pillars of sustainable development (Economic, social, and environmental dimension).

4 The Recording of the Administration Typology of Local Governments of the Member States

The concepts of governance and administration include, internationally, as their main areas of practice: *public authorities, Organizations that combine public and private sector characteristics and local authorities, such as for example Municipalities* (Askounis et al., 2016).

The local authorities shape the institution of Local Government which is an integral part of the multi-level governance within the states, *being worldwide one of the most important administrative systems for organizing and managing local affairs operating today* (Makris, 2021).

Local Government (LG) can be described as an institution of administrative Organizations (Ndreu, 2016), whose *operation is based on fiscal, legislative, and executive powers, in a region, but also in a certain population* (OECD, 2014) and their responsibilities include *a minimal amount of "self-management"* (Lidström, 1998).

The mandate of LGs is defined by the Constitution or the Laws of the Member States, with the main view that public responsibilities are ideally exercised by the authorities that are closest to the citizens. The most important is dealing with issues that affect the daily life of citizens, essentially constituting an institution that ensures the closeness of the citizen to the public administration, providing them with the possibility of control and accountability, as well as active participation (Papadimitriou, 1993).

According to Agranoff (2014), the term LG has a different meaning internationally, as it includes villages, municipalities, special authorities, states, private and public sector partnerships, modular administrations, historic areas, and many others. The most common is perhaps the institution of Municipalities, but this does not mean that it is an identical concept with common characteristics in all cases.

At the level of services provided, the Municipalities differ in the depth and breadth of the spectrum of their functions. More generally with regard to the services that provided in the context of LG, especially at the level of Municipalities, these can differ, not only from country to country, but can also differ between cities of the same country (Bulent & Nuri, 2020).

Individual state traditions determine some characteristics, just as Makris (2021) describes them resulting in four main distinct types: Napoleonic, Federal, Scandinavian, and Anglo-Saxon (Makris, 2021). Each of these types of tradition represents a different political and administrative culture, structure of the state, but also a way of connecting the state with the citizen. However, the structure of the state is not the only determining factor, as the wider national tradition, which is made up of different historical and socio-economic characteristics, also plays an important role.

The distinction of the types of government carried out by Kuhlmann and Wollmann (2019) at Kuhlmann (2020) moves in the same direction, but proceeding to an additional division of the types mentioned above. This further division is considered appropriate in order to highlight the differences that exist even within a group of states that implement the same self-governing system and is reflected in the following Table 1.

From the typology of the state organization systems and their comparison, the first conclusion that emerges is the significant degree of differentiation in terms of the presence and role of LG in the administrative structure. These differences can be attributed to the applicable historical, geopolitical and socio-economic conditions, but also to the changes that have taken place over time in these areas.

Similar changes allowed EU countries such as Italy, Sweden, and France to strengthen the institution of LG within them or on the other hand in the United Kingdom, Hungary, and partially in southern Europe to delete an opposite course of transfer of competences from the local to central administration.

Table 1 Administrative typology of local government in Europe

Administrative typology/ group of countries	Administration characteristics
French or Napoleonic type Belgium France Luxembourg *(Southern European sub-group)* Greece Italy Portugal Spain	The French Type of structuring and exercising the administration is also known as 'Napoleonic' due to the radical reforms that were attributed to Napoleon and played a decisive role, not only in the subsequent development of the French administrative system, but also of the corresponding administrative identity of neighboring states. Countries such as Belgium, France, Portugal, Spain, and Greece are characterized by a strong legal tradition that governs state functioning in all its aspects through the codification of legal rules and an extensive administrative justice In particular, the intense politicization, partisanship, and clientelism give a special and not at all widespread in other states, administration culture to the public authorities of Italy, Spain, Portugal, and Greece, with the result that in the comparative study of the countries they compose a distinct group (sub-group) of southern European countries that otherwise follow the French model (Makris, 2021) Structure wise: *Unitary-centralized; "weak" LG (decentralization in France, Italy, Greece since the 1980s and 1990s)* (Kuhlmann & Wollmann, 2019 at Kuhlmann (2020))
Federal type Germany Austria	The Federal States of Germany and Austria constitute a distinct type of administrative organization due to the particularity of their structure. Germany, through the constitutional protection of local government, the legal shielding of decentralized powers, the observance of the principle of subsidiarity and legality, the participation of citizens by strengthening their rights, territorial autonomy, and sustainability, is one of the most powerful systems of LG in Europe, without, however, missing inhibiting factors regarding the establishment of full fiscal autonomy of local authorities, especially at the county level (Makris, 2021) Structure wise: *Federal decentralized; "Strong" LG* (Kuhlmann & Wollmann, 2019 at Kuhlmann (2020))
Scandinavian type Denmark Finland Netherlands Sweden	Denmark, Sweden, and to a lesser extent the Netherlands apply a type which, on the principle of subsidiarity, gives a primary role to the relationship between the administrative system and the citizen. The Scandinavian model is the most decentralizing system where powers are transferred from the single state to the LG, ensuring it significant political, but also functional autonomy. The participation of citizens and strong LG are two key parameters that make the Nordic countries a distinct model of decentralized administrative organization that does not cease to have common origins with administrative systems of other countries, e.g., the Roman law, but to also share common principles, such as that of subsidiarity adopted by federal states (Makris, 2021) Structure wise: *Unitary-decentralized; "strong" LG/civic self-determination* Kuhlmann & Wollmann, 2019 at Kuhlmann (2020))

(continued)

Table 1 (continued)

Administrative typology/ group of countries	Administration characteristics
Anglo-Saxon type Ireland Malta United Kingdom[a] Cyprus	The Anglo-Saxon model co-shapes countries whose administrative system prioritizes both the public interest and a bourgeois culture and utilitarian tradition characterized by an instrumental concept of statism, where the differences between the state and the socio-economic spheres are small, in contrast to it applies to the rest of Europe. A more representative case of an administrative system of Anglo-Saxon tradition is the United Kingdom, followed by countries that have historically influenced it to a large extent, such as Ireland, Cyprus, and Malta (Makris, 2021) Structure wise: *Unitary-centralized; "strong" (although has weakened since the 1980s) LG* Kuhlmann & Wollmann, 2019 at Kuhlmann (2020))
Eastern European type Czech Republic Estonia Hungary Latvia Lithuania Poland Slovakia *(South-Eastern European sub-group)* Bulgaria Croatia Romania Slovenia	The Czech Republic, Estonia, Latvia, Slovakia, Lithuania, Hungary, and Poland are the Eastern European countries that compose a distinct administrative model (Eastern European model), with the last two being the most representative systems. The historical and geopolitical path of the countries of Eastern Europe and the strong influence exerted on them by the Prussian system and later by communism were a decisive factor in the formation of a socialist administrative organization and operation with a centralized character, analogous to that of the Napoleonic system It was not until the end of the twentieth century that reforms were launched, such as, e.g., primarily in Hungary, where together with the restoration of constitutional law, administrative reorganization on the standards of the rest of Europe became possible In contrast to the single state administration, the Eastern European model also includes a sub-group of countries (Bulgaria, Croatia, Romania, and Slovenia) that continues to follow a model of single centralization and, by extension, *"weak" LG* (Makris, 2021) Structure wise: *Unitary-decentralized; "strong" LG (recentralization since 2011 in Hungary) Special case South Eastern European Subgroup: unitary-centralized; "weak" LG* Kuhlmann & Wollmann, 2019 at Kuhlmann (2020))

Source The original source data (*Following Kuhlmann and Wollmann (2019, p. 24) and Heinelt et al. (2018) at* Kuhlmann (2020) *and* Makris (2021)) has been edited by the authors.
[a] Despite the recent withdrawal of the Un. Kingdom from the EU, it is nevertheless included in the recording attempted in the context of this article, as its presence is considered decisive in terms of the formation of the administrative models

However, the tendency in Eastern Europe is not that of centralization, but on the contrary the prevailing trend is that of strengthening the institution of LG through increasing its autonomy.

This autonomy is directly linked to a wider fiscal autonomy, which is found in the Scandinavian model, with the most typical example being Sweden, where autonomy is intertwined with the inextricable connection of citizens with LG and the promotion of participation.

Both this connection and fiscal autonomy are parameters of a model of administration that are absent from the Anglo-Saxon model, even when it is compared to the rest of Europe's administration systems. That is, even alongside the countries that follow the Napoleonic model (Belgium, France, Luxembourg, Italy, Portugal, Spain), with the possible exception of Greece, which to some extent combine administrative (in terms of decision-making) with economic autonomy, despite the fact that traditionally their administration is centralized.

The differentiation between the European systems, in addition to the degree of autonomy, also lies in the discrepancies in terms of the functions and responsibilities attributed between the individual levels of administration. For example, countries belonging to the federal model, such as Germany, or to the Scandinavian model, such as Sweden, have "strong" LG, a power which translates into the decentralization of key services in the areas of public utility and social welfare. In corresponding sectors, the state systems of the Napoleonic model followed a centralized policy until a few years ago, giving the central administration a primary role for their management.

In summary, despite the mosaic image that makes up the different administration systems in Europe, a common feature in recent years in the majority of cases and without missing exceptions, is the looming tendency to strengthen local autonomy in order to upgrade the institution of LG (Kuhlmann, 2020).

5 The Assessment of the Readiness of EU Countries to Proceed with the Digital Transformation and the Adoption of the Smart Sustainable Development Model in Correlation to Their Typology

The European Commission proposed the establishment of the Policy Program "Moving towards the Digital Decade" with the aim of providing the duality to countries to be guided towards their progress and digital transformation (DT). The decision was ratified in 2021, through the advisory document that was also the road map called "2030 Digital Compass: the European Way for the Digital Decade". It thus defined the digital objectives of the Member States with a time horizon of achievement in 2030. There was also a declaration on digital rights and the principles that should govern them, by the Commission in 2022, which functionally complements the objectives and is part of the guidance of agencies to shape policies and the private sector to adapt to the Digital Decade according to European values and the legal framework.

Europe's plan to implement the DT of societies and the economy should include digital sovereignty, inclusion, equality, sustainability, resilience, security, trust, improving quality of life, respect for rights and people's aspirations and should contribute to a dynamic, resource-efficient and equitable economy and society across countries.

In an effort to assess the EU's readiness to make progress in implementing DT, especially in terms of public sector service provision, there is the Digital Economy and Society Index (DESI).

It is an evaluation system used by the European Commission since 2014 in order to annually monitor the performance of the member states in terms of the main predetermined progress parameters, but also to identify thematic areas that should be a priority. The Key Indicators are (i) Human Capital, (ii) Connectivity, (iii) Digital Integration, and (iv) Digital Public Services (European Commission—Shaping Europe's Digital Future, 2023).

One of the general conclusions after analyzing the DESI results is that the EU countries as a whole maintain a trend of improving the level of digitization. In particular, the member states that in the previous decade were in the last positions are gradually recovering the lost ground by achieving higher growth rates. It is noted that countries such as Italy, Poland, and Greece have made significant progress in the last five years, both focusing their policy on Digital Transformation and making use of European financial tools and investing in this sector. This progress is also reflected in the graph below, which shows the average annual relative increase in terms of DESI rating over the period 2017–2022 (Fig. 1).

At this point, using the DESI tool, an attempt will be made to compare and analyze the overall performance of the EU countries in terms of Digital Transformation, based on the LG type they have adopted.

The following graph shows the overall performance (aggregate scores) of the Member States as a percentage of the overall DT assessment, according to DESI 2022 (Fig. 2).

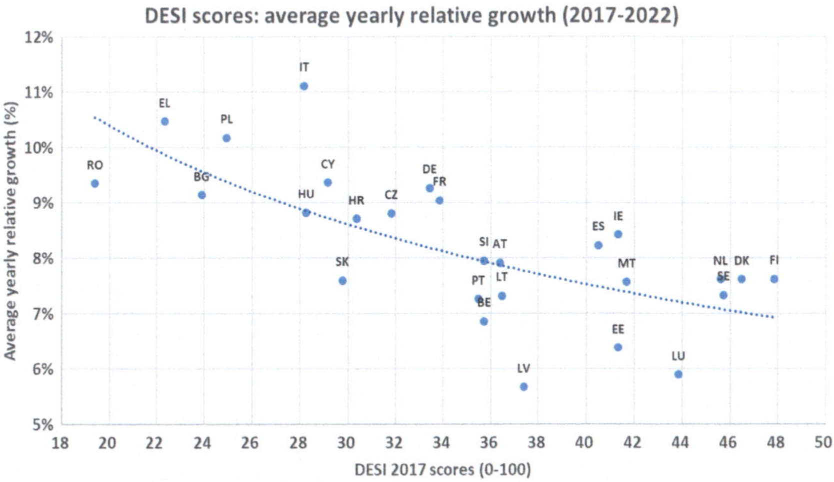

Fig. 1 DESI scores: average yearly relative growth (2017–2022). *Source* European Commission: (DESI, 2022; European Commission, 2022)

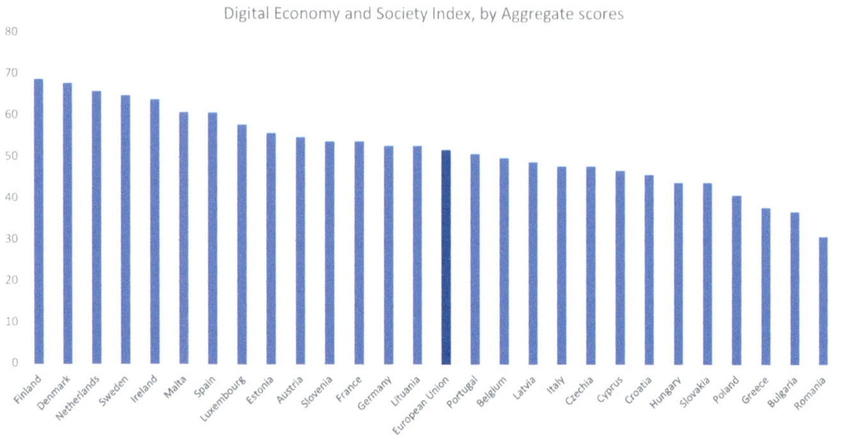

Fig. 2 Digital Economy and Society Index, by aggregate scores. *Source* The original source data (European Commission, digital scoreboard) has been edited by the authors

Based on the above chart, the graph below shows the corresponding performance according to the LG typology of the Member States as analyzed in the previous section (Fig. 3).

In the Napoleonic Type which includes a group of counties with a Unitary-centralized administrative structure and a "weak" LG the aggregate score is 51.76%, the second lower percentage among the five administrative models. 0.54% below the EU average score. Spain has the highest percentage (60.8%) between this group of countries and Greece has the lowest (38.9%) despite the fact that the growth rate is significantly high.

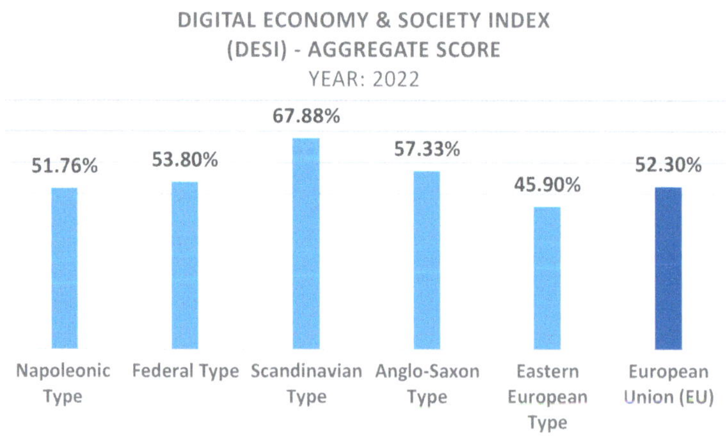

Fig. 3 Digital Economy and Society Index (DESI)—aggregate score (year 2022). *Source* The original source data (DESI, 2022) has been edited by the authors

Table 2 Digital Economy and Society Index (DESI)—dimensions

DESI dimension	DESI sub-dimension
1. Human capital	Internet user skills and advanced digital skills
2. Connectivity	Fixed broadband take-up, fixed broadband coverage, mobile broadband, and bradband prices
3. Integration of digital technology	Business digitalisation and e-commerce
4. Digital public services	e-Government

Source European Commission

In the Federal Type Germany and Austria follows a decentralized administrative model and they present a "strong" LG the aggregate DESI score is 53.8%. 1.5% over the EU member states average.

The Scandinavian group of countries has the highest score (67.88%). Member States with a unitary and decentralized administrative structure and a "strong" LG/ civic self-determination have made bigger progress on enhancing DT. The approximately 10% difference from the second ranked group of countries and the 15.58% difference from the European average show that the countries belonging to the Nordic model (Denmark 69.30%, Finland 69.60%, Netherlands 67.40%, Sweden 65.20%) show a greater degree of readiness in the implementation of digital transformation both at the level of general performance and in the individual DESI indicators that concern not only the private but also the public sector.

The Anglo-Saxon model co-shapes countries (Ireland, Malta and Cyprus) whose administrative system prioritizes both the public interest and a bourgeois culture with unitary and centralized and a "strong" LG model collects percentage of 57.33%. Approximately 5% over the EU average aggregate DESI score and the second better performance among the five administration types which are compared in the context of this paper.

The Eastern European group of countries compose a distinct administrative model with a centralized character and a weak LG system analogous to that of the Napoleonic system. The aggregate DESI score is 45.90% which is the lowest among the EU groups of countries and 6.4% lower than the EU average. A percentage that indicates the low degree of readiness in terms of the implementation of DT in comparison with the rest European administrative types of countries.

In 2021, DESI was aligned with key points and to some extent the goals of the Roadmap to the Digital Decade which was also reflected in the structure of the 2022 study (DESI, 2022, European Commission) (Table 2).

The 2022 DESI includes eleven indicators to assess progress towards a large part of the Digital Decade targets at Member State level (DESI, 2022, European Commission) (Table 3).

Table 3 Digital Economy and Society Index (DESI)—indicators related to the path to the digital decade proposal

DESI dimension	Indicators related to the path to the digital decade proposal
1. Human capital	At least basic digital skills ICT specialists Female ICT specialists
2. Connectivity	Gigabit for everyone (fixed very high capacity network coverage) 5G coverage
3. Integration of digital technology	SMEs with a basic level of digital intensity AI Cloud Big data
4. Digital public services	Digital public services for citizens Digital public services for businesses

Source European Commission

At this point the comparative analysis focuses on an indicative parameter that concerns one of the four main dimensions of the DESI evaluation system, which is the provision of '*digital public services*' and the sub-dimension of *e-Government*. The analysis we will focus on is the indicator that monitors the provision of Digital Public Services for Citizens.

In particular, the rating by type of administration and model of LG will indirectly show us the readiness of the respective member states to progress further in the DT of the public service sector for citizens and also the achievement of Smart Sustainable Development Goals (SSDGs) (Fig. 4).

In this particular area that has focused our attention, the Nordic-style countries have by far the best performance (85.77%) and seem to be more prepared for the further DT of the system of providing digital public services to the citizens. Finland, as the country with the highest score (89.83%) out of 27, has a difference from the European average of 15.23%.

Next are the countries of the Anglo-Saxon type with a percentage of 78.59%. This administrative profile seems able to follow the progress regarding the DT of public services aimed at citizens compared to the rest of the models in the countries of Europe, except for the Scandinavian model that precedes it. It is even ahead of the EU average by 1.16%.

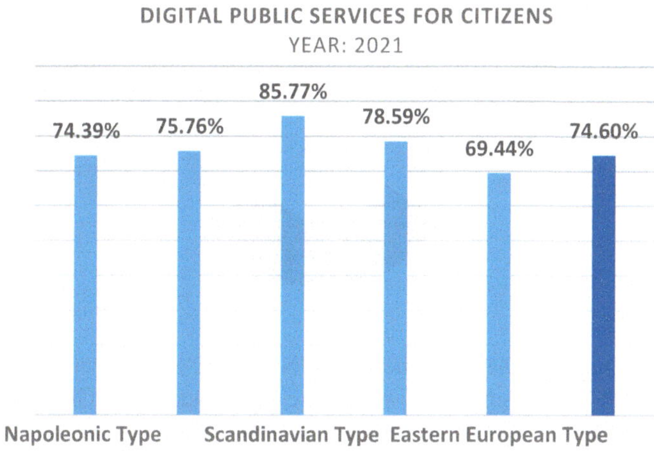

Fig. 4 Digital public services for citizens (year 2021). *Source* The original source data (DESI, 2021) has been edited by the authors

The countries of the Napoleonic type move very close to the average European rate of the DESI total score. Among the countries of this administrative profile, the percentage of Luxembourg (93.43%) stand out, which is the second highest at EU level, together with that of Malta, which records the highest performance (99.64%) within EU. In the Napoleonic Type the country with the lowest score is Greece with a percentage of 52.35%, however it is worth noting that the overall progress made during the pandemic did not manage to be recorded in its entirety during the DESI 2022 reference period.

The two countries of the federal model are slightly above (1.16%) the European average with percentages of 75.73% for Germany and 75.78% respectively for Austria.

5,16% below EU average countries belonging to the Eastern European Type.

Among these countries, the low percentage of Romania (44.24%) stands out, which brings it to the last place among the EU 27, as well as the high percentage of Estonia (92.9%) at the other end. Score reflecting the country's high degree of readiness to further digitally transform the system of providing public services to Estonian citizens.

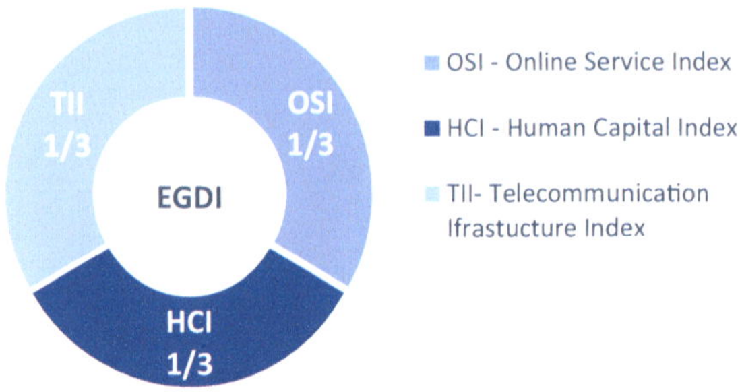

Fig. 5 The three components of the E-Government Development Index (EGDI). *Source* public administration.UN.org (2023)

The performance of the 27 in the United Nations E-Government Development Index (EGDI) 2022 assessment shows similar results. In addition, EGDI captures data regarding the development of United Nations Electronic Government. Combined with a country's assessment of website development patterns, the E-Government Development Index focuses on data on access, such as infrastructure, but also knowledge. In this way, it is able to capture more effectively how each state utilizes ICT in order to promote accessibility and by extension to deal with the exclusion of citizens. EGDI is a multidimensional tool. The three most important dimensions of e-government, which it examines, are: the provision of services via the Internet, the connection via telecommunication systems and the characteristics of human resources is intended to form a comparative picture of the degree of performance of the states and not to fully record the way in which e-government is developed in each country. The specific tool is intended to form a comparative picture of the degree of performance of the states and not to fully record the way in which e-government is developed in each country (public administration.UN.org, 2023) (Fig. 5).

The following graph shows the overall performance of the Member States based on the 2022 EGDI (Fig. 6).

Based on the above statistics provided by the United Nations Database and after processing in accordance with the proposed grouping of countries based on their administrative profile, the following diagram was produced (Fig. 7).

It is immediately noticeable that the image presented by the individual groups according to EGDI 2022 is quite similar to the canonization of DESI 2022. Therefore, according to the findings of this indicator we can conclude that the country groups show the same degree of readiness in terms of consolidation and implementation on the DT and SSDGs processes.

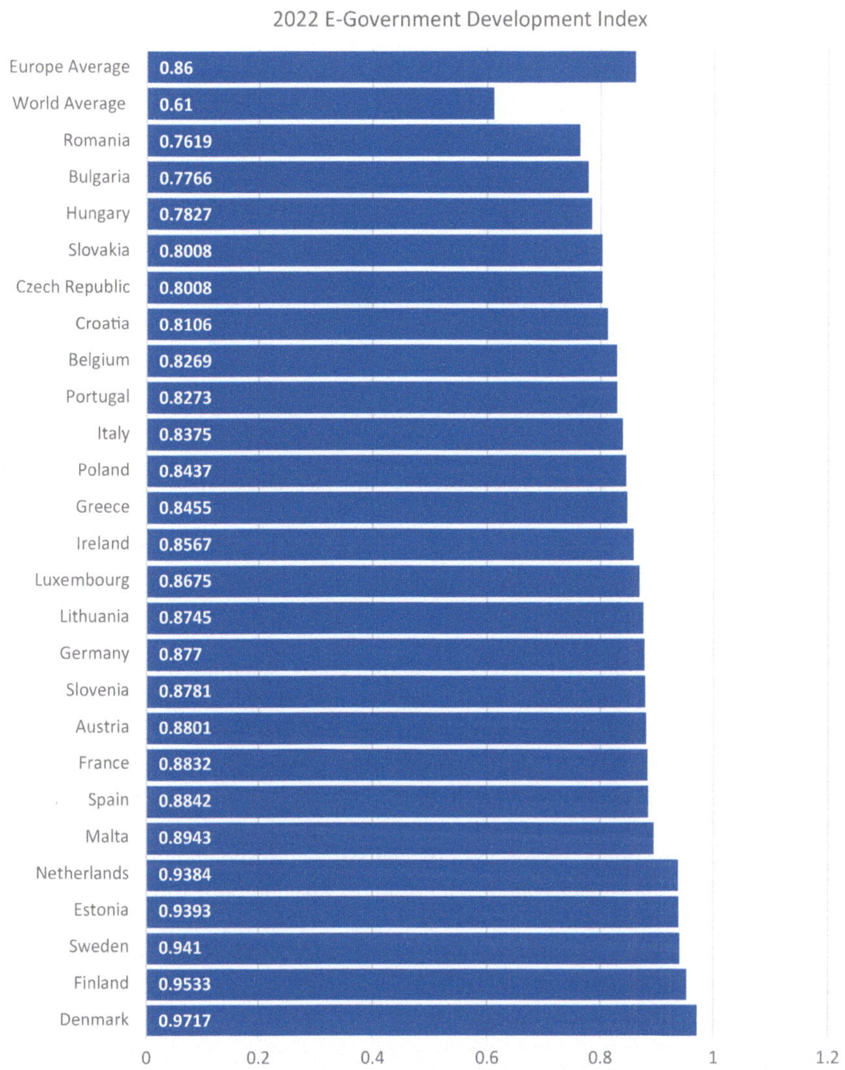

Fig. 6 2022 E-Government Development Index. *Source* public administration.UN.org (2023)

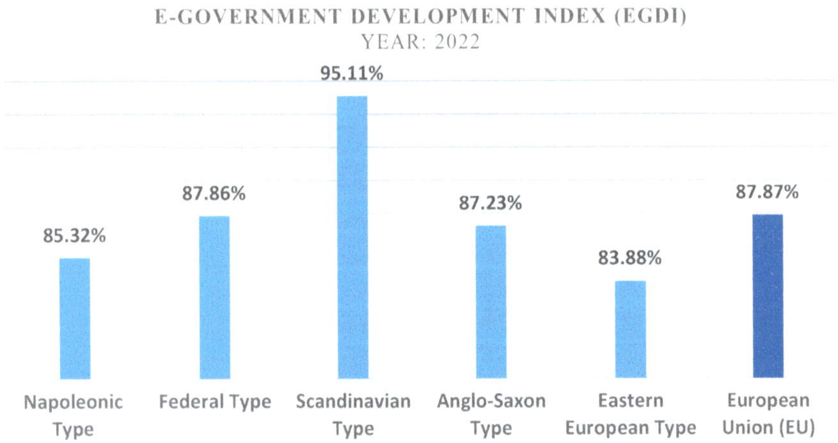

Fig. 7 E-Government Development Index (EGDI)—year: 2022. *Source* The original source data has been edited by the authors

6 Conclusion

Over the last decades the transition to the digital era is becoming imperative, especially after the COVID pandemic which accelerated the need for Digital Transformation and growth of the digital economy. Additionally, there has been given a strong emphasis on "smart growth", which was mainly achieved through the transition of cities to the digital era. Utilizing the literature related to the concept of Digital Transformation, an in-depth study was attempted regarding the application of the term t-Governance in the public sector and especially the corresponding transformation in the Local Government ecosystem. The result of this approach was to attribute to the Digital Transformation the organizational reform of the operating model in terms of processes, organizational culture, interactions, and any other critical parameter of the Organization that contributes to the improvement of the quality and efficiency of services provided to users and the citizens.

From this point of view, the SDGs were described and an attempt was made to connect them with the Smart Sustainable Development Model, which is an indicative manifestation of Digital Transformation and the application of innovations at the level of Local Government. The EU, in order to achieve economic growth, sustainable development and its dominance on the global market, had prepared a comprehensive development program, the Agenda 2030. The Smart City concept ensures sustainable environment and the key elements which identify them are in line with the principles of sustainable development and because their main purpose is the improvement of the quality of life of citizens without restricting this possibility to future generations.

An attempt was also made to define the concept of Local Government and mainly the way of its application among the Member States. In particular, the typology of Local Government was adopted through the relevant literature based on the model of administrative function followed by the EU countries. This grouping of the Member States contributed to the assessment of the comparative analysis of the degree of readiness, as reflected in Indicators such as DESI 2022 and EGDI 2023, to proceed with their Digital Transformation and adopt the Smart Sustainable Development Model in correlation to their typology.

From this comparative analysis, it is concluded that the administration model of the EU countries has an influence on the formation of the readiness to assimilate Digital Transformation processes and such applications as the Smart Sustainable Development model.

In particular, from the analysis of the quantitative data, an overall shift of the Member States to the digitization of the services provided by the state is evident. The pace of this transformation has not been the same for all countries in recent decades. However, there are some countries that they were used to make slow progress in this area, with Greece as an illustrative example that has intensified its efforts in recent years.

Using DESI quantitative data, grouping countries based on their standardization and comparative analysis of individual performance shows that countries that base their operation on more decentralized administration systems score better. This fact is verified even when the analysis delves into more specialized indicators, such as the provision of digital public services to citizens. The comparison at this level also shows that more centralized systems and types of states such as those of South Eastern Europe and the Napoleonic countries show a reduced degree of readiness. In the same direction, the comparative analysis of the data obtained from the EGDI shows that the countries belonging to the Nordic or federal type are clearly "ready" for the development of e-government. According to the assessment of the readiness of the member states carried out in the context of this study, it appears that smart and sustainable development through the digital transformation of the state and especially of the Local Government is a priority of the EU and depends to a large extent on the system of governance. Countries with a decentralized system of responsibilities, with more autonomy and self-reliance seem to be ahead in the fight to adopt smart and sustainable solutions for Local Government.

These conclusions, as well as the methodology followed, can help policymakers at the European or national level to assess the level of readiness and implement targeted measures to improve their position and cultivate those conditions that will allow the digital transformation and by extension the shift to more smart and sustainable solutions, not only at the national but also at the local level.

References

Agranoff, R. (2014). *Local governments in multilevels systems: Emergent public administration challenges.* American Review of Public Administration SAGE.

Askounis, D., Ergazakis, K., Mavri, M., & Toska, A. (2016). Estimating the performance of local authorities as a measure to overpass the financial crisis: The Greek case study. *International Journal of Public Administration, 39*(14), 1109–1124.

Berlin Declaration on Digital Society and Value-Based Digital Governement. (2020). *Ministerial Meeting During the German Presidency of the Coucil of the EU* (p. 21). eu2020.de.

Blasi, S., Ganzaroli, A., & De Noni, I. (2022). *Smartening sustainable development in cities: Strengthening the theoretical linkage between smart cities and SDG's.* Sustainable Cities and Society.

Bulent, B., & Nuri, E. (2020). *Investigating the satisfaction of citizens in municipality services using fuzzy modelling.* Socio-Economic Planning Sciences.

Calvert, M. (2021, January). *Assessing organizational readiness for digital transformation. Developing a readiness checklist for municipalities.*

(2022). *DESI 2022, European Commission.* European Commission.

Digital Economy and Society Index (DESI), Full Report, 2021. Retrieved from https://digital-strategy.ec.europa.eu/en/library/digital-economy-and-society-index-desi-2021

Directorate-General for Communications Networks, C. a. (2023, January 06). *European Commission-shaping Europe's digital future.* Retrieved from European Commission website: https://digital-strategy.ec.europa.eu/en/policies/desi

Duygan, M., Fischer, M., & Ingold, K. (2023, February). Assessing the readiness of municipalities for digital process innovation. *Technology in Society.* https://doi.org/10.1016/j.techsoc.2022.102179

European Commission. (2015). *European Commission-policies.* Retrieved from Sustainable Development Goals: https://international-partnerships.ec.europa.eu/policies/sustainable-development-goals_en

Giffinger, R., Fertner, C., Kramar, H., Kalasek, R., Pichler-Milanović, N., & Meijers, E. (2007). Smart cities: Ranking of European medium-sized cities. Centre of Regional Science (srf). Vienna University of Technology.

Giffinger, R., et al. (2023, February). *Smart cities. Ranking of European medium-sized cities.* University of Technology.

Herbert, L. (2017). *Digital transformation. Build your organization's future for the innovation age.* Bloomsbury Business.

Kohler, W. (2006). The "Lisbon Goal" of the EU: Rhetoric or substance? *Journal of Industry, Competition and Trade*, 85–113.

Kuhlmann. (2020). *The capacity of local governments in Europe: Autonomy, responsibilities and reforms.* Palgrave Macmillan.

Lidström, A. (1998). The comparative study of local government systems—A research agenda. *Journal of Comparative Policy Anaylisis: Research and Practice, 1*, 97–115.

Makris, I. (2021). *The competencies of local government as a local action structure in European countries.* Institute of Local Government (ITA).

Mebratu, D. (1998). *Sustainability and sustainable development historical and conceptual review* (pp. 6–11). Lund University.

Ndreu, A. (2016). The definition and importance of local governance. *Social and Natural Sciences Journal.*

OECD. (2014). *Public governance and territorial development.* OECD.

Papadimitriou, G. (1993). *Local government in modern democracy.* Sakkoula Publications.

public administration.UN.org. (2023). Retrieved from United Nations E-Government Knwoledge-base: https://publicadministration.un.org/egovkb/en-us/About/Overview/-E-Government-Development-Index

Rêgo, B. S., Jayantilal, S., Ferreira, J. J., et al. (2021). Digital transformation and strategic management: A systematic review of the literature. *Journal of the Knowledge Economy, 13*, 3195–3222 (2022). https://doi.org/10.1007/s13132-021-00853-3

Rosenbaum, E. (2010). Lisbon, Europe 2020, and the case for soft coordination in the EU policymaking. *Interconomics Review of European Economic Policy*, 540–542.

Tangi, L., Janssen, M., Benedetti, M., & Noci, G. (2021, April 27). Digital government transformation: A structural equation modelling analysis of driving and impeding factors. *Interantional Jouranl of Information Management.*

U.N.D.P. (2020). *Human development report.* United Nations.

United Nations. (2015). *Development, transforming our world: The agenda for sustainable, A/RES/70/1 2015.* U.N.

Vial, G. (2019, June). Understanding digital transformation: A review and a research agenda. *The Journal of Strategic Information Systems, 28*(2), 118–144.

Westerman, G., Bonnet, D., & McAfee, A. (2014). The nine elements of digital transformation. Retrieved Jan 7, 2014, from https://sloanreview.mit.edu/article/the-nine-elements-of-digital-transformation/

Wollmann, S. (2019). *Introduction to comparative public administration: Administrative systems and reforms in Europe.* Edward Elgar Publishing Ltd.

Yildiz, M. (2007, July). E-government research: Reviewing the literature, limitations, and ways forward. *Government Information Quarterly, 24*(3), 646–665. https://doi.org/10.1016/j.giq.2007.01.002

Building a Smarter Government Using Machine Learning Applications: Benefits and Challenges

Eirini Manga, Nikitas Karanikolas, and Catherine Marinagi

Abstract This paper aims to investigate the benefits and the challenges of the utilization of Machine Learning (ML) applications in public administration. The importance of ML applications to the revolutionization of public administration and the enhancement of the quality of provided services is discussed. As the volume of data available to government organizations continues to grow, ML plays a crucial role in extracting useful insights. ML can be used to analyze big data and identify patterns and trends that may not be easily discernible by human analysts, providing valuable knowledge that can be used to improve decision-making, leading to more informed and effective choices. The potentials of ML applications in the significant improvement of the efficiency and effectiveness of public administration and government operations are also discussed. ML can assist in fraud detection, crisis management, fairness in criminal justice, prediction and protection of traffic accidents, identification of risks from citizen reports, air quality prediction, water quality prediction, healthcare prediction and decision-making, energy management, forecasting crime in urban transportation, resource usage utilization, sentiment analysis, predictive maintenance, and building chatbots to support public services. Additionally, the challenges of the utilization of ML applications into government operations are addressed, including technological, ethical, and organizational issues. Technological issues concern the difficulties that arise from the deployment of ML applications on outdated legacy systems. Ethical issues concern data quality, data privacy and security, responsible and ethical design of ML algorithms, and explainable outcomes of ML algorithms that ensure accuracy, fairness, transparency, and equity. Organizational issues concern the increase of government officials' awareness and understanding of ML algorithms.

E. Manga (✉) · N. Karanikolas
Department of Informatics and Computer Engineering, School of Engineering, University of West Attica, 12243 Athens, Greece
e-mail: emanga@uniwa.gr

N. Karanikolas
e-mail: nnk@uniwa.gr

C. Marinagi
Department of Agribusiness and Supply Chain Management, School of Economics and Social Sciences, Agricultural University of Athens, 11855 Athens, Greece
e-mail: marinagi@aua.gr

M. Mavri et al. (eds.), *Digital Economy and Green Growth*, Contributions to Economics, https://doi.org/10.1007/978-3-031-66669-8_4

Keywords Machine learning · e-Government · Public administration · Big data · Chatbots

JEL Classification Codes **O33** Technological change: choices and consequences; diffusion processes · **M150** IT management

1 Introduction

In today's rapidly evolving digital age, governments are facing mounting pressure to modernize their operations and services. With the explosion of big data and the growing availability of sophisticated analytical tools, Machine Learning (ML) has emerged as a powerful technology that offers tremendous potential for public sector innovation. Through the automation of data analysis, prediction, and decision-making, ML can transform the way governments operate and deliver services to the public.

Smart government refers to the utilization of digital technologies, communication channels, and data analysis to enhance the quality, transparency, and efficiency of public services and governance (Bojovic et al., 2023). The objective is to improve citizen engagement and participation, promote innovation, and optimize resource allocation among various stakeholders. Advanced technologies like Artificial Intelligence (AI) and the Internet of Things (Constantinescu & Edu, 2022) are frequently employed in smart government initiatives to automate processes, provide real-time information to policymakers and citizens, and support decision-making. Smart government is believed to be a critical driver of creating more inclusive and responsive societies and achieving sustainable development goals.

ML is a subfield of AI that develops and studies computational systems that simulate the way humans think and learn. AI studies the broader science of mimicking human abilities, while ML studies the development of algorithms and computational models that allow machines to learn and make predictions or decisions based on data without being explicitly programmed (Xu et al., 2021). More specifically, ML is defined as the scientific field that studies the design and development of algorithms which can make predictions, make important decisions rapidly, recognize patterns, and discover correlations among data (Bishop, 2006). The goal of ML is to create systems that can automatically improve their performance and accuracy over time by learning from examples and experiences. ML can solve practical problems using programs that follow methods and algorithms that train the system to handle new data without requiring human intervention. ML can be extremely useful when dealing with large amounts of data, or big data, which come from various sources such as sensors, social media, and smart device transactions. As a wide variety of data becomes available to governments, ML plays a crucial role in evaluating their importance and making consistent decisions (Anastasopoulos & Whitford, 2019).

Two main types of ML algorithms are promising in public administration research: supervised learning and unsupervised learning (Anastasopoulos & Whitford, 2019).

In supervised learning algorithms, two phases are performed: the training phase, in which a sample (training set) is taken from the dataset and a model is created, and the testing phase, in which the model is applied to the remaining data. Examples of supervised learning algorithms are Decision Trees, Naïve Bayes, Neural Networks, and Support Vector Machines. Unsupervised learning algorithms are used to reveal hidden patterns or groupings in datasets. Examples of unsupervised learning algorithms are K-means Clustering, and Principal-Components Analysis.

This paper aims to explore the benefits and challenges involved in creating smarter governments by utilizing ML applications. Drawing on a review of existing literature and case studies, the theoretical and practical aspects of using ML in government operations are examined, with a focus on its potential benefits and the challenges that need to be addressed.

The remainder of this paper is organized as follows: Sect. 2 examines the various ML applications in public services and explores the benefits of implementing ML in public administration. Section 3 discusses the challenges associated with integrating ML into government operations. Finally, Sect. 4 summarizes the main findings of this paper.

2 Research Methodology

This paper follows a non-systematic literature review. The following research questions are posed for this study:

RQ1: Which are the benefits of utilizing Machine Learning applications in public administration?

RQ2: Which are the challenges of utilizing Machine Learning applications in public administration?

The scientific databases that were explored for articles are Scopus, Google Scholar, and Web of Science. Most of the articles were published between 2017 and 2023. Exceptionally, some articles that were published earlier were included. To identify the most relevant papers, the authors used keywords combined with the "AND" or "OR" Boolean operators. The keywords that were used include the following: "Machine Learning", "ML", "Artificial Intelligence", "AI", "smart government", "e-government", "public administration", "public sector", "benefits", and "challenges".

For each paper, firstly the title, abstract, and keywords were examined to decide the alignment with the research questions. Then, the content of the selected papers was evaluated to filter the irrelevant ones. Only papers written in English were included. The authors have considered only high-quality publications from international journals and conferences. The search in scientific databases is not exhaustive since this is not a full systematic review. Therefore, only manually selected references and manually selected citations of the included relevant papers were examined.

The following international journals were used to select the relevant papers: Public Administration Review, Public Administration, Decision Analytics Journal, Journal of Public Administration Research and Theory, Asia Pacific Journal of Public Administration, Government Information Quarterly, EJournal of EDemocracy and Open Government, International Journal of Information Management, Machine Learning and Knowledge Extraction, Artificial Intelligence Review, Applied Sciences, Mathematical and Computational Applications, Computers & Industrial Engineering, Expert Systems with Applications, Informatica, IEEE Software, IADIS International Journal on WWW/Internet, Natural Language Engineering, Sensors, IEEE Sensors Journal, Studies in Business and Economics, The Journal of Economic Perspectives, Interactions, European Journal of Interdisciplinary Studies, Journal of Biomedical Informatics, Journal of Healthcare Engineering, Transportation Research Procedia, Bioelectronic Medicine, Telecommunications Policy, Disaster Advances, Fire Technology, Journal of Hydrology, Sustainability, Energies, Natural Hazards, Computers in Biology and Medicine, Nature Reviews Drug Discovery, Nature Reviews Materials, Journal of Emergency Management, Eco-Environment & Health, and The Innovation.

3 Benefits of Utilizing Machine Learning Applications in Public Administration

With the growing volume of data available to government organizations, ML has become essential in extracting valuable insights. ML possesses the ability to scrutinize vast quantities of data and identify patterns and trends that may not be easily discernible by human analysts. This can provide valuable knowledge that can be used to make more informed and effective decisions, leading to improvements in decision-making processes. ML algorithms can identify patterns and trends that would be challenging for humans to detect, resulting in more precise and knowledgeable decision-making. This is especially beneficial in areas that are complex and data-intensive, such as environmental management, transportation, and public health (Jayatilake & Ganegoda, 2021). Furthermore, ML can assist the public sector in allocating resources such as manpower and funding by providing insights into where they are needed the most.

By using ML, public administration can improve its services, enhance citizens' trust (Barcellos et al., 2017), increase the efficiency of operations (Veale & Brass, 2019), boost productivity, simplify and accelerate processes, reduce operational expenses, and achieve better distribution of human resources. At the same time, governments must utilize ML aiming to serve the public interest and the needs of citizens, but always considering current legislation, ethical and justice issues that may arise (Oneto & Chiappa, 2020), confidentiality, and data security (Sehatbakhsh et al., 2019). In addition, the utilization of ML in public administration has the potential to foster innovation and stimulate economic growth.

The contribution of ML to decision-making optimization is particularly important. By using ML, public administration can make more accurate and reliable decisions regarding various services it is called upon to perform on a daily basis, as well as in emergency situations such as crisis and natural disasters (Lamovec et al., 2013; Zagorecki et al., 2013), prediction and prevention of traffic accidents (Chong et al., 2005; Durduran, 2010), identification of risks from citizen reports (Hirokawa et al., 2017), predictions for atmospheric pollution (Hu et al., 2017), disease forecasts (Jayatilake & Ganegoda, 2021), assistance with medical decision-making during a pandemic (Debnath et al., 2020), better management of energy efficiency (Zekić-Sušac et al., 2021), predictions of wildfires (Madaio et al., 2016), prediction of movement in areas with high crime rates (Kouziokas, 2017), and predictions for better water quality (Najah Ahmed et al., 2019).

In the following, the benefits of the utilization of ML in public services are presented.

3.1 Fraud Detection and Prevention

While traditional methods such as inspections and manual verifications are time-consuming, costly, and imprecise, ML techniques have the ability to swiftly analyze extensive financial data at a lower cost and detect fraudulent activities such as tax evasion, procurement fraud and money laundering (Ali et al., 2022). Through implementing ML powered fraud detection systems, public administrations can safeguard against financial crimes, adhere to legal requirements, and ultimately save taxpayers' funds. The utilization of ML in fraud detection and prevention includes the following cases:

Tax fraud: The governments can employ ML to detect tax fraud and evasion by analyzing extensive amounts of tax-related data (de Roux et al., 2018). The algorithms can detect unusual patterns in financial statements, identify fraudulent claims, and raise alerts to reduce overall tax fraud rates.

Financial crimes: Financial crimes like money laundering and terrorist financing can be detected using ML algorithms (Rocha et al., 2020). By analyzing large datasets from multiple sources, governments can detect unusual transactions, and suspicious activities in real-time.

Social welfare fraud: By using ML algorithms governments can detect social welfare fraud by monitoring large volumes of data related to welfare benefits claims. By recognizing patterns in the data and flagging any anomalies, governments can investigate further and prevent fraudulent activities.

Healthcare fraud: Healthcare fraud is a significant burden on government budgets. ML models can be utilized to monitor claims data, detect irregular billing patterns, and identify potentially fraudulent activities (Amponsah et al., 2022) in real-time, ultimately reducing fraud and saving taxpayers' money.

3.2 Disaster and Crisis Management

In disaster and crisis management (Zagorecki et al., 2013), ML can help governments make data-driven decisions and respond more effectively to disasters and crises, ultimately saving lives and minimizing damage. ML can be utilized in disaster and crisis management in several ways, including:

Predictive analytics: By analyzing both historical data and current conditions, ML algorithms can forecast the probability and extent of disasters. This can enable governments to be prepared for disasters ahead of time, thereby mitigating the impact of the disaster on the affected communities.

Emergency response: Governments can utilize ML to create emergency response strategies for different scenarios, such as natural disasters or pandemics. Through the application of ML methods, these plans can be optimized to maximize their efficiency and effectiveness (Linardos et al., 2022). After a disaster occurrence, ML algorithms can be utilized by autonomous robots in reach and rescue operations (Zagorecki et al., 2013).

Early warning systems: By utilizing ML algorithms, governments can analyze data from various sources such as satellites, sensors (Lamovec et al., 2013), and social media to identify early warning signs of natural disasters including earthquakes, floods, and wildfires. For example, ML algorithms can analyze data from satellite images and other factors such as wind speed, wind direction, temperature, and humidity to predict the likelihood of a wildfire (Madaio et al., 2016). Such information can then be utilized to issue alerts and warnings to the public, allowing them more time to react appropriately.

Resource allocation: Governments can use ML to optimize the allocation of resources, such as medical supplies, emergency personnel, food, and water, to areas that have been affected by disasters (Sun et al., 2020). By employing ML, resources can be distributed more efficiently to where they are most needed.

3.3 Public Safety and Fairness in Criminal Justice

ML can improve the effectiveness and efficiency of criminal justice systems by reducing bias, identifying patterns, enhancing decision-making, identifying and tracking criminal suspects through facial recognition and other biometric data, and predicting future crime hotspots. However, it's crucial to ensure ethical and responsible use of these technologies to prevent their potential misuse (Greene et al., 2019). ML has the potential to assist criminal justice as follows:

Predictive policing: ML algorithms can analyze real-time and historical crime data to identify patterns and predict where future crimes may occur (Yang, 2019). This can help law enforcement agencies allocate resources and personnel to high-risk areas and prevent crime before it happens.

Risk assessment: By analyzing various factors such as demographic information, criminal history, and mental health status, ML can assist in risk assessment. This can support judges and parole boards to make more informed decisions about release and sentencing.

Bias identification: ML algorithms can analyze vast amounts of data to identify potential biases in the criminal justice system (Ludwig & Mullainathan, 2021), such as racial disparities in sentencing. By identifying these biases, policymakers can implement reforms to ensure more equitable sentencing and parole decisions.

3.4 Transportation and Road Safety Analysis and Prediction

The use of ML technology can help governments improve transportation and road safety in various ways. ML can optimize traffic flow, improve public transportation services, predict travel times, and monitor and analyze traffic patterns to identify areas where road safety improvements are needed. With the use of ML governments can strive towards building secure and streamlined transportation networks for their inhabitants (Olugbade, 2022). ML algorithms can be utilized in the following cases:

Public transportation optimization: By analyzing data from public transportation systems to optimize schedules and routes, ML models can reduce the chances of accidents (Olugbade, 2022) resulting from overcrowding or delays, and enhance the effectiveness and safety of public transportation systems.

Speed limit detection: Speed-related accidents can be reduced with the use of ML models by detecting vehicles that are exceeding the speed limit and issue fines or warnings to drivers.

Road accident prediction: By creating prediction models capable of automatically classifying the severity of injuries in different traffic accidents, patterns associated with dangerous crashes can be identified. By detecting behavioral and roadway accident patterns, useful policies for traffic safety control can be developed (Chong et al., 2005; Durduran, 2010).

Traffic flow prediction: ML models can identify potential congestion areas and predict traffic flow patterns by analyzing historical traffic data as well as real-time data from cameras and sensors (Navarro-Espinoza et al., 2022). This data can be used by government agencies to redirect traffic to avoid accidents caused by traffic congestion and optimize traffic signals.

Road condition monitoring: ML models can analyze data from cameras and sensors to monitor road conditions (Ranyal et al., 2022) such as slippery surfaces, potholes, and cracks. Governments can reduce the risk of accidents caused by poor road conditions by exploiting the gathered information to prioritize road repairs.

3.5 Citizen Safety from Citizen Reports

ML can help governments to spot potential safety threats from citizen reports (Liu et al., 2021). By implementing such applications, public administrations can respond quickly to possible safety threats, creating a safer environment for citizens. In this context, ML algorithms can be utilized as follows:

Real-Time Data Analysis: Real-time data from multiple sources such as weather stations, traffic cameras, and sensor networks can be analyzed with the use of ML algorithms, which can detect patterns and anomalies in the data, identifying potential risks and issuing alerts to authorities.

Social Media Monitoring: Social media is a powerful tool which allow an immediate engagement with the public and can provide instant information to the authorities (Dumitrescu et al., 2011). ML algorithms can be utilized to monitor social media platforms for patterns, phrases, and keywords that indicate danger. This can help identify potential safety threats and alert relevant authorities in real-time. Governments can also use ML to detect disinformation campaigns, which could threaten public safety (Henman, 2020).

Image and Video Analysis: By using ML algorithms to examine videos and pictures provided by citizens, hazardous situations like criminal activities, fires, or accidents can be detected. This can assist public authorities in reacting promptly to prevent additional harm.

Geo-fencing: Geo-fences can be set around sensitive areas such as government buildings, hospitals, and schools. When citizens enter these areas, they can receive safety notifications and alerts on their smartphones, providing them with timely information to stay safe.

3.6 Air Quality Prediction

Public administration can utilize ML to predict air pollution levels (Subramaniam et al., 2022) and take proactive measures to decrease pollution rates, ensuring the health and safety of their citizens. Key areas of ML usability in air quality prediction include

Weather Analysis: Governments can utilize ML algorithms to forecast weather patterns that contribute to air pollution (Subramaniam et al., 2022). By analyzing meteorological data such as temperature, humidity, wind speed, and direction, algorithms can predict areas where pollution levels are likely to increase.

Traffic and Transportation Monitoring: With the use of ML algorithms governments can monitor transportation activities, traffic patterns, and industrial production activities to predict air pollution levels (Awan et al., 2020). By detecting hotspots with high pollution levels due to heavy traffic or industrial activities, governments can take preventative measures to reduce pollution.

Satellite Imaging: Satellite imagery can be utilized by ML algorithms to identify the origin of pollution and estimate its dispersion patterns. The algorithms use air pollution concentration data to anticipate areas and time frames with elevated levels of pollution.

Air Quality Monitoring: ML algorithms can assist governments in monitoring air quality by analyzing data from sensors (Hu et al., 2017) and air quality monitoring stations in real-time. These algorithms can identify patterns in the data, such as abrupt increases in pollution levels, and inform relevant authorities to take timely measures.

Citizen Reporting: Governments can use ML algorithms to analyze citizen reports of pollution levels to predict atmospheric pollution levels in real-time. By identifying patterns in the reports and prioritizing the critical alerts, governments can quickly respond to pollution incidents.

3.7 Water Quality Prediction

Governments can use ML to predict water quality (Najah Ahmedet al., 2019) and take proactive measures to prevent water contamination, enhance water quality, preserve natural resources, and safeguard public health. ML algorithms can be utilized for water quality prediction as follows:

Water Quality Analysis: ML algorithms can be utilized to analyze water quality data to identify trends and patterns in water quality. By analyzing details such as pH, turbidity, dissolved oxygen, and temperature the algorithms can identify regions with poor water quality (Zhu et al., 2022).

Environmental Data Analysis: ML algorithms can analyze environmental data, such as water flow, land use, and weather patterns to anticipate changes in water quality. The algorithms can utilize this information to recognize regions with a heightened risk for poor water quality and immediately alert relevant authorities.

Sensor Networks Analysis: ML algorithms can be used to analyze data from sensor networks to predict changes in water quality. The algorithms can analyze details such as dissolved oxygen, pH, and water temperature to recognize changes in water quality instantly and promptly alert relevant authorities.

Remote Sensing: ML algorithms can analyze remote sensing data, such as aerial photographs and satellite imagery to recognize changes in water quality. The algorithms can analyze details such as turbidity and algae blooms to recognize regions with inferior water quality.

Predictive Modeling: ML algorithms can be used to create predictive models that forecast changes in water quality based on environmental and historical data. The algorithms can utilize this information to identify regions with a high probability of inferior water quality and promptly alert the appropriate authorities.

3.8 Prediction and Decision-Making in Healthcare

In healthcare, governments can use ML to improve public health outcomes by analyzing health data and predicting illnesses (Jayatilake & Ganegoda, 2021), managing pandemics (Debnath et al., 2020), and developing personalized treatment plans for patients. Among the areas of usability of ML in healthcare are the following:

Social Media Monitoring: ML algorithms can monitor social media platforms for mentions of illness symptoms and patterns of behavior that indicate the spread of diseases (Gupta & Katarya, 2020). The algorithms can identify patterns, relevant phrases, and keywords that suggest the likelihood of an outbreak and alert authorities in real-time.

Sensor Networks Analysis: ML algorithms can analyze data from sensor networks that track the transmission of diseases. By detecting patterns in the data, such as abrupt increases in fever or coughing, these algorithms can forecast the location and timing of outbreaks.

Healthcare Data Analysis: Healthcare data, such as medical claims and patient records, can be analyzed with ML algorithms to detect potential outbreaks. By recognizing patterns in the data, such as the emergence of a new illness or a sudden increase in cases of a known disease, these algorithms can inform authorities timely.

Geo-spatial Analysis: ML algorithms can analyze geo-spatial data to recognize regions with a high risk of disease outbreaks. By analyzing factors such as environmental conditions, population density, and transportation patterns, these algorithms can forecast the location of outbreaks.

Climate and Weather Forecasting: ML algorithms can analyze climate and weather patterns to predict disease outbreaks. By analyzing data such as precipitation, temperature, and humidity, these algorithms can predict the location and timing of outbreaks.

3.9 Energy Management

Governments can utilize ML to enhance energy efficiency, reduce dependence on non-renewable sources of energy, and promote sustainability (Zekić-Sušac et al., 2021). ML algorithms can be utilized for energy management as follows:

Forecasting Energy Demand: Governments can predict energy demand through the utilization of ML algorithms. These algorithms can analyze various data sets such as population growth, weather forecasts, and historical consumption patterns to predict high-demand periods and locations. This allows for the optimization of energy supply to meet demand requirements in the short and long term.

Energy Efficiency: ML algorithms can assist governments in improving energy efficiency by predicting energy consumption and pinpointing areas where energy consumption can be minimized. These algorithms can analyze data from various sources like weather sensors and smart meters to detect usage patterns and suggest methods to reduce energy consumption.

Renewable Energy Management: Governments can leverage ML algorithms to manage their renewable energy sources, including solar and wind power (Yao et al., 2023). By analyzing data such as power generation, energy storage, and weather patterns, these algorithms can optimize the utilization of renewable energy sources and minimize the need for non-renewable sources.

Energy Storage Optimization: ML algorithms can be employed to optimize energy storage systems, such as batteries (Yao et al., 2023) and flywheels. By analyzing data such as weather forecasts, energy prices, and power consumption patterns these algorithms can optimize the storage and discharge of energy, which results in reduced costs and enhanced efficiency.

Real-Time Energy Monitoring: Governments can utilize ML algorithms to monitor energy usage in real-time and locate areas where energy consumption can be reduced. By analyzing data from sources such as sensors and smart meters, these algorithms can detect patterns in energy usage and notify the appropriate authorities for timely action.

3.10 Crime Risk Transportation Forecasting

Governments can leverage ML to predict high-risk areas for crime in urban transportation and take preventive measures to improve transportation safety, promote public safety, and enhance the overall quality of life in urban areas. A good prediction accuracy can give governments the chance to promote safer transportation policies in dangerous urban environments (Kouziokas, 2017). In this context, ML algorithms can be utilized as follows:

Crime Data Analysis: Governments can leverage ML algorithms to analyze crime data, which can assist in recognizing trends and patterns in criminal activity. By analyzing details such as type of crime, location, and time, the algorithms can identify areas with a heightened risk of crime.

Spatial Clustering: Geographic information systems (GIS) can be used for the analysis of spatial features. Then, ML algorithms can be utilized to aggregate spatial objects into clusters, where an increased concentration of incidents occurs.

Real-Time Monitoring: Governments can utilize ML algorithms to oversee crime and transportation activities in real-time and immediately inform relevant authorities when high-risk conditions are detected. The algorithms can analyze data from surveillance cameras, sensors, and social media platforms to recognize patterns and trends in transportation and criminal activity.

3.11 Resource Usage Optimization

Governments can utilize ML algorithms to optimize resource usage, decrease expenses, and improve the standard of living for their communities. Key areas of ML applications in resource usage optimization include

Resource Management: ML can support governments in improving their decision-making processes related to resource management. This includes enhancing energy efficiency in buildings (Runge & Zmeureanu, 2021), forecasting the maintenance requirements for public infrastructure, and optimizing traffic light schedules. Therefore, governments can effectively utilize their resources and make more informed decisions.

Energy Optimization: ML algorithms can aid governments in optimizing their energy resources, including fuel and electricity by analyzing patterns in energy consumption and detecting opportunities for conservation. Through effective energy optimization, governments can cut down on energy expenses and mitigate their environmental impact by reducing their carbon footprint.

Water Optimization: Governments can leverage ML algorithms to optimize their water resources by analyzing patterns in water usage and identifying opportunities for conservation. This approach can help governments to promote sustainable water use and reduce water costs.

Waste Optimization: Governments can utilize ML algorithms to optimize their waste management resources, including garbage collection and recycling (Namoun et al., 2022), by analyzing patterns in waste generation and detecting opportunities for recycling or minimizing waste. Through effective waste optimization, governments can cut down on waste disposal expenses and encourage sustainable waste management practices.

Resource Allocation: ML algorithms can enable governments to allocate their resources more efficiently by analyzing various data points (Valle-Cruz et al., 2022), such as economic activity, population demographics, and environmental conditions. This approach can help governments identify the areas where resources are most needed and ensure that resources are utilized effectively to meet the needs of their communities. Through optimized resource allocation, governments can promote greater efficiency in resource usage.

3.12 Sentiment Analysis

Governments can utilize ML for sentiment analysis (Xu et al., 2022), which involves evaluating public sentiment on various topics, such as emergency response and policy decisions. Therefore, governments can gain insight into public opinion and address concerns efficiently. ML algorithms can be applied for sentiment analysis as follows:

Social Media Monitoring: ML algorithms can assist governments in monitoring social media platforms and analyze public sentiment detected in posts and comments related to events, issues, and government policies. This approach can provide governments with valuable insights into public opinion, which they can use to adjust their policies accordingly.

Citizen Feedback Analysis: ML algorithms can aid governments in analyzing citizen complaints and feedback by identifying common issues and sentiment. This approach can enable governments to address these issues more effectively and efficiently.

News and Media Monitoring: Governments can employ ML algorithms to monitor news and media outlets and analyze public sentiment detected in news articles and broadcasts related to government policies, events, and issues. This approach can enable governments to gain valuable insights into public opinion through media analysis and use this information to adjust their policies accordingly.

Election Campaign Analysis: ML algorithms can assist governments in analyzing public sentiment detecting in speeches, debates, and advertisements during election campaigns. This approach can provide governments with valuable insights into public opinion during election campaigns, which they can use to adjust their campaigns accordingly.

Public Health Monitoring: Governments can leverage ML algorithms to analyze public sentiment regarding health issues detected in social media posts, news articles, and other sources. This approach can enable governments to gain a better understanding of public perception and address concerns related to health issues more effectively (Kowalski et al., 2020).

3.13 Predictive Maintenance

Predictive maintenance is considered one of the most promising applications of ML in the public sector. ML algorithms can analyze data from public assets, facilities, vehicle fleets, equipment, and power grids (Carvalho et al., 2019), to identify patterns and trends that could indicate potential maintenance issues. Evaluating the results, government agencies can take preventive measures to avoid costly repairs in the future. The application areas of ML algorithms for predictive maintenance are as follows:

Fleet Maintenance: Governments can employ ML algorithms to anticipate the maintenance requirements of their vehicle fleets (Eisler & Holmes, 2021), including ambulances, police cars, and buses. These algorithms can examine data such as usage patterns, mileage, and fuel consumption to forecast when maintenance is required. By anticipating maintenance needs, governments can decrease vehicle downtime and ensure that their fleet is always operational.

Public Facilities Maintenance: Governments can utilize ML algorithms to anticipate maintenance requirements for public facilities such as community centers, parks, and libraries. The algorithms can analyze past maintenance history, usage patterns, and weather conditions, to anticipate when repairs are necessary. By forecasting maintenance needs, governments can decrease maintenance expenses and guarantee that public facilities are always in excellent condition for the public to use.

Infrastructure Maintenance: Governments can utilize ML algorithms for predicting maintenance requirements for their infrastructure, which includes roads, buildings, and bridges. These algorithms analyze various factors such as usage patterns, material degradation, and weather patterns to determine when maintenance is necessary. By anticipating maintenance needs, governments can ensure the safety of their infrastructure while also reducing maintenance costs.

Equipment Maintenance: ML algorithms can forecast maintenance requirements for equipment, such as HVAC systems (heating, ventilation, and air conditioning), pumps, and generators. These algorithms can analyze data such as sensor readings, performance metrics, and usage patterns, and to anticipate when maintenance will be necessary. By anticipating maintenance requirements, governments can decrease equipment downtime and ensure the smooth operation of their equipment.

Power Grid Maintenance: Governments can utilize ML algorithms to anticipate maintenance requirements for their power grids. The algorithms can examine data such as equipment performance, usage patterns, and weather patterns to identify when maintenance is necessary. Through anticipating maintenance requirements, governments can decrease power outages and guarantee the reliable operation of power grids.

3.14 Chatbots in the Public Sector

Chatbots are software applications created to mimic human-like conversation, primarily on the internet. They can use text or sound to communicate with humans (Henman, 2020). There has been a noteworthy increase in the use of chatbots in various forms, including mobile platforms, social media, and websites, across both public and private sectors (Mohasses, 2019). They have a range of uses, including customer service, providing information, and entertainment (Brandtzaeg & Følstad, 2017). Chatbots vary from basic rule-based systems to more complex AI-powered models (Androutsopoulou et al., 2019) that can analyze and learn from user interactions to enhance their performance. A chatbot based on AI technology is a dialogue system that can simulate human chatting, not just answering a question but learning how to converse more naturally. ML methods, data mining, and Natural Language Processing (NLP) can be applied to implement such chatbots that can give informative answers in human language, recommending the most appropriate options for individuals based on their unique needs (Zumstein & Hundertmark, 2017).

Chatbots can aid in improving the efficiency of public administration (Henman, 2020; Makasi et al., 2022). They provide 24/7 information and personalized services to citizens regarding public services (Androutsopoulou et al., 2019; Zumstein & Hundertmark, 2017) that are similar to what a public service representative would provide (Antoniadis & Tambouris, 2022). Most of the inquiries that the public sector receives are repetitive in nature and could be anticipated and automated for chatbots to respond to (Lommatzsch, 2018). This is particularly beneficial in situations where there is a significant amount of data, as chatbots can more easily identify high-frequency topics and handle complicated policies and legislation (Henman, 2020). In case where a chatbot cannot address an issue, there is the option to submit a specific request to be dealt by a knowledgeable staff member.

Chatbots offer more benefits for both citizens and public administration. Chatbots provide citizens with simplified access to information without having to navigate multiple websites, access information from any device and location, round-the-clock service, straightforward communication that does not require technical expertise, chat-based interface that citizens are familiar with thanks to messaging apps (Dale, 2016; Følstad & Brandtzaeg, 2017), and multilingual support. Moreover, citizens find it easy to communicate with chatbots as they would with a public service officer making this form of communication very user-friendly, they receive immediate resolution to simple or routine issues, and they save time and effort (Brandtzaeg & Følstad, 2017) as they do not need to navigate through frequently asked questions. Also creating chatbots with voice functionality can serve people with visual or mobility impairments.

From the administrative viewpoint, chatbots free up employees from help desks and reduce administrative workload (Lommatzsch, 2018; van Noordt & Misuraca, 2019). Data collected from chatbots can later be analyzed and services can be created/modified according to citizens' needs. Recently, most security issues related to chatbots have been identified and addressed, so chatbots are considered quite secure

(PwC EU Services, 2019). Moreover, the implementation of a chatbot may cost less than developing other multiple-platforms applications which need trained human operators to work.

4 Challenges of Utilizing Machine Learning Applications in Public Administration

Although ML has the potential to offer numerous benefits in governments, there are also various challenges that need to be addressed. In the following the challenges of integrating ML into government operations are discussed. These can be classified into three groups: ethical, technological, and organizational challenges.

The use of ML in the public domain poses ethical challenges, particularly in terms of data quality, data privacy, and ethical design of ML systems, as it is crucial to ensure that ML systems are used responsibly in order to build public trust (Greene et al., 2019). The effectiveness of ML algorithms relies on the quality of data on which they are trained (Vamathevan et al., 2019). If that data is biased inaccurate, incomplete, and hard to access, the outcomes may also be biased or incorrect (Henman, 2020). This can lead in discrimination against certain groups, exacerbating existing social inequalities. ML algorithms can accidentally maintain existing prejudices or act in a discriminatory manner towards certain groups, such as minorities or low-income individuals (Agarwal, 2018). Governments must ensure that their ML applications are open, interpretable (Graziani et al., 2023), and responsible to prevent these concerns. ML algorithms have the capacity to intensify existing biases and prejudices in datasets, resulting in unjust or discriminatory consequences. This highlights the significance of conscientious and ethical utilization of ML in government management, as well as the necessity of tackling issues of bias and discrimination in government datasets to ensure administrative justice.

Data privacy and security pose significant ethical challenges in utilizing ML in public administration (Agarwal, 2018; Henman, 2020; Thapa & Camtepe, 2021). The large amounts of data needed for ML algorithms to function can cause considerable privacy concerns, particularly if data is personal, sensitive, or confidential. Therefore, it is essential to ensure that ML systems are secure and protected against cyber threats. Since governments are responsible for safeguarding confidential information, they impose stringent regulations that dictate how data can be utilized. ML systems must comply with these rules to guarantee the protection and confidentiality of the data they utilize.

Another ethical challenge of using ML in public administration concerns the interpretation and elucidation of the outcomes of ML algorithms. Unlike traditional decision-making processes, which are often transparent and comprehensible to the public, the algorithms used in ML are often complicated and difficult to become explainable (Graziani et al., 2023; Pi, 2021). This can result in a lack of confidence in government decisions and may make it challenging to hold government officials accountable for their actions. Government officials should be able to evaluate the consequences of ML algorithms on the public values of accuracy, fairness, transparency, and equity (Veale & Brass, 2019). This is a crucial issue for the public sector since the decisions made by ML systems can significantly impact citizens' lives. The public sector finds itself in a challenging predicament, as it must balance its duty to protect citizens from potential harms caused by algorithms with its desire to improve its own efficiency. In other words, it must navigate the competing goals of governing algorithms while being governed by algorithms (Kuziemski & Misuraca, 2020).

An additional difficulty involves the requirement for investing in both technology and personnel, which can be a complicated and time-consuming process. Technological challenges are related with the available infrastructure. Government organizations may rely on outdated legacy systems that are not compatible with new technologies (Veale & Brass, 2019). In this case, they experience difficulties in developing ML models and realize their intended benefits.

Concerning organizational challenges, a skills gap may be observed when ML is introduced in public administration (Agarwal, 2018). Many government agencies may lack the expertise required to develop and implement ML applications, making it difficult to realize their full potential benefits and their constraints. The limited awareness of how ML can transform public services and understanding of the ML algorithms could result in misconceptions, unrealistic expectations, and improper use of the technology (Kuziemski & Misuraca, 2020). Moreover, implementing ML may necessitate considerable changes to current processes and workflows, which could be met with opposition from staff and other stakeholders that are resistant to change.

Despite the ML potential for transforming public administration and enhancing government services, it is essential to confront the obstacles linked to its implementation and guarantee principled and judicious use of the technology. Governments must create distinct policies and protocols, guarantee data quality and precision, and establish supervisory procedures to ensure sensible and responsible use of ML with a high level of accountability.

5 Conclusions

In this paper, we examined the benefits and challenges in applying ML in public administration. We presented the key areas of applications of ML in the public sector and highlighted the great potential of ML algorithms in improving government operations, decision-making, and citizen services. ML assists in fraud detection by uncovering fraudulent activity in areas like welfare, tax, and healthcare. In public safety, crime data analysis helps allocate resources and prevents crime. For disaster response, information is evaluated, and the speed and efficiency of public administration's actions are improved. In the criminal justice system, bias in decision-making can be limited. Transportation also benefits from ML by optimizing traffic flow, reducing congestion, and improving mobility. Healthcare sees improvement through analysis of patient data and prediction of disease outbreaks. ML also helps in environmental protection by monitoring and predicting changes in the natural environment to mitigate climate change. Chatbots and virtual assistants can offer citizens fast and efficient service, reducing wait times and increasing satisfaction.

Then we discussed the numerous challenges of integrating ML into government operations, including technological, ethical, and organizational issues. Technological issues concern the difficulties that arise from the deployment of ML applications on outdated legacy systems. Ethical issues include several challenges such as low data quality that may lead to potential biases and discrimination of ML algorithm results, less responsible and ethical implementation of ML applications, difficulties in interpreting and explaining ML algorithm results, and threats of data privacy and security. Organizational issues are related with the lack of awareness of ML algorithms and probably a skills gap in government agencies. To address these challenges, governments must invest in necessary infrastructure, human resources and expertise, develop best practices and standards for ML use, increase transparency and accountability in decision-making processes, and ensure data privacy and security.

By embracing ML technology, governments can build a more intelligent, efficient, and responsive government for their citizens. As the use of ML continues to grow in the public sector, governments have the potential to move from the e-government phase to Smart Government. This transition would involve the implementation of an increasing number of smart areas such as smart disaster management, smart transportation, smart urban planning, and smart medicare.

References

Agarwal, P. K. (2018). Public administration challenges in the world of AI and bots. *Public Administration Review, 78*(6), 917–921. https://doi.org/10.1111/puar.12979

Ali, A., et al. (2022). Financial fraud detection based on machine learning: A systematic literature review. *Applied Sciences, 12*(19), 9637. https://doi.org/10.3390/app12199637

Amponsah, A. A., et al. (2022). A novel fraud detection and prevention method for healthcare claim processing using machine learning and blockchain technology. *Decision Analytics Journal, 4*, 100122. https://doi.org/10.1016/j.dajour.2022.100122

Anastasopoulos, L. J., & Whitford, A. B. (2019). Machine learning for public administration research, with application to organizational reputation. *Journal of Public Administration Research and Theory, 29*(3), 491–510. https://doi.org/10.1093/jopart/muy060

Androutsopoulou, A., et al. (2019). Transforming the communication between citizens and government through AI-guided chatbots. *Government Information Quarterly, 36*(2), 358–367. https://doi.org/10.1016/j.giq.2018.10.001

Antoniadis, P., & Tambouris, E. (2022). PassBot: A chatbot for providing information on getting a Greek passport. In *Proceedings of the 14th International Conference on Theory and Practice of Electronic Governance (ICEGOV '21)* (pp. 292–297). Association for Computing Machinery. https://doi.org/10.1145/3494193.3494233

Awan, F. M., et al. (2020). Improving road traffic forecasting using air pollution and atmospheric data: Experiments based on LSTM recurrent neural networks. *Sensors, 20*(13), 3749. https://doi.org/10.3390/s20133749

Barcellos, R., et al. (2017). Transparency in practice: Using visualization to enhance the interpretability of open data. In *Proceedings of the 18th Annual International Conference on Digital Government Research* (pp. 139–148). Association for Computing Machinery. https://doi.org/10.1145/3085228.3085294

Bishop, C. M. (2006). *Pattern recognition and machine learning. Information science and statistics.* Springer.

Bojovic, Ž, et al. (2023). Interconnected government services: An approach toward smart government. *Applied Science, 13*, 1062. https://doi.org/10.3390/app13021062

Brandtzaeg, P. B., & Følstad, A. (2017). Why people use chatbots. In I. Kompatsiaris, et al. (Eds.), *Internet Science. INSCI 2017.* Lecture notes in computer science (Vol. 10673, pp. 377–392). Springer. https://doi.org/10.1007/978-3-319-70284-1_30

Carvalho, T. P., et al. (2019). A Systematic literature review of machine learning methods applied to predictive maintenance. *Computers & Industrial Engineering, 137*, Article ID: 106024. https://doi.org/10.1016/j.cie.2019.106024

Chong, M., et al. (2005). Traffic accident analysis using machine learning paradigms. *Informatica. An International Journal of Computing and Informatics, 29*(1), 89–98.

Constantinescu, R., & Edu, T. (2022). Internet of Things (IoT) as an instrument to improve business and marketing strategies. A literature review. *European Journal of Interdisciplinary Studies, 14*(2), 143–154. https://doi.org/10.24818/ejis.2022.26

Dale, R. (2016). The return of the chatbots. *Natural Language Engineering, 22*, 811–817. https://doi.org/10.1017/S1351324916000243

Debnath, S., et al. (2020). Machine learning to assist clinical decision-making during the COVID-19 pandemic. *Bioelectronic Medicine, 6*(1), 1–8. https://doi.org/10.1186/s42234-020-00050-8

de Roux, D., et al. (2018). Tax fraud detection for under-reporting declarations using an unsupervised machine learning approach. In *Proceedings of the 24th ACM SIGKDD International Conference on Knowledge Discovery & Data Mining* (KDD '18) (pp. 215–222). Association for Computing Machinery. https://doi.org/10.1145/3219819.3219878

Dumitrescu, L., et al. (2011). Disclosing the promising power of social media—An important digital marketing tool. *Studies in Business and Economics, 6*(1), 37–45. https://magazines.ulbsibiu.ro/eccsf/publicatii.html

Durduran, S. (2010). A decision making system to automatic recognize of traffic accidents on the basis of a GIS platform. *Expert Systems with Applications, 37*(12), 7729–7736. https://doi.org/10.1016/j.eswa.2010.04.068

Eisler, C., & Holmes, M. (2021). Applying automated machine learning to improve budget estimates for a naval fleet maintenance facility. In *Proceedings of the 10th International Conference on Pattern Recognition Applications and Methods* (ICPRAM 2021) (pp. 586–593). https://doi.org/10.5220/0010302205860593

Følstad, A., & Brandtzaeg, P. (2017). Chatbots and the new world of HCI. *Interactions, 24*, 38–42. https://doi.org/10.1145/3085558

Graziani, M., et al. (2023). A global taxonomy of interpretable AI: Unifying the terminology for the technical and social sciences. *Artificial Intelligence Review, 56*, 3473–3504. https://doi.org/10.1007/s10462-022-10256-8

Greene, D., et al. (2019). Better, nicer, clearer, fairer: A critical assessment of the movement for ethical artificial intelligence and machine learning. In *Proceedings of the 52nd Hawaii International Conference on System Sciences* (pp. 2122–2131). https://doi.org/10.24251/hicss.2019.258

Gupta, A., & Katarya, R. (2020). Social media based surveillance systems for healthcare using machine learning: A systematic review. *Journal of Biomedical Informatics, 108*, 103500. https://doi.org/10.1016/j.jbi.2020.103500

Henman, P. (2020). Improving public services using artificial intelligence: Possibilities, pitfalls, governance. *Asia Pacific Journal of Public Administration, 42*(4), 209–221. https://doi.org/10.1080/23276665.2020.1816188

Hirokawa, S., et al. (2017). Machine learning is better than human to satisfy decision by majority. In *Proceedings of the International Conference on Web Intelligence* (WI '17) (pp. 694–701). Association for Computing Machinery. https://doi.org/10.1145/3106426.3106520.

Hu, K., et al. (2017). HazeEst: Machine learning based metropolitan air pollution estimation from fixed and mobile sensors. *IEEE Sensors Journal, 17*(11), 3517–3525. https://doi.org/10.1109/jsen.2017.2690975

Jayatilake, S. M. D. A. C., & Ganegoda, G. U. (2021). Involvement of machine learning tools in healthcare decision making. *Journal of Healthcare Engineering, 2021*, 6679512. https://doi.org/10.1155/2021/6679512

Kouziokas, G. N. (2017). The application of artificial intelligence in public administration for forecasting high crime risk transportation areas in urban environment. *Transportation Research Procedia, 24*, 467–473. https://doi.org/10.1016/j.trpro.2017.05.083

Kowalski, R., et al. (2020). Improving public services by mining citizen feedback: An application of natural language processing. *Public Administration, 98*, 1011–1026. https://doi.org/10.1111/padm.12656

Kuziemski, M., & Misuraca, G. (2020). AI governance in the public sector: Three tales from the frontiers of automated decision-making in democratic settings. *Telecommunications Policy., 44*(6), 101976. https://doi.org/10.1016/j.telpol.2020.101976

Lamovec, P., et al. (2013). Detection of flooded areas using machine learning techniques: Case study of the Ljubljana Moor floods in 2010. *Disaster Advances, 6*(7), 4–11.

Linardos, V., et al. (2022). Machine learning in disaster management: Recent developments in methods and applications. *Machine Learning and Knowledge Extraction, 4*(2), 446–473. https://doi.org/10.3390/make4020020

Liu, Z. G., et al. (2021). Identifying community fire hazards from citizen communication by applying transfer learning and machine learning techniques. *Fire Technology, 57*, 2809–2838. https://doi.org/10.1007/s10694-020-01035-4

Lommatzsch, A. (2018). A next generation chatbot-framework for the public administration. In M. Hodoň, G. Eichler, C. Erfurth, G. Fahrnberger (Eds.), *Innovations for community services. I4CS 2018. Communications in computer and information science* (Vol. 863, pp. 127–141). Springer. https://doi.org/10.1007/978-3-319-93408-2_10

Ludwig, J., & Mullainathan, S. (2021). Fragile algorithms and fallible decision-makers: Lessons from the justice system. *The Journal of Economic Perspectives, 35*(4), 71–96. https://www.jstor.org/stable/27074126.

Madaio, M., et al. (2016). Firebird: Predicting fire risk and prioritizing fire inspections in Atlanta. In *Proceedings of the 22nd ACM SIGKDD International Conference on Knowledge Discovery and Data Mining (KDD '16)* (pp. 185–194). Association for Computing Machinery. https://doi.org/10.1145/2939672.2939682

Makasi, T., et al. (2022). A typology of chatbots in public service delivery. *IEEE Software, 39*(3), 58–66. https://doi.org/10.1109/MS.2021.3073674

Mohasses, M. (2019). How AI-chatbots can make Dubai smarter? In *Amity International Conference on Artificial Intelligence* (AICAI), Dubai, United Arab Emirates (pp. 439–446). https://doi.org/10.1109/AICAI.2019.8701413

Najah Ahmed, A., et al. (2019). Machine learning methods for better water quality prediction. *Journal of Hydrology, 578*, 124084. https://doi.org/10.1016/j.jhydrol.2019.124084

Namoun, A., et al. (2022). Solid waste generation and disposal using machine learning approaches: A survey of solutions and challenges. *Sustainability, 14*(20), 13578. https://doi.org/10.3390/su142013578

Navarro-Espinoza, A., et al. (2022). Prediction for smart traffic lights using machine learning algorithms. *Technologies, 10*(5). https://doi.org/10.3390/technologies10010005

Olugbade, S. (2022). A review of artificial intelligence and machine learning for incident detectors in road transport systems. *Mathematical and Computational Applications, 27*, 77. https://doi.org/10.3390/mca27050077

Oneto, L., & Chiappa, S. (2020). Fairness in machine learning. In *Recent trends in learning from data, studies in computational intelligence* (Vol. 896, pp. 155–196). Springer. https://doi.org/10.1007/978-3-030-43883-8_7

Pi, Y. (2021). Machine learning in governments: Benefits, challenges and future directions. *JeDEM—EJournal of EDemocracy and Open Government, 13*(1), 203–219. https://doi.org/10.29379/jedem.v13i1.625

PwC EU Services. (2019). *Architecture for public service chatbots*. ISA^2 programme, European Commission. https://joinup.ec.europa.eu/sites/default/files/news/2019-09/ISA2_Architecture%20for%20public%20service%20chatbots.pdf

Ranyal, E., et al. (2022). Road condition monitoring using smart sensing and artificial intelligence: A review. *Sensors, 22*(8), 3044. https://doi.org/10.3390/s22083044

Rocha, J., et al. (2020). Money laundering and terrorism financing detection using neural networks and an abnormality indicator. *Expert Systems with Applications, 169,* 114470. https://doi.org/10.1016/j.eswa.2020.114470

Runge, J., & Zmeureanu, R. (2021). A review of deep learning techniques for forecasting energy use in buildings. *Energies, 14*(3), 608. https://doi.org/10.3390/en14030608

Sehatbakhsh, N., et al. (2019). Security and privacy considerations for machine learning models deployed in the government and public sector. In *Proceedings of the AAAI Conference on Artificial Intelligence, Fall Symposium Series (AAAI-FSS)* (pp. 1–4). https://doi.org/10.48550/arXiv.2010.05809

Subramaniam, S., et al. (2022). Artificial intelligence technologies for forecasting air pollution and human health: A narrative review. *Sustainability, 14*, 9951. https://doi.org/10.3390/su14169951

Sun, W., et al. (2020). Applications of artificial intelligence for disaster management. *Natural Hazards, 103*, 2631–2689. https://doi.org/10.1007/s11069-020-04124-3

Thapa, C., & Camtepe, S. (2021). Precision health data: Requirements, challenges and existing techniques for data security and privacy. *Computers in Biology and Medicine, 129*, 104130. https://doi.org/10.1016/j.compbiomed.2020.104130

Valle-Cruz, D., et al. (2022). From E-budgeting to smart budgeting: Exploring the potential of artificial intelligence in government decision-making for resource allocation. *Government Information Quarterly, 39*(2), 101644. https://doi.org/10.1016/j.giq.2021.101644

Vamathevan, J., et al. (2019). Applications of machine learning in drug discovery and development. *Nature Reviews Drug Discovery, 18*(6), 463–477. https://doi.org/10.1038/s41573-019-0024-5

van Noordt, C., & Misuraca, G. (2019). New wine in old bottles: Chatbots in government. In P. Panagiotopoulos, et al. (Eds.), *Electronic Participation. ePart 2019.* Lecture notes in computer science (Vol. 11686, pp. 49–59). Springer. https://doi.org/10.1007/978-3-030-27397-2_5

Veale, M., & Brass, I. (2019). Administration by algorithm? Public management meets public sector machine learning. In K. Yeung & M. Lodge (Eds.), *Algorithmic regulation* (pp. 1–30). Oxford University Press.

Xu, Q. A., et al. (2022). A systematic review of social media-based sentiment analysis: Emerging trends and challenges. *Decision Analytics Journal, 3*, 100073. https://doi.org/10.1016/j.dajour.2022.100073

Xu, Y., et al. (2021). Artificial intelligence: A powerful paradigm for scientific research. *The Innovation, 2*(4), 100179. https://doi.org/10.1016/j.xinn.2021.100179

Yang, F. (2019). *Predictive policing. Oxford research encyclopedia. Criminology and criminal justice.* Oxford University Press. https://doi.org/10.1093/acrefore/9780190264079.013.508

Yao, Z., et al. (2023). Machine learning for a sustainable energy future. *Nature Reviews Materials, 8*, 202–215. https://doi.org/10.1038/s41578-022-00490-5

Zagorecki, A. T., et al. (2013). Data mining and machine learning in the context of disaster and crisis management. *International Journal of Emergency Management, 9*(4), 351–365. https://doi.org/10.1504/ijem.2013.059879

Zekić-Sušac, M., et al. (2021). Machine learning based system for managing energy efficiency of public sector as an approach towards smart cities. *International Journal of Information Management, 58*, 102074. https://doi.org/10.1016/j.ijinfomgt.2020.102074

Zhu, M., et al. (2022). A review of the application of machine learning in water quality evaluation. *Eco-Environment & Health, 1*(2), 107–116. https://doi.org/10.1016/j.eehl.2022.06.001

Zumstein, D., & Hundertmark, S. (2017). Chatbots—An interactive technology for personalized communication, transactions and services. *IADIS International Journal on WWW/Internet, 15*(1), 96–109.

Cloud Governance in the European Union: Unlocking the Power of Data in the Era of the Digital Economy

Panagiotis Kitsos and Paraskevi Pappa

Abstract The unprecedented increase of activity in the digital domain, which was significantly developed during the pandemic, made clear that the new environment should be carefully regulated. In the advent of the global health crisis, several policy and regulatory initiatives are adopted by the EU in relation to the evolution of cloud computing as means of innovation, economic growth, and digital sovereignty. The pivotal transition of economic and societal activities to cloud computing services created numerous policy and legal issues that derive from the fact that non-European cloud service providers dominate the cloud market. In response to developments EU faces the enormous challenge to increase its presence on the market, cloud uptake and boost user confidence by facilitating access and use of Cloud computing infrastructure and services through a new set of EU rules.

Keywords Cloud computing · Cyber-security · Data economy · EU regulation · Data protection · GAIA-x · Data spaces

JEL Classification Codes K21 · K24 · K33

1 Introduction

The unprecedented conditions that have arisen during the pandemic had an enormous impact on the development and usage of digital tools since almost every sector and industry had to accelerate their digital transformation in order to adapt their functions to the new dystopian reality. From public health to global economy, the need to continue to offer efficient and resilient services resulted in a widespread

P. Kitsos (✉)
Hellenic Open University, Syrrakou 2, 45221 Ioannina, Greece
e-mail: kitsos.panagiotis@ac.eap.gr

P. Pappa
University of Ioannina, Psathaki, 48100 Preveza, Greece
e-mail: pvpappa@uoi.gr

M. Mavri et al. (eds.), *Digital Economy and Green Growth*, Contributions to Economics, https://doi.org/10.1007/978-3-031-66669-8_5

adoption of Cloud computing[1] which serves as a foundation for organizations across various industries so as to modernize their IT infrastructure, operate remotely, and improve their efficiency. In the meantime, the cloud infrastructure market in Europe is dominated by U.S. tech companies and that means that European data can be stored in servers that are either located outside its borders or that belong to undertakings of foreign interests (European Commission COM/2014/214, 2014). This raises concerns not just because Europeans have lost grasp over their personal and non-personal data, but also because EU tech companies seem unable to compete with the US tech industry, achieve a level of digital autonomy, and foster digital innovation and growth in Europe.

The issue of transatlantic personal data flows was highlighted in 2015 with ruling C-362/14, of Court of Justice of European Union (CJEU) which invalidated the European Commission Decision 2000/520 on the adequacy of the EU-U.S Safe Harbour framework drawn up to facilitate personal data transfers from E.U. to U.S.A. (Monteleone et al., 2015).· This led to the creation of the Privacy Shield framework as an alternative data transfer mechanism which was also invalidated by the CJEU with ruling C-311/18 (Mildebrath, 2020). In both cases, the Court found that despite the adequacy decisions the US surveillance laws do not allow for a sufficient protection of EU citizens personal data seriously disrupting the transatlantic data flows.

In order to address these issues, the EU is launching a digital ecosystem along with the creation of a regulatory "fortress". In particular, the EU has been developing policies and legislation aimed at assisting Europe towards the digital transition of its economy. In 2018 the Commission launched the "Digital Europe" program, which aimed at enhancing the EU's digital economy, adopting and assisting the growth of digital technologies (i.e., supercomputers, Artificial Intelligence, Cybersecurity) for the period 2021–2027 (European Commission Communication 443, 2018), shaping it's digital capabilities and technologies that could transform the Public Administration and establish a Network of European Digital Innovation Hubs for industry, business, and administration (Green, 2020).

On 19 February 2020, the European Commission published the Communication "A European strategy for data" as a part of its digital strategy. This initiative aims to position the EU at the forefront of a data-driven society and enabling the seamless flow of data across all sectors in the EU market. Such an initiative is expected to benefit businesses, researchers, and public administrations alike. For the purpose of accomplishing its aims, the European Strategy for Data focuses among other things

---

[1] A definition of cloud computing is provided by the National Institute of Standards and Technology (NIST) as "a model for enabling ubiquitous, convenient, on-demand network access to a shared pool of configurable computing resources (e.g., networks, servers, storage, applications and services) that can be rapidly provisioned and released with minimal management effort or service provider interaction." The NIST identifies five key aspects of cloud computing, namely: on-demand self-service, broad network access, resource pooling, rapid elasticity or expansion, and measured service. It also identifies three "service models" (software, platform, and infrastructure), and four "deployment models" (private, community, public, and hybrid) that constitute the ways of cloud services deliverance together categorize ways to deliver cloud services. See Mell et al. (2011).

on reshaping the digital policy environment by adopting legislation on data management, access, and reuse, investing in European projects to develop data processing infrastructures, data sharing tools, architectures and governance mechanisms for thriving data sharing and bringing together energy-efficient and trusted cloud infrastructures and related services. It aims to facilitate the establishment of a procurement marketplace for data processing services and provide clarity on the applicable regulatory framework for cloud services to ensure access to secure, fair, and competitive cloud services (European Commission COM 2020/66, 2020).

In March 2021, the European Commission announced the Digital Decade policy program which covered targets related to skills, government, infrastructure, and business for 2030 in order for Europe to manage its digital transformation and grow its economy with cloud computing being at the heart of this transformation (European Commission COM 2021/118, 2021).

These initiatives would ensure that the EU tech industry would lead the way in the new digital environment towards a single European data space in order to create a level playing field for businesses, researchers, and public administration (European Commission COM/2020/66, 2020). In the context of these initiatives, EU is building more specialized policy and legislative instruments related to cloud computing.

This paper aims to serve as a bird's eye view of the current regulatory attempts in fields related to technical aspects of cloud computing in EU and shed some light to the different aspects of cloud computing design and implementation policies and regulations. It seeks to raise the degree of comprehension required to recognize current legislation and offer perspectives into the European Union's regulatory priorities.

Doctrinal legal methodology has been applied, focusing on the analysis of existing legal rules, principles, and regulations. Comprehensive research was performed to gather all the relevant legal sources, including regulations, guidelines, legal commentary, and scholarly articles. Legislative history has been considered. In addition, empirical legal scholarship has been used as a research tool incorporating qualitative methods, namely case observation.

To highlight the regulatory and policy environment of Cloud computing in the European Union, we rely on desk research and textual legal analysis, based on sources including legislation, its appendices and accompanying policy documentation, grey literature (EU Institutions' and national reports, briefs, policy documents, etc.) and academic literature. In particular, the paper focuses on the GAIA-X project, the European Federated Cloud, European Cybersecurity Certification Scheme for Cloud Services, European Alliance on Industrial Data, Edge and Cloud, the publication of Codes of Conduct and the European Open Science Cloud. Furthermore, it presents significant EU legal initiatives, related to the evolution of cloud computing nominally the "General Data Protection Regulation" (GDPR), the "Regulation on the free flow of non-personal data", together with the "EU Cybersecurity, Act Digital Operational Resilience Act" and the "Data Act".

2 Cloud Computing Market

The Cloud computing market in Europe has experienced significant growth and is expected to continue expanding. More and more European enterprises are migrating their IT infrastructure and services to the cloud. This trend is driven by benefits such as increased flexibility, agility, scalability, and cost savings. The contribution of cloud computing in fostering the data economy is crucial and its significance in a data–driven economy has been stressed since 2012 (European Commission Com/2012/0529, 2012). In 2017, the European Commission adopted a "Staff Working Document on the free flow of data and emerging issues of the European data economy", in which the importance of investing in Cloud computing technologies is stressed as a means to foster data-driven economy (European Commission SWD/2017/02, 2017). In a study published in February 2022, the Commission underlined the importance of cloud computing presenting an overview of volume and types of cloud data inflows and outflows per economic sector, location, size of enterprises, and type of cloud services across the 27 Member States, Iceland, Norway, Switzerland, and the UK. The study found, among other things, that in 2020, the largest data flows to cloud came from the health sector, retail, and education, estimating that by 2030, the flow of data stemming from European enterprises buying cloud services will be 15 times higher than in 2020 (European Commission Mapping Data Flows, 2022).

The diffusion of cloud computing in EU companies is steadily increasing, but there is still growth potential. In 2014, 18% of all European companies used cloud computing but according to recent studies in 2021 this percentage rose to 41%, mainly for email hosting and file storage while 73% of these used advanced cloud services related to application security, company database hosting, and computing platform usage for application development, testing, and debugging. It is worth noting the major differences in cloud adoption between EU countries with the Scandinavian countries at the top with the highest adoption rates and the Balkan countries and Greece at the bottom (Carlo, 2023). This evolution makes cloud computing one of the most continually disruptive forces in IT markets since the early days of the digital age. As shown in Fig. 1 in 2021 the share increased to 41% in Sweden (75%), Finland (75%), the Netherlands (65%), and Denmark (65%) at least 65% of enterprises used cloud computing. On the other hand, in Greece (22%), Romania (14%), and Bulgaria (13%) less than 25% of enterprises did so.

It is predicted that by 2024 these numbers will rise with more than 45% of IT spending to shift to cloud (Gartner, 2019).

3 Regulatory Framework

As noted, COVID-19 health crisis speeded up the adoption of Internet technologies and the extensive adoption of cloud computing. Societies shifted to Internet tools, (i.e., cooperation platforms, virtual events, virtual entertainment, ecommerce,

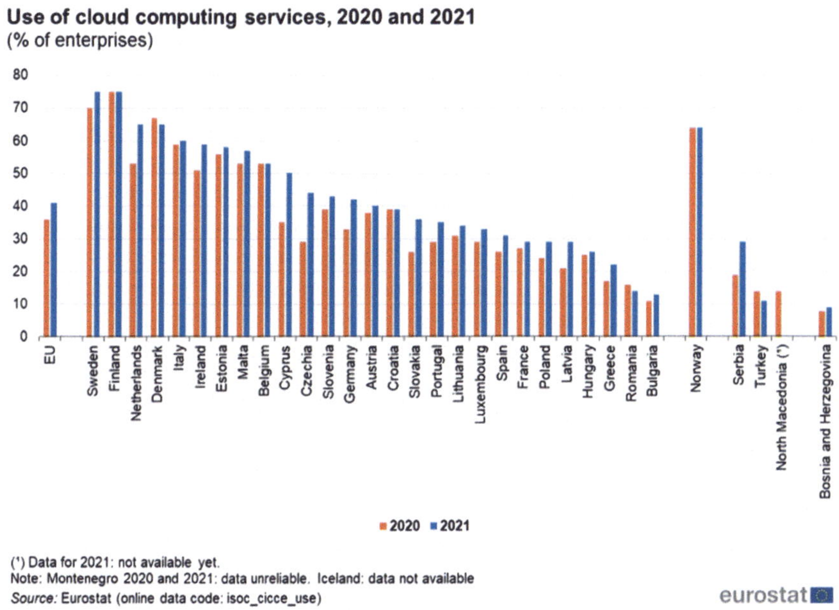

Fig. 1 Use of cloud computing service

eHealth solutions, and online education) which resulted in a broadened adoption of cloud computing services, accompanied by a rise in the establishment of data centers and private cloud infrastructures (IDC, 2022; IFBD, 2020).

The fact that cloud infrastructure market in Europe is dominated by non-European, mainly U.S, companies raise concerns in Europe not only about the ability of European tech companies to compete against the U.S ones technologically but also about the ability to protect EU personal and non-personal data since under the present circumstances EU data is kept on servers based in the United States, external to the European jurisdiction. This has resulted in Europeans relinquishing authority over their personal and non-personal data, undermining user confidence and impeding the adoption of cloud services, intensifying the ongoing discussion on the need for the EU to be able to shape its own Internet governance models and achieve a level of digital independence and autonomy in order to determine Europe's digital future.

A new package of regulatory interventions by the European Commission is being shaped regarding the protection of personal data (El-Gazzar et al., 2020), the need to facilitate the cross-border exchange of data, and the need for increased security of network and information systems. This regulatory framework aims to ensure that data is processed in the most efficient way to guarantee that enterprises and the public sector within the EU can access resilient and competitive capacities for the storage and processing of extensive datasets using Big Data Analytics and to ensure that businesses and the public sector in the EU have access to robust and competitive capabilities to store Big Data and process it through Big Data Analytics.

3.1 Processing of Personal Data

As more and more activities are moving to the cloud, numerous privacy concerns emerge concerning the gathering, retention, and handling of personal data stored within data centers positioned outside the EU, subject to distinct legal jurisdictions. Given the lack of control the client possesses over various factors impacting the security of the cloud infrastructure, security apprehensions hold equal significance. The fact that cloud service providers are becoming data processors since they process personal data stored in their servers and the clients (undertakings or individual users) assume the role of the controller also create complex accountability issues. To deal with the problems a new legislation that replaced the older Data Protection Directive, namely the General Data Protection Regulation, commonly referred to as the GDPR. This meticulously constructed framework enhances individuals' rights and imposes stringent obligations technical and organizational protocols for data controllers and data processors alike. This has led to a multitude of implementation requirements especially in the context of cloud computing. It is recognized that the new regulation to safeguard personal data in response to the rise of novel digital landscape, a revised approach was imperative (Hon et al., 2011, 2012). This approach aims to guarantee the protection of the personal data of EU citizens regardless of the storage and processing location, thereby confidence in the use of cloud computing services (European Parliament and Council, Regulation 2016/619).

3.2 Facilitating Cross-border Exchange of Data

Regulation (2018/1807) on free flow of non-personal data (IDC, 2022) came into force on 28 May 2019 (European Parliament and the Council, 2018). The Regulation stipulates that every organization will have the capacity to retain and handle data across the EU, aiming to eliminate the need for "data localization requirements." This is intended to streamline data sharing among different parties, regardless of whether the data is stored in a different EU Member States or within a cloud environment. Consequently, professionals will have the capability to move data from cloud service providers to their own organizational framework. As a result, professionals will be able to transfer data between cloud providers and their own infrastructure. In most of the cases though, data sets are a mix containing personal data along with non-personal data since the new digital technologies are blurring the lines between personal and non-personal data. Under these circumstances companies are trying to correctly identify their datasets and determine the appropriate legislation to be employed (European Commission Communication Establishing Digital Europe, 2021).

In 2022, the European Commission adopted a proposal for a regulation on fair access to and use of data, also known as the Data Act (European Commission, Data Act, 2022). This new regulation, which is only one part of a broader package of measures in the European data strategy, complementary of the Data Governance

Act, aims to firstly untap the potential of industrial data, increase legal certainty for companies and consumers who generate data so as to facilitate the transfer of data between service providers, eliminate contractual imbalances created by abusive contractual terms imposed by parties with stronger market power, create means for private sector data to be accessed and used by public sector bodies for public interest purposes and also shape rules to facilitate user mobility and switching of providers in order to unlock the EU's cloud market. In addition, the Data Act clarifies the right to protect the content of certain databases and its application to databases resulting from data generated or received from IoT devices (Kerber, 2023). This new proposal is considered as one of the main pillars of European Strategy for Data that will create a new environment for data architecture designers who will again be called upon to help shape a new data strategy so that businesses can update policies, processes, and data flows in the new regulatory environment leading to a gradual strengthening of cloud computing technologies.

3.3 Security of Networks and Information Systems

The updated EU cybersecurity framework encompassed the "Directive on the security of network and information systems" (NIS) which was introduced in 2016, however, new legislation is in the process of development. The EU Cybersecurity Act was enacted in June 2019 aiming to enhance cybersecurity in the European Union's digital landscape taking into consideration the shift of businesses to cloud-based environments and the growing number of cybersecurity challenges (European Parliament, 2019). The EU Cybersecurity Act has two main objectives. First, it strengthens ENISA by providing a mandate to the agency, with new duties, allocating more resources to enhance its role in achieving cybersecurity. Second, it introduces an EU-wide cybersecurity certification framework for ICT products which will be services and processes. Thus, a common cybersecurity certification for digital products and services circulating in the EU is established, which will help ensure consistent standards across the EU, promoting higher levels of trust and security in the digital single market. Secure and trusted cloud services in EU require a European cloud certification scheme be adopted, a scheme that would overcome the current fragmentation of cloud certification schemes in the European Union and strengthen the sense of security for businesses, the public sector, as well as for citizens.

The increased dependence on information and communication technologies (ICT) in the financial sector, particularly highlighted by the ongoing COVID-19 pandemic, underscores the importance of maintaining seamless remote access to financial services. Nevertheless, the adoption of digital technologies and cloud computing also raises apprehensions, as businesses must possess the resilience to withstand potential disruptions in ICT to effectively address digital incidents and ensure the continuity of services (Scott, 2021). In 2020 European Commission proposed a new Regulation the Digital Operational Resilience Act (Regulation (EU) 2022/2554) or in short, "DORA" (European Commission No 648/2012, (EU) No 600/2014 and

(EU) No 909/2014 COM/2020/595 final) together with the directive (EU) 2022/2556 (European Parliament and Council, 2022) to harmonize digital operational resilience rules for financial organizations in the EU so as to upgrade existing EU financial sector legislation and introduce new requirements with the main scope to create a more coherent and consistent incident reporting mechanism and therefore reduce the administrative burden on financial institutions and enhance the efficiency of supervision.

4 Building a Sovereign Cloud

4.1 Secure and Federated Data Infrastructure

In 2019, the GAIA-X project was launched by France and Germany aiming at the creation of a cloud computing ecosystem that would strengthen Europe's digital capacity and reduce its reliance on the dominant U.S. cloud providers (IFBD, 2022). It has been described as the backbone of the EU's digital transformation (Green, 2020). Its objective is to set uniform rules for the storage and processing of data on servers situated in the EU, adhere to stringent European Union privacy rules while at the same time adhering to the European principles and ideals. GAIA-x is based on the principles of data protection, transparency, trust, free market access decentralization, interoperability, and usability. Current data infrastructure forms a link between centralized and decentralized existing infrastructures under a common system which serves as a tool for the efficient control and management of data and applications. At the same time, it fosters transparency in the markets and provides widespread adoption of customized services. The proposed infrastructure will be open-source based in order to facilitate the adaption on behalf of EU cloud providers. The adoption of common standards would contribute to the increased competitiveness of European cloud providers, allowing for the production of improved easily accessible products and models. GAIA-X is designed to serve as an instrument for the EU to retain its digital sovereignty and to lay the groundwork for the advancement of the EU's digital economy.

4.2 A Common Approach to Building the Next Generation Cloud

Following the GAIA-X project, the EU Member States, in October 2020 adopted a Joint Declaration on the establishment of a central Cloud Computing infrastructure across the EU, a "next generation cloud" towards the creation of cloud infrastructure and cloud services which will be based on the principles of transparency, cybersecurity, data protection, interoperability, energy efficiency, performance, and reliability.

The significance of digital technologies for a productive economy and functional society, along with the necessity for the public sector, small and medium businesses, and start-ups to decrease their dependence on foreign cloud computing providers, was recognized by the EU Member States, especially in light of the COVID-19 crisis (European Commission press release on EU Cloud Federation, 2020). In order to succeed in their goals, decision was made by the Member States to collaboratively pool various private and domestic investments to foster the growth of interoperable, secure, and energy-efficient cloud services and infrastructure.

Building of a European cloud infrastructure will stimulate the European businesses growth and innovation as well as building confidence in the storage and processing of data within Europe, while at the same time observing EU regulations and principles.

In December 2021, the European Commission launched the "European Alliance on Industrial Data, Edge and Cloud". Any organization from Member States, or third country (Reinsel et al., 2018), cloud providers and industrial-scale cloud users can join the Alliance by signing up to the Alliance Declaration (European Commission, 2021). Its scope is to support the adoption of cloud and edge technologies by EU industry, businesses, and public administrations. To succeed, all relevant stakeholders will be brought together in order to develop "horizontal and technology-specific" investment roadmaps for future cloud technologies. Moreover, it will provide recommendations to ensure the coherent integration of investments for the deployment of EU-wide Common Data Spaces" (European Commission European Data Strategy, 2020), advise the European Commission on requirements and standards for cloud services, including for public procurement.

4.3 *Harmonization of National Certification Schemes*

In December 2020, ENISA set up a Working Group to prepare a candidate scheme on cloud services, as part of the European Cybersecurity Certification Framework. A public consultation was launched on a new draft candidate cybersecurity certification scheme (EUCS) in order to harmonize the fragmented national certification schemes already in place in various EU member states and boost trust in cloud computing services across Europe (ENISA, 2021). In particular the EUCS scheme has a number of characteristics that distinguish it from other certification schemes. It covers three assurance levels: "Basic", "Substantial", and "High". It is a voluntary scheme. It is applicable for all kinds of cloud services—from infrastructure to applications. It is a new approach based on current national schemes and international standards. It grants a 3-year certification that can be renewed while it includes transparency requirements.

In March 2021 the European Data Protection Board (EDPB) issued a set of recommendations on the draft EUCS Scheme. Among other, EDPB recommended that, personal data and special categories of personal data should be introduced into the EUCS scheme, the CSPs should choose a level of security already adapted to the risks of the personal data processing taking place in their cloud service, include the requirements of data processing in all assurance levels in order to facilitate compliance with GDPR, the indication that the portability control under the EUCS Scheme is not the same as the right to data portability under the GDPR. Furthermore, the EDPB suggested the involvement of the cloud service provider's data protection officer (DPO) "in the early stages of designing the cloud service to monitor the provider's internal compliance with the GDPR and the obligation of Data Protection by Design" (ENISA, 2021). This Letter was followed by a second one where EDPB stressed the need for *Schrems II* to be addressed by EUCS in order to ensure protection against "access from authorities not subject to EU legislation and not offering a level of protection of personal data" essentially equivalent to the one offered by GDPR (SWIPO, 2021).

4.4 Codes of Conduct

In 2020 the so-called SWIPO (Switching Cloud Providers and Porting Data), a multi-stakeholder association facilitated by the European Commission, announced the publication of the 2020 versions of its IaaS and SaaS Codes of Conduct (European Commission, 2017). SWIPO Codes of Conduct are expected to provide voluntary guidance for Cloud Providers and Cloud Customers to prevent "vendor lock-in" by facilitating the portability of their customer's non-personal data according to article 6 of the Free Flow of Non-Personal data regulation towards an open and transparent market of cloud services. Members of the Cloud Infrastructure Service Providers in Europe (CISPE) (European Commission, 2022a, 2022b) who already submitted these Declarations to the SWIPO Secretariat are OVHcloud, 3DS Outscale, Amazon Web Services, Aruba, Irideos, Infoclip, Scaleway and CoreTech (SWIPO, 2021).

The GDPR in Article 40 provides that the "Member States, the supervisory authorities, the Board and the Commission shall encourage the drawing up of codes of conduct intended to contribute to the proper application" of the Regulation. Moreover it provides that the codes of conduct may be prepared, amended, or extended by associations and other bodies representing categories of controllers or processors for the same purpose (European Commission, 2022).

In May 2021, the Belgian Data Protection Authority and the European Data Protection Board (EDPB, 2021a, 2021b, 2021c) approved the "EU Data Protection Code of Conduct for Cloud Service Providers" (General Secretariat of the Belgian DPA, 2021), a transnational voluntary code of conduct which was developed by Cloud Infrastructure Services Providers in Europe (CISPE) with the scope to provide legal certainty for cloud service providers, demonstrating compliance with GDPR in order to be used as an approved transfer mechanism or as an alternative to standard contractual clauses. It addresses all types of cloud services (Iaas, Paas, Saas) so it applies to large players like Microsoft, Alibaba, Dropbox, Cisco, Google and IBM, and provides practical guidance and defines specific requirements (regarding the obligations of sub-processors, transparency audits, compliance with data subject rights requests, etc.) for the CSPs where the CSP acts as a processor in order to help CSPs to comply with Article 28 GDPR and facilitate customers to analyze whether cloud services are appropriate for their use case in line with Article 28.1 GDPR.

4.5 Access to and Reuse of Data and Services by Researchers

The facilitation of scientific research and researchers access to data, is a sine qua non, for innovation across all sectors of the European data-driven economy. In 2021, the Commission in order to build a modern scientific ecosystem launched the European Open Science Cloud (EOSC) portal. A legal entity which lays the foundations of European ecosystem with the scope to manage user identity and access and put together standards, tools, and services allowing researchers to find, access, and reuse results stored in the European Open Science Cloud (EOSC) (Lewis, 2020) following FAIR (Findable, Accessible, Interoperable, and Reusable) principles (Wilkinson et al., 2016). Sharing data is a key digital transformation enabler across industries. The European Commission has acknowledged the importance of funding and supporting of European Open Science Cloud in its European data strategy document stressing that the EU would "continue to facilitate discovery, sharing of, access to and reuse of data and services by researchers through the European Open Science Cloud (EOSC)".

5 Conclusions

The adoption of cloud computing holds immense importance for the European economy due to its potential to be the engine of digital transformation across private and public sector industries providing the infrastructure and tools necessary for businesses to adopt emerging technologies, fostering innovation and competitiveness. The adoption of cloud computing in Europe has the potential to stimulate economic growth and job creation. Cloud services and platforms offer opportunities for startups and small businesses to compete globally, enabling them to scale their operations and reach a broader customer base. Concerning the importance of Cloud computing adoption for the Central and Eastern European (CEE's) countries a recent joint statement by Central and Eastern European (CEE's) countries digital industry, highlights the need for a stable regulatory framework that will support and sustain the cloud computing adoption, contribute to the development of the CEE countries on their way to digital transition and enhance the competitive advantage of their businesses. From a geopolitical perspective Cloud computing has become a "battlefield" of transatlantic tension where EU is exercising its digital and political power aiming to ensure that EU member states regain control over citizens privacy rights, security, and economy (Lewis, 2020). The imperative for the European Union to establish its autonomy in the realms of system design, application development, and utilization lies at the core of these policies and legal endeavors (Autolitano et al., 2021). This includes the capacity to exert control over and exert influence upon various aspects such as the ability to influence, check and correct "data, software (e.g., AI), standards and protocols (e.g., 5G, domain names), processes (e.g., cloud computing), hardware (e.g., mobile phones), services (e.g., social media, e-commerce), and infrastructures (e.g., cables, satellites, smart cities), in short, for the control of the "digital" (Floridi, 2020).

To achieve its goals, the EU has put in place a regulatory and policy framework to ensure that foreign tech companies that store and process EU data are accountable under EU laws and that EU companies can innovate and compete using freely and easily circulated data under the prerequisites of EU legislation. The initiatives can have important implications for non-EU cloud providers operating within the EU market. These providers will need to comply with EU regulations to offer their services to EU customers. This raises concerns from across the Atlantic since these initiatives could result in additional compliance costs and requirements for U.S providers and potentially influence their competitiveness in the EU market (Wirth A et al.). The rise of GDPR as a global regulatory standard and a compliance "sine qua non" equally for EU and non-EU companies is a striking example of how regulation has changed the business models of U.S. companies like Microsoft which are now building data centers around Europe in order to store and process customer data for commercial enterprise online services. Microsoft enables residency options for it's on line services such as Azure, Dynamics 365, Power Platform, and Microsoft 365 within EU the so-called Microsoft's Data boundaries (Brill, 2022).

Meanwhile, Google is launching a new Google workspace in EU in order for public and private sector organizations to control the flow of data from and to EU (Soltero, 2022) while Oracle has launched its EU Sovereign Cloud (Twaddle, 2022).

There is a lot to be gained for the EU as well as for Member States from the adoption of regulations and initiatives related to cloud computing.

Regulations that promote cloud computing adoption can stimulate economic growth within the region. By creating a conducive environment for businesses to adopt cloud technologies, governments can attract investments, foster innovation, and generate new job opportunities (Haucap et al., 2022).

Cloud adoption contributes to the digital transformation of government services. Regional governments can streamline their operations, offer digital public services, and improve the efficiency of public administration through cloud-based solutions.

As underlined, EU regulations prioritize data security, building thus trust in digital services, and minimizing the risk of data breaches or cyberattacks.

By fostering cloud adoption, an environment conducive to innovation is created. Local start-ups and tech companies are more likely to emerge and thrive, driving technological advancements and competitiveness in the region (Theby, 2022).

In addition to the above, regulations that promote cloud computing often lead to the development of digital infrastructure, including data centers and high-speed internet connectivity. This infrastructure benefits not only businesses but also citizens who gain access to better internet services.

By aligning with EU regulations and global standards, regional governments can position their countries as attractive destinations for international businesses. This can enhance global competitiveness and encourage foreign direct investment (Fournier, 2015).

Regulations that mandate robust cybersecurity measures help governments protect critical infrastructure and sensitive information. Strengthened cybersecurity can prevent cyberattacks and security breaches that may disrupt public services or harm national security (Ilves et al., 2023).

Still the main issue for the EU is how to realize the vision of a single market for data in order to boost innovation and create a safe environment for EU companies and citizens. The question that arises among policy makers and scholars is whether the EU should follow a strict policy of sovereign cloud infrastructure or could simply rely on foreign cloud infrastructure which will be closely monitored in order to comply with EU legislation and values. Should it be feasible to secure EU–US data flows through a proper transatlantic agreement would seem like a realistic policy decision to create a regulatory environment where the US and other companies offer their services. Nevertheless, if the EU wishes to grow as a player in the global technology landscape, it should continue to pursue its digital sovereignty goals so as to improve competitiveness, and foster its digital economy.

References

Journals

El-Gazzar, R., et al. (2020). Examining how GDPR challenges emerging technologies. *Journal of Information Policy, 10*, 237–275. https://doi.org/10.5325/jinfopoli.10.2020.0237

Floridi, L. (2020). The fight for digital sovereignty: What it is, and why it matters, especially for the EU. *Philosophy and Technology, 33*, 369–378. Retrieved February 2, 2022, from https://doi.org/10.1007/s13347-020-00423-6

Fournier, J. (2015). *The negative effect of regulatory divergence on foreign direct investment*. OECD Economics Department Working Papers, No. 1268. OECD Publishing. https://doi.org/10.1787/5jrqgvg0dw27-en

Haucap, J., et al. (2022). The economic impact of cloud computing in Europe. *Dice Consult*, 1–11.

Hon, W. K., et al. (2011). The problem of 'personal data' in cloud computing: What information is regulated?—The cloud of unknowing. *International Data Privacy Law, 1*(4), 211–228.

Hon, W. K., et al. (2012). Who is responsible for 'personal data' in cloud computing?—The cloud of unknowing, Part 2. *International Data Privacy Law, 2*(1), 3–18.

Ilves, L. K., et al. (2023). European Union and NATO global cybersecurity challenges: A way forward. *Prism, 6*(2), 126–141.

Kerber, W. (2023). Governance of IoT data: Why the EU data act will not fulfill its objectives. *GRUR International, 72*(2), 120–135.

Lewis, J. (2020). *Sovereignty and the evolution of internet ideology*. CSIS research report. https://csis-website-prod.s3.amazonaws.com/s3fs

Mildebrath, H. (2020). *The CJEU judgment in the Schrems II case*. EPRS: European Parliamentary Research Service. https://www.europarl.europa.eu/thinktank/en/document/EPRS_ATA(2020)652073

Monteleone, S., et al. (2015). *At a glance The CJEU's Schrems ruling on the safe harbor*. EPRS: European Parliamentary Research Service. https://www.europarl.europa.eu/thinktank/en/document/EPRS_ATA(2015)569050
Scott, H. S. (2021). *The EU's digital operational resilience act: Cloud services & financial companies 2021*. Available at SSRN: https://ssrn.com/abstract=3904113 or https://doi.org/10.2139/ssrn.3904113
Theby, M. (2022). Public sector cloud computing adoption and utilization during COVID-19: An agenda for research and practice. In *Public sector cloud computing adoption and utilization during COVID-19: An agenda for research and practice: Theby, Mark*. [Sl]: SSRN.
Wilkinson, M., et al. (2016). The FAIR guiding principles for scientific data management and stewardship. *Scientific Data, 3*, 160018. https://doi.org/10.1038/sdata.2016.18

Official EU Material

EDPB, Letter to ENISA regarding the European cybersecurity certification scheme for cloud services, 2021. Retrieved February 28, 2022, from https://edpb.europa.eu/system/files/2021-03/letteredpbtoenisa_feedbackooneucsscheme.pdf
EDPB. 2nd Letter to ENISA regarding the European cybersecurity certification scheme for cloud services, 2021. Retrieved February 28, 2022, from https://edpb.europa.eu/system/files/2021-11/edpb_letter_to_enisa_out2021-00157.pdf
EDPB, Opinion 16/2021 on the draft decision of the Belgian Supervisory Authority regarding the "EU data protection code of conduct for cloud service providers" submitted by Scope Europe, 2021. Retrieved February 28, 2022, from https://edpb.europa.eu/system/files/2021-05/edpb_opinion_202116_eucloudcode_en.pdf
ENISA, EUCS—Cloud service schemes—Draft. Technical report. European Union Agency for Cybersecurity (ENISA), 2021. Retrieved February 21, 2022, from https://www.enisa.europa.eu/publications/eucs-cloud-service-scheme
European Commission 2012, Unleashing the potential of cloud computing in Europe, communication to the European Parliament, the Council, the European Economic and Social Committee and the Committee of the Regions, COM/2012/0529 final 2012. Retrieved February 28, 2022, from https://eur-lex.europa.eu/legal-content/en/TXT/?uri=CELEX:52012DC0529
European Commission, 2014 Towards a thriving data-driven economy, Communication COM (214) final 2014. Retrieved December 9, 2021, from https://eur-lex.europa.eu/legal-content/EN/TXT/?uri=celex%3A52014DC0442
European Commission, On the free flow of data and emerging issues of the European data economy *Commission staff working document accompanying the document building a European data economy communication*, SWD/2017/02 final 2017. Retrieved February 28, 2022, from https://eur-lex.europa.eu/legal-content/EN/TXT/?uri=CELEX%3A52017SC0002
European Commission, Establishing the Digital Europe program for the period 2021–2027, communication from the Commission to the European Parliament and the Council, COM(2018) 443 final, June 2018. Retrieved February 10, 2022, from https://eur-lex.europa.eu/legal-content/EN/TXT/?uri=COM%3A2018%3A434%3AFIN
European Commission, GAIA-X: a federated data infrastructure for Europe, 2020. Retrieved December 2, 2021, from https://www.data-infrastructure.eu/GAIAX/Navigation/EN/Home/home.html
European Commission, The European data strategy, *Factsheet* 2020. Retrieved December 12, 2021, from https://ec.europa.eu/commission/presscorner/detail/en/fs_20_283
European Commission. (2020, February 19), Communication from the commission to the European Parliament, The Council, The European Economic and Social Committee and the Committee of the Regions. *A European Strategy For Data.* Com/2020/66 Final.

European Commission, Commission welcomes Member States' declaration on EU cloud federation, Press Release, 2020. https://ec.europa.eu/digital-single-market/en/news/commission-welcomes-member-states-declaration-eu-cloud-federation
European Commission, European Alliance for Industrial Data, Edge and Cloud. Retrieved February 28, 2022, from https://digital-strategy.ec.europa.eu/en/policies/cloud-alliance
European commission, 2021 Communication from the Commission to the European Parliament, the Council, the European Economic and Social Committee and the Committee of the Regions. 2030 Digital Compass: The European Way for the Digital Decade Com/2021/118 Final.
European Commission, 2020 Communication from the Commission to the European Parliament, the Council, the European Economic and Social Committee and the Committee of the Regions a European Strategy for Data, COM/2020/66 final, 2020. Retrieved February 10, 2022, from https://eur-lex.europa.eu/legal-content/EN/TXT/?uri=CELEX%3A52020DC0066
European Commission, 2022 mapping data flows *Study* 2022. Retrieved February 28, 2022, from https://digital-strategy.ec.europa.eu/en/policies/european-data-flow-monitoring
European Commission, Proposal for a Regulation of the European Parliament and of the Council on digital operational resilience for the financial sector and amending Regulations (EC) No 1060/2009, (EU) No 648/2012, (EU) No 600/2014 and (EU) No 909/2014 COM/2020/595 final.
European Parliament and the Council 2016, Regulation (EU) 2016/679 of the European Parliament and of the Council of 27 April 2016 on the protection of natural persons with regard to the processing of personal data and on the free movement of such data, and repealing Directive 95/46/EC (OJ L 119, 4.5.2016, pp. 1–88). https://eur-lex.europa.eu/eli/reg/2016/679/oj
European Commission, 2022 Proposal for a regulation of the European Parliament and of the Council on harmonized rules on fair access to and use of data (Data Act) {SEC(2022) 81 final—SWD(2022) 34 final}—SWD(2022) 35 final.
European Parliament and the Council 2019 Regulation (EU) 2018/1807 of the European Parliament and of the Council of 14 November 2018 on a framework for the free flow of non-personal data in the European Union (OJ L 303, 28.11.2018, pp. 59–68). https://eur-lex.europa.eu/legal-content/EN/TXT/?uri=CELEX%3A32018R1807
European Parliament and the Council, 2019 Regulation (EU) 2019/881 of 17 April 2019 on ENISA (the European Union Agency for Cybersecurity) and on Information and Communications Technology Cybersecurity Certification and Repealing Regulation (EU) No 526/2013 (Cybersecurity Act) (OJ L 151/15).
European Parliament and the Council, 2022, Directive (EU) 2022/2556 of the European Parliament and of the Council of 14 December 2022 amending Directives 2009/65/EC, 2009/138/EC, 2011/61/EU, 2013/36/EU, 2014/59/EU, 2014/65/EU, (EU) 2015/2366 and (EU) 2016/2341 as regards digital operational resilience for the financial sector (OJ L 333, 27.12.2022, pp. 153–163).
General Secretariat of the Belgian Data Protection Authority, 2021 Approval decision of the "EU data protection code of conduct for cloud service providers, 2021". Retrieved February 21, 2022, from https://www.dataprotectionauthority.be/publications/decision-n05-2021-of-20-may-2021.pdf
IDC, 2022. Spending on public cloud IT infrastructure surpasses spending on traditional IT infrastructure for the first time in the second quarter of 2020, *IDC Press Release.* Retrieved February 14, 2022, from https://www.idc.com/getdoc.jsp?containerId=prUS46895020
IDC, 2020. Spending on public cloud IT infrastructure surpasses spending on traditional IT infrastructure for the first time in the second quarter of 2020, [Press Release]. Retrieved February 2, 2022, from https://www.idc.com/getdoc.jsp?containerId=prUS46895020
IFBD International Finance business desk, 2020 Has AWS beat the likes of Google in the Cloud? *International Finance,* 2020. Retrieved February 28, 2022, from https://internationalfinance.com/has-aws-beat-likes-google-cloud/
Retrieved February 2, 2022, from public/publication/201030_Lewis_Sovereignty_Evolution_Internet_Ideology_1.pdf

SWIPO, Cloud companies move forward declaring adherence to SWIPO Codes of Conduct, Blog, 2021. Retrieved February 28, 2022, from https://swipo.eu/blog/cloud-companies-move-forward-declaring-adherence-to-%E2%80%8Eswipo-codes-of-conduct-%E2%80%8E/

Other Publications

Autolitano, S., et al. (2021). *Europe's quest for digital sovereignty: GAIA-X as a case study [working paper].* Retrieved February 2, 2022, from https://www.iai.it/sites/default/files/iaip2114.pdf

Brill, J. (2022). Microsoft announces the phased rollout of the EU Data Boundary for the Microsoft Cloud begins January 1, 2023. *Microsft EU Policy Blog.* https://blogs.microsoft.com/eupolicy/2022/12/15/eu-data-boundary-cloud-rollout/?culture=en-us&country=us

Carlo, D. (2023, February 23). *The state of cloud computing in Europe and the UK.* https://kinsta.com/blog/cloud-computing-in-europe/

Gartner. (2019, November 5). *Cloud shift impacts all IT markets.* https://www.gartner.com/smarterwithgartner/cloud-shift-impacts-all-it-markets

Green, A. (2020). Europe's Gaia-X looks to challenge Big Tech's cloud dominance. *Financial Times.* Retrieved February 10, 2022, from https://www.ft.com/content/6ac505fd-5b90-4979-8c3c-b5ba756e9089

Mell, P., et al. (2011). *The NIST definition of cloud computing, special publication (NIST SP).* National Institute of Standards and Technology [online]. Retrieved May 25, 2023, from https://doi.org/10.6028/NIST.SP.800-145

Reinsel, D., et al. (2018). The digitization of the world-from edge to core. Framingham: *IDC Corporate USA.* https://www.seagate.com/files/www-content/ourstory/trends/files/idc-seagate-dataage-whitepaper.pdf

Soltero, J. (2022). Announcing sovereign controls for Google workspace. *Google Digital Sovereignty Blog.* https://workspace.google.com/blog/product-announcements/duet-ai-now-available-preorder

The Economist. (2017). The world's most valuable resource is no longer oil, but data. *The Economist.* Retrieved December 9, 2021, from https://www.economist.com/leaders/2017/05/06/the-worlds-most-valuable-resource-is-no-longer-oil-but-data

Twaddle, S. (2022). Introducing Oracle's sovereign cloud regions for the European Union. *Oracle Blog.* https://www.oracle.com/uk/news/announcement/introducing-oracle-sovereign-cloud-regions-for-european-union-2022-07-11/

Wirth, A., et al. Clouds on the horizon: Europe's cloud policy threatens transatlantic digital harmony. *CEPA.* https://cepa.org/article/clouds-on-the-horizon-europes-cloud-policy-threatens-transatlantic-digital-harmony

Citizens' Attitudes Towards E-government Applications

Lambros Tsourgiannis, Stavros Valsamidis, Sotirios Papadopoulos, and Polina Karagianni

Abstract Electronic government (e-gov) consists of information and communication technologies applied in government issues. The new digital era contributed to the evolution of the use of e-gov applications to a more transactional and integrated operational level. Public managers use them a problem-solving tool whilst citizens and stakeholders in order to control public servants. The recent pandemic of COVID-19 forced the public sector to adopt e-gov applications extensively and Internet, telework, remote work, distance learning, online transactions are now part of everyday life in society. This study aims to explore the attitudes of Greek citizens to-wards the use of e-government applications. A primary survey conducted in November–December of 2022 to a random sample of 1200 Greek citizens. Principal component analysis (PCA) conducted to identify the main attitudes of Greek citizens towards the use of e-government applications. Therefore, Principal Component Analysis indicated two main attitudes: (a) E-gov applications contribute to the improvement of the efficiency and effectiveness of public sector, and (b) E-gov applications contribute to the better citizens' service. Cluster analysis is used to group those citizens into clusters according to their attitudes towards the use of e-government applications. It

L. Tsourgiannis (✉)
General Directorate of Internal Operation, Region of Eastern Macedonia and Thrace, 1 Dimokratias Ave, Komotini, Greece
e-mail: ltsourgiannis@gmail.com

L. Tsourgiannis · S. Valsamidis · P. Karagianni
Department of Accounting and Finance, Campus of Kavala, International Hellenic University, Kavala, Greece

L. Tsourgiannis
School of Social Sciences, Management Studies, Hellenic Open University, Patra, Greece

S. Papadopoulos
General Directorate of Agricultural Economy of Eastern Macedonia and Thrace, 1 Dimokratias Ave, Komotini, Greece

Department of Oinology and Biotechnology, Campus of Drama, International Hellenic University, Drama, Greece

M. Mavri et al. (eds.), *Digital Economy and Green Growth*, Contributions to Economics, https://doi.org/10.1007/978-3-031-66669-8_6

identified three groups of citizens: (a) those who believe that e-government applications contribute to better citizens' service (b) those who believe that e-gov applications contribute to the improvement of the efficiency and effectiveness of public sector and (c) those who are indifferent. Nonparametric tests including chi-square performed to develop the profile of each of the identified group of citizens towards the main reasons they use e-gov applications and their demographic characteristics.

Keywords E-government · Digital marketing · Public sector · Internet · Citizens' attitudes

1 Introduction

The Internet is a necessary tool for the social and economic inclusion of a person and may reinforce the respective relationships and inequalities at the cultural, economic and social level (Van Deursen & Van Dijk, 2015).

E-government is more than a single website; it is a concept that combines the intensive use of ICT with forms of management, planning and management (Concha & Naser, 2012), aimed at creating a more efficient and effective public sector to meet the needs of citizens optimally, by developing new electronic services (e-services) (Justice et al., 2006).

The evolution of e-Government in the developing countries appears to be rapid as it goes beyond mere service delivery and is directed to a framework for smart, sustainable, and inclusive growth with a predominant role of the citizen as an "active customer" of public services (Ferelis et al., 2022).

Electronic Government (E-government or E-Gov) refers to the use of information and delivery of services through the use of digital and electronic tools and applications in order to enhance transparency and accountability (Al-Hujran et al., 2015; Panagiotopoulos & Al-Debei, 2010; West, 2004). Therefore, this kind of Government is nonhierarchical, nonlinear, two-way and can be used 24 h a day, seven days a week (West, 2004).

E-Government has assumed an important role in today's society and is even considered a key instrument for a modern, open, agile and collaborative Public Administration (Hammerschmid et al., 2023; Katsonis & Botros, 2015; Malodia et al., 2021).

The adoption of E-government applications by citizens is voluntary and is affected by many factors related to the sociocultural, political and economic environment (Al-Hujran et al., 2015). Therefore, it is necessary for the stakeholders to find out the motives of the public that make it to adopt e-government services and tools, otherwise the governments could not make informed strategic decisions to increase the e-government adoption and use (Al-Huhjran et al., 2015; Carter et al., 2012; Gilbert et al., 2004).

According to Capgemini (2012) report there is a big gap between the supply and the usage of E -government services in most European Countries. The main reasons people do not use E- Government according to Savoldelli et al. (2014) are the lack of: (i) citizens' participation, (ii) legal bases, (iii) policy cycle management, (iv) measurement and evaluation and (v) trust and transparency, as well as the digital divide.

In 2020, Greece aimed to develop a more efficient and effective public administration through the use of E-Government applications. Citizen's reconnection with public administration was one of the main strategic pillar of the Greek e-Government strategy for the years 2014–2020. Thus, the Greek State adopted policies, regulations and business practices that promote the adoption by the Greek Citizens E-Government applications and tools (Gounopolos et al., 2019). However, Greece is underperforming in the use of e-government services, compared to the other EU countries (Gounopoulos et al., 2019).

This study aims to explore the attitudes of Greek citizens towards the use of e-government applications. The remainder of the paper is constructed as following: The second section presents the baseline. The third section proposes the research methodology. The fourth section presents the results and the discussion of the investigation, and fifth section highlights the findings of the results and draws useful implications for the public administration.

2 Baseline

Several theories on technology acceptance and use have been developed over the last 60 years (Oliveira & Martins, 2011). Some studies focus on how adoption is disseminating. Other studies examine the characteristics of technologies that tend to be quickly assimilated, while others focus on the application characteristics of that lead to such quick acceptance (Venkatesh et al., 2012).

Although many of the researchers have explored the supply-side e-government adoption, relatively very few examined is the reasons citizens adopt e-government services (Gauld et al., 2010; Reddick, 2005). Most of the researchers in order to understand or predict users' adoption and acceptance of technologies adopted the Technology Acceptance Model (TAM) (Davis, 1993), Theory of Reasoned Action (TRA) (Fishbein & Ajzen, 1975), Theory of Planned Behavior (TPB) (Ajzen, 1985). In particular, the TAM is an adaptation of the TRA from psychology specifically tailored to model user acceptance of Information Technology (IT). TAM examines how by two specific belief factors: (a) perceived usefulness, and (b) perceived ease of use affects behavioral intentions. On the other hand, the TAM does not take under consideration social and human factors (Al-Huhjran et al., 2015). Gilbert et al. (2004) also identified that citizen willingness to use e-government services is affected by saving citizens' time and money as well as by the enhancements in the accessibility and convenience of government services and information (Alhujran, 2009). Moreover, trust is also an important factor leading to E-Governance applications acceptance. Venkatesh et al. (2003) based on the above models developed the Unified Theory of Acceptance and Use of Technology (UTAUT) that contains five main pillars of behavioral intention and use behavior including the performance expectancy, effort expectancy, social influence, facilitating conditions and behavioral intention. UTAUT also takes into consideration factors such as gender, age, experience, and voluntariness of use.

Citizens' attitudes towards-commerce as well as digital marketing and e-government applications are affected by four main demographic characteristics such as age, education, occupation and income, their previous experience in the use of Internet (Karavasilis, 2012; Valili, 2007; Venkatesh et al., 2003). Furthermore, factors included relative advantage, compatibility, ease of use and image, perceived usefulness, trustworthiness, cultural consideration and demographic characteristics such as gender, education, occupation and age have significant impact on citizens' use of e-government services as Akman et al. (2005), Al Awadhi and Morris (2009), Carter and Belanger (2004), Carter and Belanger (2005), Chen and Dimitrova (2006), Hung et al. (2006) argue.

Therefore, this study aims to explore which attitudes affect citizens to the adoption of E-Government applications and how these attitudes are interrelated with their preferences towards the use of those applications and their demographic characteristics. In particular the researchers developed a questionnaire based on the questionnaire used by Al Awadhi and Morris (2009). The variables used in the questionnaire derived from the model UTAUT; its suitability, validity and reliability in technology adoption studies in different contexts have been proven as well as the variables adopted to explore the use of e-government applications applied in the Greek State (Anderson & Schwager, 2004; Al Awadhi & Morris, 2009; Lin et al., 2004; Venkatesh et al., 2003).

More specifically, this work aims to investigate the null research hypotheses are presenting bellow:

Ho1: "Greek citizens cannot be classified into similar groups according to their attitudes towards the use of e-government applications".

Ho2: "The demographic and personal characteristics of Greek citizens are not significantly related to their attitudes towards the use of e-government applications".

Ho3: "The attitudes of the Greek citizens towards the use of e-government applications are not significantly related to main reasons they use these applications".

3 Methodology

The researchers of the current study elaborated a primary survey during November and December of 2022 to a random representative sample of 1400 people using the methodology of Tsourgiannis et al. (2023) and Oppermann (1995). In particular, the researchers in their effort to achieve a representative sample for the geographical area of Greece, chose at random seven regions from a total of thirteen. In the next phase, they selected at random two prefectures from each study region whilst in the last stage volunteer enumerators used to send a structured questionnaire to citizens of their area through their social networks. In particular, the questionnaire should be sent to 100 people by each enumerator.

A preliminary survey was performed to a total of 50 citizens. Next a pilot survey conducted in October 2022 to check if the research objectives were met by the designed questionnaire. The results of the pilot survey indicated that the questionnaire was considered adequate to be used in the final survey with no further modification.

The researchers by using the methodology of Siardos (1997) checked the proportion of the members of the sample who declared that have an account and use social networks with those of the pilot survey, in order to assess the representativeness of the sample. The researchers used the above methodology as they could not know how many respondents are from each region (and this consist of one limitation of the current study.

In particular, the proportion of the of the citizens (p) in the pilot survey who indicated that used e-government applications for tax issues is 65%, whilst the total population of the Greece (N) is 10,816,286 according to Greek Census data (ELSTAT, 2020). Therefore, in order to achieve a representative sample, the sample size should be at least 350 citizens (in order have $z = 3$ and $d = 5\%$). The researchers to secure a representative sample, sent the questionnaire electronically to 1400 persons. The productive sample reached the 1201 persons (85% response rate) and is reasonable representative according to Siardos (1997) methodology ($z = 1.96$ and $d = 5\%$). Additionally, a power analysis ($\beta = 0.95$) was conducted using the software package G*POWER 3.1.9.2 (Faul et al., 2009; Tsourgiannis et al., 2015), indicating a minimum sample size of 111 people for a medium effect size (Cohen, 1988). Therefore, a sample size of 1201 people has been considered as fully representative of the whole Greek population.

Besides, the researchers performed the statistical methodology used by Tsourgiannis et al. (2023). More specifically they conducted factor analysis conducted to identify the main attitudes of Greek citizens towards the use of e-government applications and k-means cluster analysis to classify those citizens into groups according to their attitudes the use of such applications. Nonparametric tests including chi-square and Friedman nonparametric test performed to develop the profile of those citizens regarding their demographic characteristics and the reasons they use e-government applications.

4 Results and Discussion

Principal component analysis employed by the researchers in order to identify the key variables describing the attitudes of the Greek citizens towards the use of e-government applications. The latent root criterion (eigenvalue = 1) as well as the percentage of variance were used to determine the number of factors (Table 1). Several different trial rotations were conducted to compare factor interpretability as by Hair et al. (1998).

The above analysis indicated that two key factors explain the 62.6% of the total volatility. The interpretation of the loading scores in each factor by researchers make

Table 1 Results of principal component analysis

Component	Initial eigenvalues			Extraction sums of squared loadings		
	Total	% of variance	Cumulative %	Total	% of variance	Cumulative %
1	7.554	47.211	47.211	7.554	47.211	47.211
2	2.465	15.409	62.619	2.465	15.409	62.619
3	0.841	5.253	67.873			
4	0.727	4.544	72.417			
5	0.525	3.284	75.701			
6	0.477	2.983	78.683			
7	0.464	2.901	81.585			
8	0.403	2.519	84.104			
9	0.387	2.421	86.525			
10	0.354	2.215	88.740			
11	0.338	2.111	90.851			
12	0.330	2.062	92.913			
13	0.310	1.935	94.848			
14	0.296	1.848	96.696			
15	0.279	1.744	98.440			
16	0.250	1.560	100.00			

them to define the two factors (Table 2) as follows: (a) Improvement of the effectiveness and efficiency of the public authorities (b) E-gov applications contribute to the better citizens' service.

The conduction of cluster analysis classified the Greek citizens into the following three groups according to their attitudes towards E-government applications as Table 3 represents: (a) those who believe that e-government applications contribute to better citizens' service (b) those who believe that e-gov applications contribute to the improvement of the efficiency and effectiveness of public sector and (c) those who are indifferent.

More specifically, those who believe that e-government applications contribute to better citizens' service mainly think that their daily routine will become easier as E-Gov applications will contribute significantly in solving issues regarding:

i. the lack of trust for the safety of personal data,
ii. the incomplete interoperability of the operating systems among the public authorities, the provision of incomplete services by public authorities
iii. the lack of efficient free training of the public relative to the use of E-Government applications
iv. the use of old information systems by the public authorities
v. the lack of public awareness regarding the E-government applications and websites
vi. the long waiting time in the web, phone and the misunderstanding instructions.

Table 2 The main factors affecting attitudes of the Greek citizens towards the use of e-government applications

	Component	
	1	2
To which extend the benefits of the E-governance contribute to the reduction of corruption and misgovernment	0.786	0.188
To which extend the benefits of the E-governance contribute to the quality improvement of the provided services	0.783	0.213
To which extend the benefits of the E-governance contribute to the cost reduction of provided services	0.777	0.194
To which extend the benefits of the E-governance contribute to possible development of isolated and degraded areas	0.774	0.182
To which extend the benefits of the E-governance contribute to the control and apportion responsibilities in Public Administration	0.766	0.205
To which extend the benefits of the E-governance contribute to less bureaucracy	0.749	0.233
To which extend the benefits of the E-governance contribute to the promotion of electronic democracy and transparency with electronic vote	0.742	0.195
To which extend the benefits of the E-governance contribute to time reduction	0.732	0.189
To which extend the benefits of the E-governance contribute to the participation of the society to the formulation of the public policies	0.714	0.229
To which extend E-governance will make your daily routine easier by solving issues regarding the lack of trust for the safety of personal data	0.165	0.793
To which extend E-governance will make your daily routine easier by solving issues regarding the incomplete interoperability of the operating systems among the public authorities	0.203	0.790
To which extend E-governance will make your daily routine easier by solving issues regarding the provision of incomplete services by public authorities	0.252	0.781
To which extend E-governance will make your daily routine easier by solving issues regarding the lack of efficient free training of the public relative to the use of E-Government applications	0.184	0.776
To which extend E-governance will make your daily routine easier by solving issues regarding the use of old information systems by the public authorities	0.223	0.774
To which extend E-governance will make your daily routine easier by solving issues regarding the lack of public awareness regarding the E-government applications and websites	0.199	0.771
To which extend E-governance will make your daily routine easier by solving issues regarding the long waiting time in the web, phone and the misunderstanding instructions	0.225	0.709

KMO MSA = 0.938, Bartlett test of Sphericity = 1174.396, $P < 0.001$

Table 3 Classification of the Greek citizens regarding their attitudes towards E-Government applications

Factors affecting Greek citizens regarding their attitudes towards E-Government applications	Cluster			
	Those who believe that e-government applications contribute to better citizens' service	Those who believe that e-gov applications contribute to the improvement of the efficiency and effectiveness of public sector	Indifferent	P
E-gov applications contribute to the improvement of the efficiency and effectiveness of public sector,	0.34574	1.05564	−1.00892	0.001
E-gov applications contribute to the better citizens' service	0.64521	−1.17947	−0.31187	0.001
$N = 1201$	579	207	415	

On the other hand, most of the citizens who believe that e-gov applications contribute to the improvement of the efficiency and effectiveness of public sector have the opinion that E-governance contribute to:

i. reduction of corruption and misgovernment
ii. quality improvement of the provided services
iii. cost reduction of provided services
iv. possible development of isolated and degraded areas
v. the control and apportion responsibilities in Public Administration
vi. less bureaucracy
vii. promotion of electronic democracy and transparency with electronic vote
viii. to time reduction
ix. participation of the society to the formulation of the public policies.

Besides the third group, the indifferent citizens, do not pay attention to any of the identified factors.

Thus, *Ho1: "Greek citizens cannot be classified into similar groups according to their attitudes towards the use of e-government applications"* can be rejected.

The researchers performed chi-square analysis in order to develop the demographic profile of each identified group and identified as Table 4 represent that both groups: (a) "those who believe that e-government applications contribute to better citizens' service" and (b) "those who believe that e-gov applications contribute to the improvement of the efficiency and effectiveness of public sector" are mainly female, hold a bachelor degree, belong to Generation X and are private employees. On the other hand, most of the "indifferent" hold a bachelor degree, are millennials (Gen Y) and students.

Therefore, the research hypothesis Ho2: "*The demographic and personal characteristics of Greek citizens are not significantly related to their attitudes towards the use of e-government applications*" can be rejected.

Furthermore, the chi-square analysis indicated (Table 5) that most citizens of the "those who believe that e-government applications contribute to better citizens' service" and "those who believe that e-gov applications contribute to the improvement of the efficiency and effectiveness of public sector" have similar preferences regarding the use of E-Gov applications. In particular, they mostly use those applications for tax issues, paying bills, issuing certificates issue, social insurance issues, job searching and unemployment benefits, education and health matters, issuing Identity card or Passport, retirement issues, online/remote education and teleconferences,

Table 4 Profiling each group according to their demographics

Demographic characteristics		Those who believe that e-government applications contribute to better citizens' service		Those who believe that e-gov applications contribute to the improvement of the efficiency and effectiveness of public sector A		Indifferent	
Gender	Male	$x^2 = 7.753$ $(P < 0.05)$	44.21%	$x^2 = 5.918$ $(P < 0.05)$	41.55%	n.s	50.60%
	Female		55.79%		58.45%		49.40%
Education	Primary school	$x^2 =$ 237.366 $(P < 0.001)$	3.97%	$x^2 =$ 95.126 $(P < 0.001)$	3.86%	$x^2 =$ 141.000 $(P < 0.001)$	11.57%
	High school		27.98%		39.13%		23.37%
	University degree		48.36%		43.96%		49.16%
	Postgraduate degree		19.69%		13.04%		15.90%
Generation	Gen Z	$x^2 =$ 85.283 $(P < 0.001)$	19.17%	$x^2 =$ 95.126 $(P < 0.001)$	25.60%	$x^2 =$ 11.786 $(P < 0.01)$	25.78%
	Gen Y		32.30%		28.02%		30.36%
	Gen X		36.10%		30.92%		25.30%
	BabyBoomers		12.44%		15.46%		18.55%
Occupation	Civil servant	$x^2 =$ 41.383 $(P < 0.001)$	17.27%	$x^2 =$ 26.478 $(P < 0.001)$	15.46%	$x^2 =$ 40.292 $(P < 0.001)$	12.53%
	Private employee		25.22%		24.64%		18.31%
	Free licensed		14.85%		15.94%		12.29%
	Student		16.41%		23.19%		25.06%
	Unemployed		16.06%		14.01%		20.96%
	Retired		10.19%		6.76%		10.84%

and searching in library. On the other hand, they do not use those apps for asking information/data by the National Statistical Agency.

Moreover, most of the indifferent citizens use the E-Government applications for tax issues, paying their bills, issuing certificates from public authorities and for health issues. They do not prefer to use those applications for social insurance issues, job searching and unemployment benefits, education, issuing Identity card or Passport, retirement issues, online/remote education and teleconferences, searching in library as well as asking for information/data by the National Statistical Agency.

Hence, the research hypothesis Ho3: *"The attitudes of the Greek citizens towards the use of e-government applications are not significantly related to main reasons they use these applications"* can be rejected.

5 Conclusions

This study indicated that Greek citizens are influenced to the use of E- Government applications by two main factors: (a) Improvement of the effectiveness and efficiency of the public authorities (b) E-gov applications contribute to the better citizens' service. Moreover, they were classified into three groups according to their attitudes towards the use of E-Government applications: (i) those who believe that e-government applications contribute to better citizens' service (ii) those who believe that e-gov applications contribute to the improvement of the efficiency and effectiveness of public sector and (ii) those who are indifferent.

Those who believe that e-government applications contribute to better citizens' service mainly think that their daily routine will become easier as E-Gov applications will contribute significantly in solving issues regarding the lack of trust for the safety of personal data, the incomplete interoperability of the operating systems among the public authorities, the provision of incomplete services by public authorities, the lack of efficient free training of the public relative to the use of E-Government applications, the use of old information systems by the public authorities, the lack of public awareness regarding the E-government applications and websites and the long waiting time in the web, phone and the misunderstanding instructions. On the other hand, most of the citizens who believe that e-gov contribute to the improvement of the efficiency and effectiveness of public sector have the opinion that E-governance contributes to the reduction of corruption and misgovernment, quality improvement of the provided services, cost reduction of provided services, possible development of isolated and degraded areas, control and apportion responsibilities in Public Administration, less bureaucracy, promotion of electronic democracy and transparency with electronic vote, time reduction and participation of the society to the formulation of the public policies. The indifferent citizens do not pay attention to any of the identified factors.

Moreover, most citizens who believe that e-government applications contribute to better citizens' service and those who believe that e-gov applications contribute to the improvement of the efficiency and effectiveness of public sector mostly use

Table 5 Profiling each group of Greek citizens according to their preferences about the use of E-Gov applications

Preferences about E-Gov Apps		Those who believe that e-government applications contribute to better citizens' service		Those who believe that e-gov applications contribute to the improvement of the efficiency and effectiveness of public sector a		Indifferent	
Use of E-gov app for tax issues	No	$x^2 =$ 184.679 ($P < 0.001$)	22%	$x^2 =$ 15.696 ($P < 0.001$)	36%	$x^2 = 24.000$ ($P < 0.001$)	43%
	Yes		78%		64%		57%
Use of E-gov app for paying bills	No	$x^2 =$ 205.570 ($P < 0.001$)	20%	$x^2 =$ 119.077 ($P < 0.001$)	12%	$x^2 = 24.000$ ($P < 0.001$)	41%
	Yes		80%		88%		59%
Use of E-gov app for issuing certificate	No	$x^2 =$ 97.010 ($P < 0.001$)	30%	$x^2 =$ 49.280 ($P < 0.001$)	26%	$x^2 = 39.185$ ($P < 0.001$)	50%
	Yes		70%		74%		50%
Use of E-gov app for social insurance issues	No	$x^2 =$ 10.779 ($P < 0.001$)	43%	$x^2 = 4.063$ ($P < 0.001$)	43%	$x^2 = 24.000$ ($P < 0.001$)	63%
	Yes		57%		57%		37%
Use of E-gov app for job searching and unemployment benefits issues	No	$x^2 =$ 13.680 ($P < 0.001$)	42%	$x^2 = 3.019$ ($P < 0.001$)	44%	$x^2 = 39.185$ ($P < 0.001$)	58%
	Yes		58%		56%		42%
Use of E-gov app for education issues	No	$x^2 =$ 41.494 ($P < 0.001$)	37%	$x^2 =$ 17.976 ($P < 0.001$)	35%	$x^2 = 42.667$ ($P < 0.001$)	51%
	Yes		63%		65%		49%
Use of E-gov app for health issues	No	$x^2 =$ 33.370 ($P < 0.001$)	38%	$x^2 =$ 10.671 ($P < 0.001$)	39%	$x^2 = 39.185$ ($P < 0.001$)	49%
	Yes		62%		61%		51%
Use of E-gov app for issuing identity card or Passport	No	$x^2 =$ 19.041 ($P < 0.05$)	41%	n.s	53%	$x^2 = 42.667$ ($P < 0.001$)	59%
	Yes		59%		47%		41%
Use of E-gov app for retirement issues	No	$x^2 = 9.204$ ($P < 0.001$)	44%	n.s	44%	$x^2 = 42.667$ ($P < 0.001$)	56%
	Yes		56%		56%		44%

(continued)

Table 5 (continued)

Preferences about E-Gov Apps		Those who believe that e-government applications contribute to better citizens' service		Those who believe that e-gov applications contribute to the improvement of the efficiency and effectiveness of public sector a		Indifferent	
Use of E-gov app for online/remote education and teleconferences	No	$x^2 =$ 49.328 ($P < 0.001$)	35%	$x^2 =$ 25.744 ($P < 0.001$)	32%	$x^2 = 39.185$ ($P < 0.001$)	52%
	Yes		65%		68%		48%
Use of E-gov app for asking information/data by the National Statistical Agency	No	$x^2 = 5.611$ ($P < 0.001$)	55%	$x^2 =$ 15.696 ($P < 0.001$)	64%	$x^2 = 42.667$ ($P < 0.001$)	63%
	Yes		45%		36%		37%
Use of E-gov app for searching in library	No	$x^2 =$ 19.774 ($P < 0.001$)	41%	n.s	47%	$x^2 = 42.667$ ($P < 0.001$)	57%
	Yes		59%		53%		43%

those applications for tax issues, paying bills, issuing certificates issue, social insurance issues, job searching and unemployment benefits, education and health matters, issuing Identity card or Passport, retirement issues, online/remote education and teleconferences, and searching in library. On the other hand, they do not use those apps for asking information/data by the National Statistical Agency. Besides, most of the indifferent citizens use the E-Government applications for tax issues, paying their bills, issuing certificates from public authorities and for health issues. They do not prefer to use those applications for social insurance issues, job searching and unemployment benefits, education, issuing Identity card or Passport, retirement issues, online/remote education and teleconferences, searching in library as well as asking for information/data by the National Statistical Agency.

This study also identified that both "those who believe that e-government applications contribute to better citizens' service" and "those who believe that e-gov applications contribute to the improvement of the efficiency and effectiveness of public sector" are mainly female, hold a bachelor degree, belong to Generation X and are private employees. On the other hand, most of the "indifferent" hold a bachelor degree, are millennials (Gen Y) and students.

The findings of this study support the arguments of other researchers that factors including relative advantage, compatibility, ease of use and image, perceived usefulness, trustworthiness, cultural consideration and demographic characteristics such as gender, education, occupation and age have significant impact on citizens' use of e-government services (Akman et al., 2005; Al Awadhi & Morris, 2009; Carter & Belanger, 2004; Carter & Belanger, 2005; Chen & Dimitrova, 2006; Hung et al., 2006).

The above conclusions should be taken into consideration by policy makers and executives in public service organizations and institutions. For example, the fact that citizens are particularly concerned about security, trust, interoperability of the operating systems, reduction of corruption and misgovernment, quality improvement and cost reduction of the provided services, development of isolated and degraded areas, less bureaucracy, more transparency, time reduction and participation of the society to the formulation of the public policies should be a goal for those who are responsible. These insights are very helpful for managers i.e., development, optimization and customization of E-Government applications according to the needs of the citizens. In addition, necessary emphasis should be placed on the demographic factors that play the quite important role in how respondents' views are shaped in relation to their attitudes towards E- Government applications. The use of questionnaires designed for citizens after the completion of their transactions to determine the completeness of the service provided to them would be very helpful. Informing citizens during their transactions in the physical points of service regarding the available electronic services and the benefits of their use. Organizing information events with the participation of local bodies and committees.

However, there are some limitations regarding the data analysis. In particular, we analyzed data from seven regions which were randomly selected from a total of thirteen. Nevertheless, the regions of Attica and Thessaloniki among the selected ones. The place of residence and the availability of fast internet were not examined whether affected the results. Thus, caution needs to be taken when generalizing the findsings. Another limitation of the present study is that the survey was performed after the COVID-19 outbreak in Greece. Undoubtedly, it had positive effect on E-Governance.

In this regard, the results of this work should lead to further research, both in Greece and in other countries with similar characteristics. Longitudinal studies are also worth conducting.

References

Ajzen, I. (1985). From intentions to actions: A theory of planned behavior. In J. Kuhl & J. Beckmann (Eds.), *Action-Control: From Cognition to Behavior* (pp. 11–39). Springer.

Akman, I., Yazici, A., Mishra, A., & Arifoglu, A. (2005). E-government: A global view and an empirical evaluation of some attributes of citizens. *Government Information Quarterly, 22*(2), 239–257.

AlAwadhi, S., & Morris, A. (2009). Factors influencing the adoption of e-government services'. *Journal of Software, 4*(6), 584–590.

Al-Hujran, O., Al-Debei, M., Chatfield, A., & Migdadi, M. (2015). The imperative of influencing citizen attitude toward e-government adoption and use. *Computers in Human Behavior, 53*, 189–203.

Alhujran, O. (2009). *Determinants of e-government services adoption in developing countries: A field survey and a case study*. Ph.D. thesis, School of Information Systems and Technology, Faculty of Informatics, University of Wollongong, Australia

Anderson, J. E., & Schwager, P. H. (2004). SME adoption of wireless LAN technology: applying the UTAUT model. In *Proceedings of the 7th Annual Conference of the Southern Association for Information Systems*, vol 7 (pp. 39–43).

Capgemini. (2012). *Public services online 'digital by default or by detour?' Assessing user centric Egovernment performance in Europe eGovernment benchmark 2012*. Final Background Report. Brussels: Delivered for the European Commission, DG Connect.

Carter, L., & Belanger, F. (2004). The influence of perceived characteristics of innovating on e-government adoption. *Electronic Journal of E-Government, 2*(1), 11–20.

Carter, L., & Belanger, F. (2005). The utilization of e-government services: Citizen trust, innovation and acceptance factors. *Information Systems Journal, 15*(1), 5–25.

Carter, L., Christian, S. L., Hobbs, J., & Campbell, R. (2012). The role of security and trust in the adoption of online tax filing. *Transforming Government: People, Process and Policy, 5*(4), 303–318.

Chen, Y. C., & Dimitrova, D. V. (2006). Electronic government and online engagement: Citizen interaction with government via web portals. *International Journal of Electronic Government Research (IJEGR), 2*(1), 54–76.

Cohen, J. (1988). *Statistical power analysis for the behavioral sciences* (2nd edn.) (pp. 273–406). Erlbaum.

Concha, G., & Naser, A. (2012). *CEPAL – Colección Documentos de proyectos, El desafío hacia el gobierno abierto en la hora de la igualdad* (pp. 11–14). Santiago de Chile, Impreso en Naciones Unidas.

Davis, F. D. (1993). User acceptance of information technology: system characteristics, user perceptions and behavioral impacts. *International Journal of Man-Machine Studies, 38*, 475–487.

ELSTAT. (2020). Retrieved Feb 12, 2022, from https://www.statistics.gr/el/statistics/-/publication/SAM03/.

Faul, F., Erdfelder, E., Buchner, A., & Lang, A. (2009). Statistical power analyses using G*Power 3.1: Tests for correlation and regression analyses. *Behavior Research Methods, 41*(4), 1149–1160.

Ferelis, V., Chatzoudes, D., Valsamidis, S. I., & Chatzoglou, P. (2022). A framework for identifying the factors affecting the use of e-government services. *International Journal of Information Systems and Social Change (IJISSC), 13*(1), 1–22.

Fishbein, M., & Ajzen, I. (1975). *Belief, attitude, intention and behavior: An introduction to theory and research*. Addison-Wesley Publishing Company.

Gauld, R., Goldfinch, S., & Horsburgh, S. (2010). Do they want it? Do they use it? The 'Demand-Side' of e-Government in Australia and New Zealand. *Government Information Quarterly, 27*(2), 177–186.

Gilbert, D., Balestrini, P., & Littleboy, D. (2004). Barriers and benefits in the adoption of e-government. *International Journal of Public Sector Management, 17*(4), 286–301.

Gounopoulos, E., Kontogiannis, S., Kazanidis, I., & Valsamidis, S. (2019). The Impact of the digital divide on the adoption of e-government in Greece, *KnE Social Sciences*, 401–411.

Hair, J. F., Anderson, R. E., Tatham, R. L., & Black, W. C. (1998). *Multivariate data analysis*. Prentice Hall Inc.

Hammerschmid, G., Palaric, E., Rackwitz, M., & Wegrich, K. (2023). A shift in paradigm? Collaborative public administration in the context of national digitalization strategies. *Governance*.

Hung, S. Y., Chang, C. M., & Yu, T. J. (2006). Determinants of user acceptance of thc e-government services: The case of online tax filing and payment system. *Government Information Quarterly, 23*(1), 97–122.

Justice, J., Melitski, J., & Smith, D. (2006). E-government as an instrument of fiscal accountability and responsiveness: Do the best practitioners employ the best practices? *American Review of Public Administration., 36*(3), 301–322.

Karavasilis, I. (2012). *The electronic governance in Public Organizations' Management. The case of Greece within the framework of European Union*. Ph.D. Thesis, Department of International and European Studies, School of Economic Studies, University of Macedonia.

Katsonis, M., & Botros, A. (2015). Digital government: A primer and professional perspectives. *Australian Journal of Public Administration, 74*(1), 42–52.

Lin, J., Chan, H., & Jin, Y. (2004). Instant messaging acceptance and use among college students. *PACIS 2004 Proceedings, 15*.

Malodia, S., Dhir, A., Mishra, M., & Bhatti, Z. A. (2021). Future of e-Government: An integrated conceptual framework. *Technological Forecasting and Social Change, 173*, 121102.

Oliveira, T., & Martins, M. (2011). Literature review of information technology adoption models at firm level. *The Electronic Journal Information Systems Evaluation, 14*(1), 110–121.

Oppermann, M. (1995). Family life cycle and cohort effects: A study of travel patterns of German residents. *Journal of Travel & Tourism Marketing, 4*(1), 23–44.

Panagiotopoulos, P., & Al-Debei, M. M. (2010). Engaging with citizens online: Understanding the role of ePetitioning in local government democracy. *Internet, Politics, Policy*, 16–17.

Reddick, C. (2005). Citizen interaction with e-government: From the streets to servers? *Government Information Quarterly, 22*(1), 38–57.

Savoldelli, A., Codagnone, C., & Misuraca, G. (2014). Understanding the egovernment paradox: Learning from literature and practice on barriers to adoption. *Government Information Quarterly, 31*, S63–S71.

Siardos, G. (1997). *Methodology of agricultural sociological research* (p. 367). Ziti Publications.

Tsourgiannis, L., Valsamidis, S., Karagianni, P., & Tassos, K. (2023). The use of internet and social networks during covid-19 in Greece in economies of the Balkan and Eastern European Countries. *KnE Social Sciences*, 360–374.

Tsourgiannis, L., Delias, P., Polychronidou, P., Karasavvoglou, A., & Valsamidis, S. (2015). Profiling tourists who have holidays in the region of Eastern Macedonia and Thrace in Greece. *Procedia Economics and Finance, 33*, 450–460. Elsevier.

Valili, A. (2007). *The attitudes of employees of citizens service centers towards computers*. Master Thesis, Panteio University.

Van Deursen, A. J., van Dijk, J. A., & Peter, M. (2015). Increasing inequalities in what we do online: A longitudinal cross sectional analysis of Internet activities among the Dutch population (2010 to 2013) over gender, age, education, and income. *Telematics and Informatics, 32*(2), 259–272.

Venkatesh, V., Morris, M. G., Davis, G. B., & Davis, F. D. (2003). User acceptance of information technology: Toward a unified view. *MIS Quarterly, 27*(3), 425–478.

Venkatesh, V., Thong, J. Y., & Xu, X. (2012) Consumer acceptance and use of information technology: Extending the unified theory of acceptance and use of technology. *MIS quarterly*, 157–178.

West, D. M. (2004). E-government and the transformation of service delivery and citizen attitudes. *Public Administration Review, 64*(1), 15–27.

Digitization and E-government: A Systematic Literature Review for the European Union (EU 27) and The United Kingdom

Konstadina Kasabali, Persefoni Polychronidou, and Dimitrios Kydros

Abstract The subject of digitization, both in the public and private sectors, seems to have attracted the interest of many researchers in recent years. The increase in the number of investigations related to this specific issue has become more intense since the emergence of the covid-19 pandemic, which brought about significant changes in the way of working, in the operation of the public administration, but also in the everyday life of citizens both in Europe and in Greece. In this research, a systematic literature review is carried out in the field of digitization in countries of the European Union (EU 27) as well as the United Kingdom. The purpose of the research is to make a categorization of the researches, to study the evolution of the number of studies in recent years, to highlight the countries that were most involved as well as the collaborations between the countries in the specific researches.

Keywords Digitization · European Union · e-government · Quantitative methods · Social network analysis

JEL Classification Codes C10 · D85 · H5

1 Introduction

In the last 10 years more countries have gradually started to provide digital services to their citizens. An improved government through digitization not only has an increasing effect on business, but will also be able to engage citizens' participation and contribute to economic growth (Alvarenga et al., 2020). Information and

K. Kasabali · P. Polychronidou (✉) · D. Kydros
Department of Economic Sciences, International Hellenic University, Serres, Greece
e-mail: polychr@ihu.gr

K. Kasabali
e-mail: konskasa2@ihu.gr

D. Kydros
e-mail: dkydros@ihu.gr

M. Mavri et al. (eds.), *Digital Economy and Green Growth*, Contributions to Economics, https://doi.org/10.1007/978-3-031-66669-8_7

Communication Technologies (ICT) as a tool for public sector reform, efficiency and effectiveness is a key theme in the Public Administration, Information Technology (IT) governance and e-Government literature (Martins & Nielsen, 2020).

Measuring the degree of digitization is also considered important as there must be effective strategic public policies to regulate the digital transition (Bánhidi et al., 2020).In recent years, a very popular tool for researchers of the digital effectiveness of countries is the Digital Economy and Society Index (DESI), which is a complex combination of key indicators that depict the digital performance of each European Union (EU) member state and through their score a comparison of digital competitiveness between Member States can be realized (Polychronidou et al., 2021).

However, despite significant amounts of public investment devoted to enhancing e-government over the past ten years, the use of this service by citizens is still limited, posing a challenge to national governments. Citizens' use of e-government services is influenced by supply-side e-government evaluations, citizens' trust in governments, and the digital divide linked to income and education (Pérez-Morote et al., 2020). Nevertheless, the digitization of public services, due to the Covid-19 pandemic, has become an essential necessity for many governments around the world (Alvarenga et al., 2020).

Using a systematic literature review in the field of digitization in countries of the European Union (EU 27) as well as the United Kingdom, the primary objective of the research work is to make a categorization of the researches, to study the evolution of the number of studies in recent years and to highlight the countries that were most involved. In addition, using social network analysis, the collaborations between the countries in the specific surveys are studied, as well as the frequency and proximity of the keywords that appear and the relationship between them in order to highlight which keywords are more closely connected.

2 Methodology

Bibliometric analysis is a popular and rigorous method for exploring and analyzing large volumes of scientific data (Donthu et al., 2021). Due to information and communication technologies, nowadays, it is possible to observe a growing interest in bibliometric analysis. Large amounts of data can be processed using it, and bibliometric maps are additionally provided as a way of visualizing the results (Zyoud et al., 2015). An analysis that can be realized is keyword analysis that identifies the most popular topics covered, highlights countries that contribute more to each theme of the bibliometric analysis and conducts results related to the provision and receipt of references (Ellegaard & Wallin, 2015).

A consequence of the increasing number of empirical studies in digitization is the need to adopt systematic approaches to the evaluation and aggregation of research results in order to provide a balanced and objective summary of the research evidence on a particular issue. The use of a review protocol prior to a review activity is particularly valuable (Brereton et al., 2007). The standard method of systematic literature review involves the use of non-automatic searching (Kitchenham et al., 2009). Systematic reviews are important tools for an objective approach to the literature, the synthesis and critical analysis of the results of primary studies, with an excellent contribution to the clarification of issues and the search for new research directions (Patelarou & Brokalaki, 2010). The systematic review of the literature draws conclusions using quantitative methods, while techniques and methods of Social Network Analysis can also be used (Kydros & Filenta, 2022).

Network analysis is presented as a useful extension of conventional forms of analysis; it can complement standard modes of analysis to broaden and deepen the application of theories, and has great potential in research (Streeter & Gillespie, 1992). A quantitative approach to social network analysis involves the application of mathematics, statistical techniques and graphical presentation of results (Yousefi Nooraie et al., 2020). Social Network Analysis (SNA) is used to analyze, create and shape communities within the subject of analysis in order to identify the interaction between them. Essentially it is a complex adaptive socio-economic system. It shares many of the characteristics usually associated with such entities that is non-linear relationships between components, self-organization and organizational structures as well as their relationship with external factors (Valeri & Baggio, 2021). VOS Viewer is a software tool for creating and displaying bibliometric networks. It can be used to evaluate the relationships between keywords. VOS Viewer describes the frequency and proximity of keywords occurring as well as the relationship between them and, as a result, summarize which keywords are most closely linked. In addition, conclusions can be drawn regarding collaboration between authors and countries (Gajdosikova & Valaskova, 2021). Another network analysis tool, also used in this research, is Gephi. It is a complex software that offers complex data analysis for the purpose of powerful data organization and visualization (Yang et al., 2017). Gephi is an open source software for graph and network analysis. It uses a 3D render engine to display large networks in real-time and to speed up the exploration. A flexible and multi-task architecture brings new possibilities to work with complex data sets and produce valuable visual results. It provides easy and broad access to network data and allows for specializing, filtering, navigating, manipulating and clustering (Bastian et al., 2009).

In the present research, a systematic review of the literature is presented with the use of Google Scholar using the following keywords: "digitization", "European Union", "e-government", "questionnaire", "regression", "statistical analysis" and "index". The results were 3.120 documents. Then a first filtering was done and documents were retained covering the time period from January 2010 to February 2023. A total of 2.880 documents were retrieved. Afterwards, a second filtering was performed and only those created by authors in European Union countries and the United Kingdom were kept and, with this filtering, the sample number became 943. Finally, a final filtering was done and only articles, books, conference proceedings and the collective volumes were kept. The filtering process finally yielded 595 documents. The sample selection process is indicated in Fig. 1.

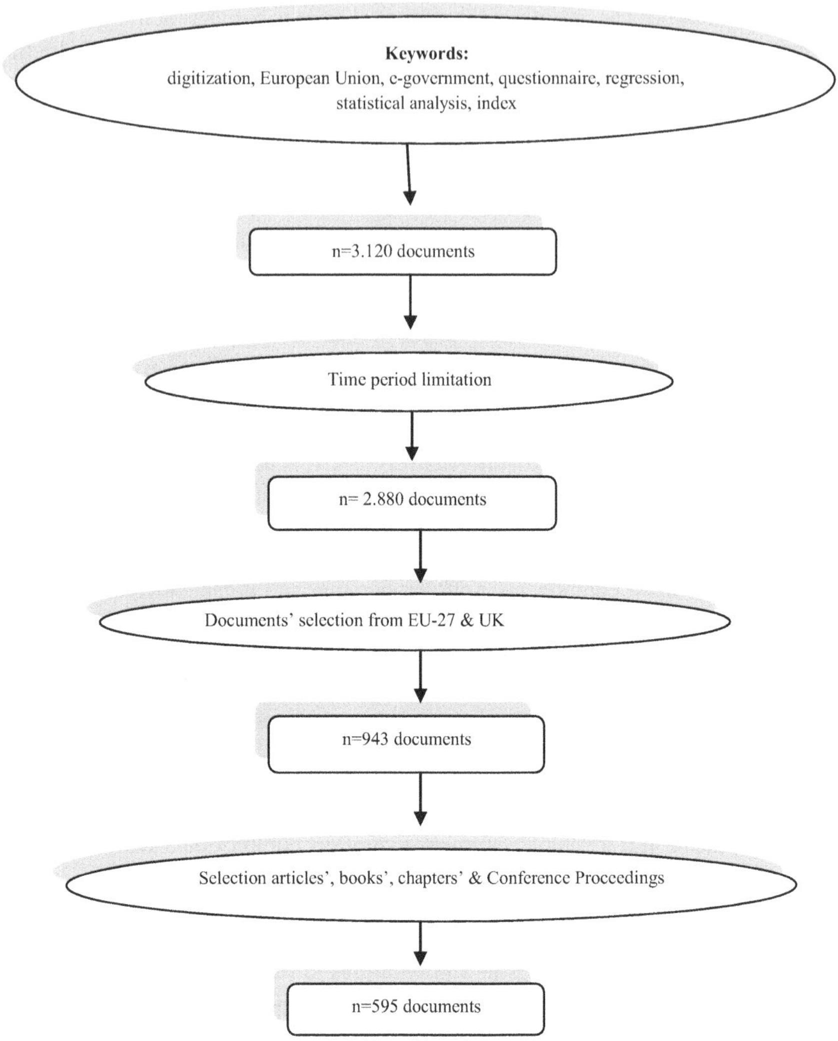

Fig. 1 Sample selection process. *Source* Own elaboration

The information collected from the sample to be analyzed is:

- Title
- Year
- References
- Type of document
- Keywords
- Countries.

Finally, it was done with personal judgment, a categorization of the data.

3 Results

Digitization is a large and influential trend that is rapidly and extensively transforming economic spaces worldwide (Haefner & Sternberg, 2020). Scientific research on digitization has grown exponentially in recent years. This became particularly evident from 2010 onwards (Caputo et al., 2021). COVID-19 has caused a dramatic impact on the global economy, business activities and people. However, digitization is helping many companies to adapt and overcome the current situation caused by COVID-19.The increase in the use of technology in the daily lives of people and companies to cope with this extraordinary situation is evidence of the digital acceleration process (Almeida et al., 2020). In the analyzed sample, see Fig. 2, the exponential increase in documents over the last five years is evident. From 2010 to 2012 the documents did not exceed 10 per year. In 2013 they reached 11, while in 2014 their number doubled. Until 2017 no significant fluctuations are observed. In 2018 there is again a slight increase to almost double. In 2019 the price remains almost the same while a rapid increase from 2020 onwards is observed. In 2022 the number of documents reached 176.

The bar diagram below (Fig. 3) illustrates an analysis of published documents by country. That the United Kingdom has the largest number with 92 publications is observed. Spain, Italy, Romania and Germany follow with small differences, with around 70 publications each. Greece, the Czech Republic and France have about 30 publications each in the period under study. Portugal, Hungary and Finland are close to 20, followed by all the others. The number of documents does not match the number of the sample because collaborations were also taken into account.

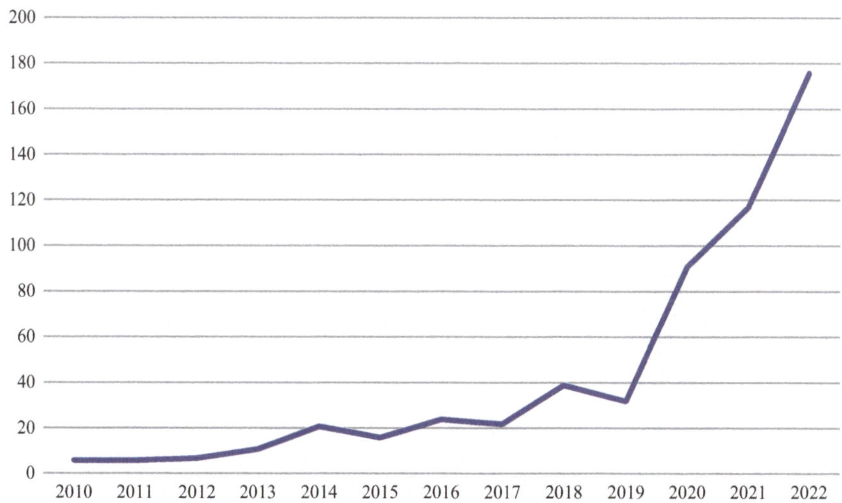

Fig. 2 Annual growth of documents. *Source* Own elaboration

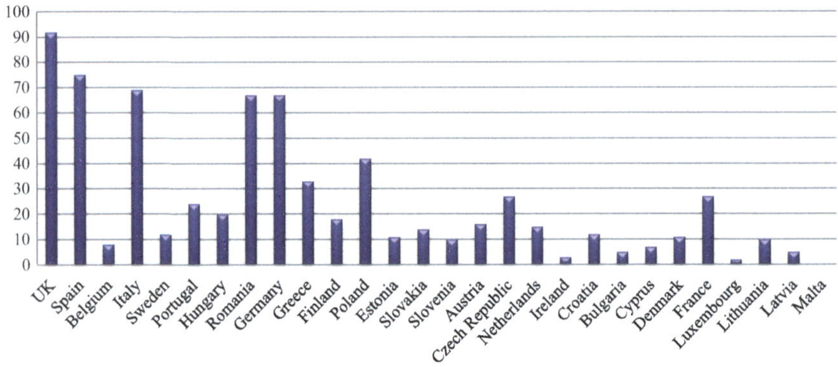

Fig. 3 Number of documents by country. *Source* Own elaboration

In Fig. 4, a separation is made according to the type of document. The majority of the sample concerns articles as it covers a percentage of 68.9%.

The COVID-19 pandemic has presented challenges and opportunities to the required digital transformation. However, there was also the effect of the factor of reliability and technology acceptance on the use of e-government services during the pandemic (Balaskas et al., 2022). Another aspect of digitization is that in recent decades, experts from all over the world have become increasingly interested in illegal behavior and corruption in financial institutions (Zafeiriou et al., 2023). The digitization of public services is also an important pillar. An improved government through digitization will not only have an increasing effect on business, but will also be able to intensify citizen participation and contribute to economic growth (Alvarenga et al., 2020). Another issue that arises due to Digital Transformation is legal coverage. Technologies such as big data, artificial intelligence, machine learning, blockchain,

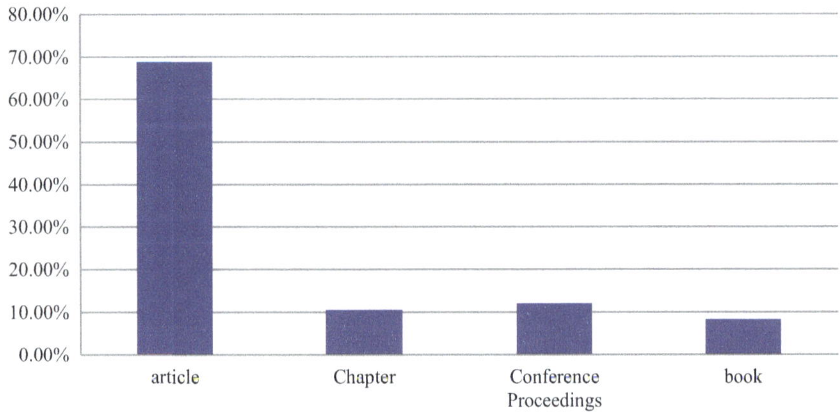

Fig. 4 Document type. *Source* Own elaboration

3D promise to have a profoundly disruptive effect on industry, business models, governance models and the way we interact with each other in society. However, there is no legal information system capable of supporting the legislation of all countries in order to facilitate the above function but there are many initiatives to develop legal ontologies (Loutsaris & Charalabidis, 2020). E-health for citizens, patients, health providers, governments and other stakeholders has also been given particular importance due to the pandemic (Wynn et al., 2020). The problems of distance education instead of in-person education that arose due to the COVID-19 pandemic were also studied (Vlasov, 2020). Digitization, however, directly concerns and to a large extent the modern entrepreneurship. Research has been done on the emergence of companies increasingly involved in digital entrepreneurship with digitized activities (Vadana et al., 2020).

It was therefore considered important to classify the sample documents by subject area. The results shown in Fig. 5 show that e-government arouses interest at a rate of 17.14%.The three categories that follow and also seem to be of particular concern to the research community are smart city and innovation (13.61%), e-business (12.94%) and degree of digitization (11.09%).With a small difference, but at a level of less than 10%, follow the surveys that report to the economic impact of digitization.

Another criterion worth analyzing when processing information is the number of reports of scientific documents (Kydros & Filenta, 2022). Table 1 presents the five documents with the most references, authors, date, type of document and subject area of document. The first place with 2.499 reports is observed in an article on smart city and innovation, followed, with 1.954 citations in an article on the challenges of large data analysis, followed by an article on e-government. In the fourth and fifth place books with 530 and 528 references respectively can be found. The first refers to the economic influence of government reforms and the last one to the digital divide.

A network analysis of the keywords collected from the sample is then performed. The analyzed file consists of 493 lines. The number does not match the number of the sample as there were files for which the keywords were not available. In each line there are the keywords of each document. In order to create our network, we used each line as an adjacency list. Hence, a network of key-phrases is created. Edges are formed between keywords that reside on the same line. Hence, at this point we have formed a semantic network. This process of network formation gave 1917 nodes and 2317 edges. And can be seen in Fig. 6.

After the network formation we proceed our analysis, first by an attempt to cluster these keywords. Modularity measures the strength of division of a network into clusters or communities. Networks with high modularity have dense connections between the nodes within the modules and sparse connections with the nodes in different modules (Hussain et al., 2018). We applied such a clustering through Gephi and filtered out clusters with small numbers of nodes, for reasons of simplicity. This procedure yielded five clusters. And can be seen in Table 2.

In Fig. 7, the bibliometric map is presented and consists of 591 nodes and 660 edges.

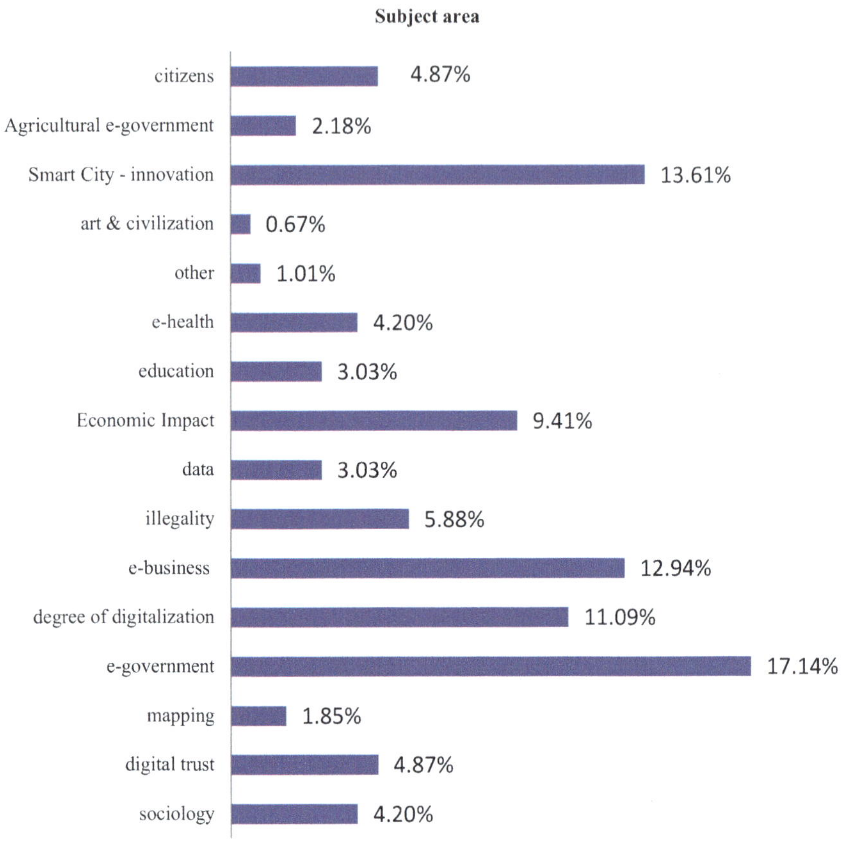

Fig. 5 Subject area. *Source* Own elaboration

The first cluster (purple) includes 163 keywords. Most central (with respect to betweenness) keywords are "digitalization", "European Union", "public administration", "DESI" and "sustainable development". The second cluster (green) includes 146 elements and the keywords with the greatest betweenness centrality that we find are "e-government", "adoption", "e-participation" and "e-services". The third cluster (blue) includes 126 keywords and the most important of these (with respect to betweenness) are "ICT", "digital divide" and "internet". The fourth cluster (yellow) includes 79 keywords and most central (using as a measure the betweenness) are "smart city", "sustainability", "sensor city" and "smart people". Finally, the fifth cluster (orange) includes 77 keywords and the most important (with the greatest betweenness) are "covid-19", "Greece", "emotional", "EMU countries", "e-government services" and "citizen engagement".

In a network graph, degree centrality is measured by the total amount of direct links with the other nodes (Zhang & Luo, 2017). Closeness centrality, first considered by Bavelas (1948), is an importance measure of a node in a network which is based

Table 1 Top 5 most cited documents

	Title	Authors	Citations	Type	Subject area
1	Current trends in Smart City initiatives: Some stylised facts	Neirotti et al. (2014)	2499	Article	Smart city–innovation
2	Critical analysis of Big Data challenges and analytical methods	Sivarajah et al. (2017)	1954	Article	Data
3	Technology Ecosystem Governance	Wareham et al. (2014)	916	Article	E-government
4	A Government that Worked Better and Cost Less?: Evaluating three decades of reform and change in UK central Government	Hood and Dixon (2015)	530	Book	Economic impact
5	The digital divide	Van Dijk (2020)	528	Book	Degree of digitalization

Source Own elaboration

Fig. 6 Random visualization of keywords. *Source* Own elaboration

Table 2 Clusters

Cluster	Color of cluster	Number of documents	Keywords with the greatest betweenness centrality
1st	Purple	163	Digitalization, European Union, public administration, DESI and sustainable development
2nd	Green	146	E-government, adoption, e-participation and e-services
3rd	Blue	126	ICT, digital divide and internet
4th	Yellow	79	Smart city, sustainability, sensor city and smart people
5th	Orange	77	Covid-19, Greece, emotional, EMU countries, e-government services and citizen engagement

Source Own elaboration

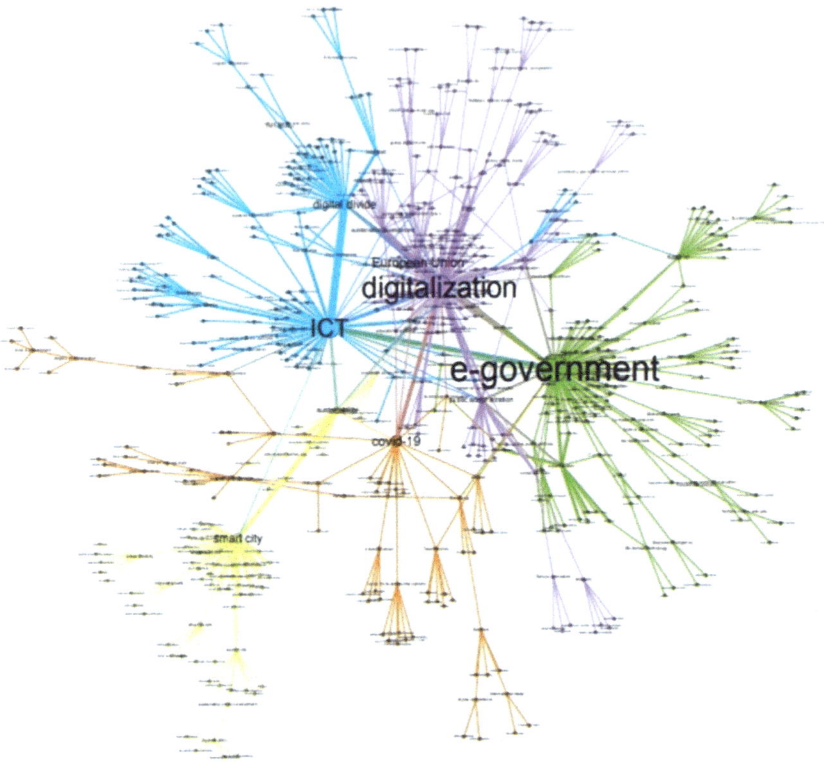

Fig. 7 Network visualization of keywords. *Source* Own elaboration

on the distances from the node to all other nodes (Cohen et al., 2014). Betweenness is a measure of the centrality of a node in a network, and is normally calculated as the fraction of shortest paths between node pairs that pass through the node of interest. Betweenness is, in some sense, a measure of the influence a node has over the spread of information through the network (Newman, 2005). Table 3 shows the 5 keywords with the highest values in the above variables among all the keywords in the sample.

Table 3 Top 5 keywords in terms of degree, closeness and betweenness centrality

Degree centrality	Closeness centrality	Betweenness centrality
E-government	Digitalization	E-government
Digitalization	E-government	Digitalization
ICT	ICT	ICT
Digital divide	European Union	Covid-19
Smart city	Digital divide	European Union

Source Own elaboration

A final analysis using again the network analysis method is done in order to visualize the network between countries that collaborated to write the sample files. In Fig. 8, the bibliometric map is presented. The analysis yielded 83 nodes and 202 edges. In addition, Table 4 shows the results of countries co-authorship. The first cluster (purple) includes 19 countries. Most central (with respect to betweenness) countries are UK, Italy and USA. The second cluster (green) includes 19 elements and the countries with the greatest betweenness centrality that we find are Romania, Poland and Russia. The third cluster (blue) includes 14 countries and the most central, with the same measure of the centrality, are Germany, China, Croatia and Slovakia. The fourth cluster (orange) includes 13 elements and the countries with the greatest betweenness centrality that we find are Spain and Portugal. The fifth cluster (brown) includes 8 countries. Most central (with respect to betweenness) country is France, followed by a significant difference, India, Brazil and Tunisia. The sixth cluster (red) includes 7 elements and the most important of these (with respect to betweenness) are Finland, Sweden and South Africa. Finally, the seventh cluster (dark green) includes 3 countries which are Greece, Turkey and Cyprus with the first having the greatest betweenness centrality than the other two.

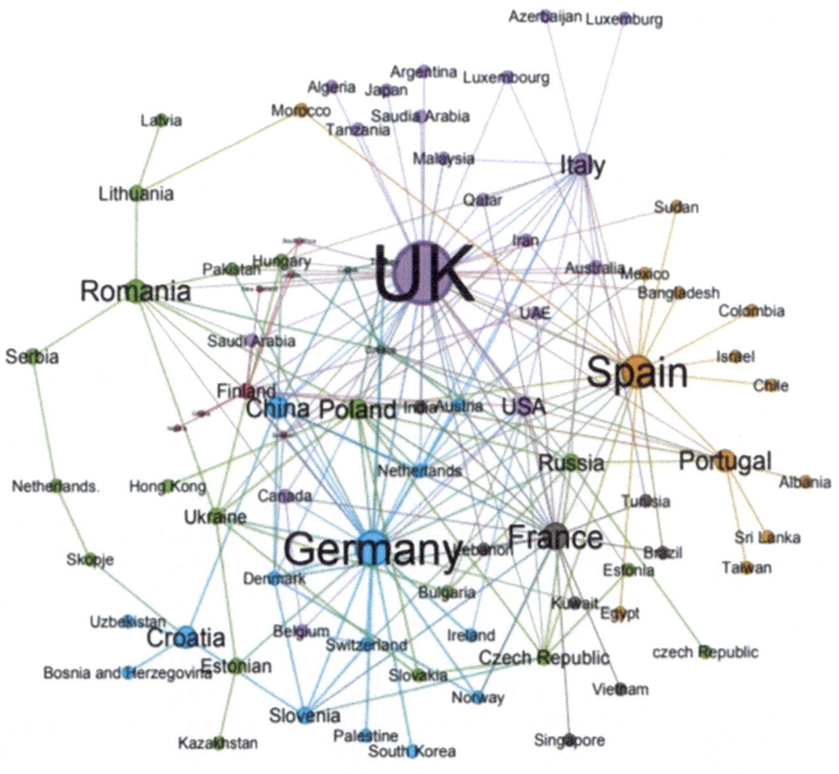

Fig. 8 Network visualization of countries co-authorship. *Source* Own elaboration

Table 4 Countries co-authorship

Cluster	Color of cluster	Number of documents	Countries with the greatest betweenness centrality
1st	Purple	19	UK, Italy and USA
2nd	Green	19	Romania, Poland and Russia
3rd	Blue	14	Germany, China, Croatia and Slovakia
4th	Orange	13	Spain and Portugal
5th	Brown	8	France, India, Brazil and Tunisia
6th	Red	7	Finland, Sweden and South Africa
7th	Dark green	3	Greece, Turkey and Cyprus

Source Own elaboration

In addition, top 3 countries in terms of degree, closeness and betweenness centrality are UK, Germany and Spain.

4 Conclusion

In this research, the method of systematic literature review was used in order to analyze the research related to the issue of digitization and e-government through quantitative methods and analyses. The results show that this theme began to concern the research community very strongly from the outbreak of the covid-19 pandemic onwards, as in 2020 the number of files doubled compared to 2019 and since then every year there has been an increase of almost 50%. The countries that were most involved in research related to the specific topic are the United Kingdom, followed by Spain, Italy, Germany and Romania with small differences. The majority of the sample at 70%, are articles. Regarding the subject area of researches, e-government is studied the most, followed by smart city and innovation, e-business and the degree of digitization. With a small difference, but at a level of less than 10%, follow the surveys that report the economic impact of digitization. Given that most of the sample are researches conducted after the Covid-19 pandemic, it is partly logical that the study of ways to improve e-government and e-business as well as solve problems that arose due to the digital divide or between countries, or between regions of the same country. The five documents with the most references are three articles in the first three positions with the topic category smart city and innovation, data and e-government respectively, while in the fourth and fifth positions we find two books with the topic category economic results and degree of digitization respectively. The results of the network analysis of the keywords collected from the sample showed that top 5 keywords with the biggest betweenness centrality are "e-government", "digitalization", "ICT", "Covid-19" and "European Union". Of these keywords, "digitalization" is more connected with "public administration", "DESI" and "sustainable development", "e-government" connects with "adoption", "e-participation" and "e-services", "ICT" with "digital divide" and "internet" and "Covid-19" is more connected with "emotional", "e-government services" and "citizen engagement". The researched issue was the most widespread in the UK in the monitored period. Important co-author relations have developed with the UK, Italy and USA.

References

Almeida, F., Santos, J. D., & Monteiro, J. A. (2020). The challenges and opportunities in the digitalization of companies in a post-COVID-19 World. *IEEE Engineering Management Review, 48*(3), 97–103.

Alvarenga, A., Matos, F., Godina, R., & Co Matias, J. (2020). Digital transformation and knowledge management in the public sector. *Sustainability, 12*(14), 5824.

Balaskas, S., Panagiotarou, A., & Rigou, M. (2022). The Influence of trustworthiness and technology acceptance factors on the usage of e-government services during COVID-19: A case study of post COVID-19 Greece. *Administrative Sciences, 12*(4), 129.

Bánhidi, Z., Dobos, I., & Nemeslaki, A. (2020). What the overall digital economy and society index reveals: A statistical analysis of the DESI EU28 dimensions. *Regional Statistics, 10*(2), 42–62.

Bastian, M., Heymann, S., & Jacomy, M. (2009). Gephi: An open source software for exploring and manipulating networks. In *International AAAI Conference on Weblogs and Social Media.*

Brereton, P., Kitchenham, B. A., Budgen, D., Turner, M., & Khalil, M. (2007). Lessons from applying the systematic literature review process within the software engineering domain. *Journal of Systems and Software, 80*(4), 571–583.

Caputo, A., Pizzi, S., Pellegrini, M. M., & Dabić, M. (2021). Digitalization and business models: Where are we going? A science map of the field. *Journal of Business Research, 123*, 489–501.

Cohen, E., Delling, D., Pajor, T., & Werneck, R. F. (2014). Computing classic closeness centrality, at scale. In *Proceedings of the Second ACM Conference on Online Social Networks* (pp. 37–50).

Donthu, N., Kumar, S., Mukherjee, D., Pandey, N., & Lim, W. M. (2021). How to conduct a bibliometric analysis: An overview and guidelines. *Journal of Business Research, 133*, 285–296.

Ellegaard, O., & Wallin, J. A. (2015). The bibliometric analysis of scholarly production: How great is the impact? *Scientometrics, 105*, 1809–1831.

Gajdosikova, D., & Valaskova, K. (2021). Bibliometric analysis of debt financing semiotics. *The Slovak Research and Development Agency—Grant Vega 1/0121/20*.

Haefner, L., & Sternberg, R. (2020). Spatial implications of digitization: State of the field and research agenda. *Geography Compass, 14*(12), e12544.

Hood, C., & Dixon, R. (2015). *A government that worked better and cost less? Evaluating three decades of reform and change in UK central Government*. OUP Oxford.

Hussain, S., Muhammad, L. J., & Yakubu, A. (2018). Mining social media and DBpedia data using Gephi and R. *Journal of Applied Computer Science & Mathematics, 12*(1), 14–20.

Kitchenham, B., Brereton, O. P., Budgen, D., Turner, M., Bailey, J., & Linkman, S. (2009). Systematic literature reviews in software engineering–A systematic literature review. *Information and Software Technology, 51*(1), 7–15.

Kydros, D., & Filenta, P. (2022). Literature review of economic and regional development through quantitative methods and social network analysis. *European Journal of Interdisciplinary Studies*, (01).

Loutsaris, M. A., & Charalabidis, Y. (2020). Legal informatics from the aspect of interoperability: A review of systems, tools and ontologies. In *Proceedings of the 13th International Conference on Theory and Practice of Electronic Governance* (pp. 731–737).

Martins, J., & Nielsen, M. M. (2020). ICT development in the public sector and the small island states context-evidence from across the world. In *2020 Seventh International Conference on eDemocracy & eGovernment (ICEDEG)* (pp. 67–73). IEEE.

Neirotti, P., De Marco, A., Cagliano, A. C., Mangano, G., & Scorrano, F. (2014). Current trends in Smart City initiatives: Some stylised facts. *Cities, 38*, 25–36.
Newman, M. E. (2005). A measure of betweenness centrality based on random walks. *Social Networks, 27*(1), 39–54.
Patelarou, E., & Brokalaki, H. (2010). The methodology of the systematic review and meta-analysis. *Nosileftiki, 49*(2).
Pérez-Morote, R., Pontones-Rosa, C., & Núñez-Chicharro, M. (2020). The effects of e-government evaluation, trust and the digital divide in the levels of e-government use in European countries. *Technological Forecasting and Social Change, 154*, 119973.
Polychronidou, P., Zoumpoulidis, V., & Valsamidis, S. (2021). Labor digitalization in Europe. *Intellectual Economics, 15*(2), 6–21. ISSN 1822-8038 (online)
Sivarajah, U., Kamal, M. M., Irani, Z., & Weerakkody, V. (2017). Critical analysis of Big Data challenges and analytical methods. *Journal of Business Research, 70*, 263–286.
Streeter, C. L., & Gillespie, D. F. (1992). Social network analysis. *Journal of Social Service Research, 16*(1–2), 201–222.
Vadana, I. I., Torkkeli, L., Kuivalainen, O., & Saarenketo, S. (2020). Digitalization of companies in international entrepreneurship and marketing. *International Marketing Review, 37*(3), 471–492.
Valeri, M., & Baggio, R. (2021). Social network analysis: Organizational implications in tourism management. *International Journal of Organizational Analysis, 29*(2), 342–353.
Van Dijk, J. (2020). *The digital divide.*
Vlasov, I. (2020). Legal and pedagogical aspects of e-education. In *2020 International Conference Engineering Technologies and Computer Science (EnT)* (pp. 144–151). IEEE.
Wareham, J., Fox, P. B., & Cano Giner, J. L. (2014). Technology ecosystem governance. *Organization Science, 25*(4), 1195–1215.
Wynn, R., Gabarron, E., Johnsen, J. A. K., & Traver, V. (2020). Special issue on e-health services. *International Journal of Environmental Research and Public Health, 17*(8), 2885.
Yang, J., Cheng, C., Shen, S., & Yang, S. (2017). Comparison of complex network analysis software: Citespace, SCI 2 and Gephi. In *2017 IEEE 2nd International Conference on Big Data Analysis (ICBDA)* (pp. 169–172). IEEE.
YousefiNooraie, R., Sale, J. E., Marin, A., & Ross, L. E. (2020). Social network analysis: An example of fusion between quantitative and qualitative methods. *Journal of Mixed Methods Research, 14*(1), 110–124.
Zafeiriou, E., Garefalakis, A., Passas, I., & Ragazou, K. (2023). Illicit and corruption mitigation strategy in the financial sector: A study with a hybrid methodological approach. *Sustainability, 15*(2), 1366.
Zhang, J., & Luo, Y. (2017). Degree centrality, betweenness centrality, and closeness centrality in social network. In *2017 2nd International Conference on Modelling, Simulation and Applied Mathematics (MSAM2017)* (pp. 300–303). Atlantis Press.
Zyoud, S. E. H., Al-Jabi, S. W., & Sweileh, W. M. (2015). Scientific publications from Arab world in leading journals of integrative and complementary medicine: A bibliometric analysis. *BMC Complementary and Alternative Medicine, 15*(1), 1–10.

Regional, Sustainable and Smart Growth

Technological Transformations and Global Value Chains: Strategic Challenges for Europe and Its Territory

Roberta Capello and Andrea Caragliu

Abstract Over the past decade, Europe faced multiple challenges that have already caused structural changes in the way regional growth patterns have been taking place. Among many, these challenges include a substantial restructuring of Global Value Chains, with a reversal of the process of offshoring production towards the EU, and the technological transformations induced by the pervasive diffusion of Industry 4.0 and the digital service economy. Both challenges exert effects that are ex ante expected to be intertwined with other driving forces, most notably related to the structural changes associated with the COVID-19 restrictions, and the presently ongoing Russia-Ukraine conflict. Thus, the well-entangled nature of these challenges makes it hard to separate out their net impacts at the local level. The aim of this paper is to simulate the net effects of technological transformations and global value chains, and isolate their local effects on GDP growth, thanks to a regional macro-econometric forecasting model, called *MAcroeconometric, Social, Sectoral, Territorial model* in its fifth version (*MASST5*). Results are presented against the backdrop of a reference scenario, modeling both the long-run trends characterizing the EU economy over the past decade, as well as the long-lasting consequences of both COVID-19 restrictions, and the presently ongoing Russia-Ukraine conflict. Results hint at a remarkable spatial heterogeneity of the impacts of these challenges, both in absolute terms, as well as in terms of regional disparities.

Keywords Macroeconometric regional growth models · Regional growth · Territorial disparities · Industry 4.0 · Digital service economy · Global value chains

This paper has been presented at the 15th International Conference *Economies of the Balkan and Eastern European Countries EBEEC 2023*. May 12–14, 2023. Chios, Greece. We would like to thank the organizers of the conference for inviting the paper, and the crowd for useful comments and remarks. All remaining errors are our own.

R. Capello · A. Caragliu (✉)
ABC Department, Politecnico Di Milano, Piazza Leonardo da Vinci, 32, BLD 5, 20133 Milan (MI), Italy
e-mail: andrea.caragliu@polimi.it

R. Capello
e-mail: roberta.capello@polimi.it

M. Mavri et al. (eds.), *Digital Economy and Green Growth*, Contributions to Economics, https://doi.org/10.1007/978-3-031-66669-8_8

JEL Classification Codes R11 · O18 · O47 · O52

ἔσσεται ἦμαρ ὅτ᾽ ἄν ποτ᾽ ὀλώλη Ἴλιος ἱρὴ
καὶ Πρίαμος καὶ λαὸς ἐϋμμελίω Πριάμοιο.
(Iliad, book VI, 447–449)

1 Setting the Scene

Over the past decade, Europe faced multiple challenges that have already caused structural changes in the way regional growth patterns have been taking place. Among many, these challenges include a substantial restructuring of Global Value Chains (henceforth, GVCs), with a partial reversal of the process of offshoring production towards the EU and the technological transformations induced by the pervasive diffusion of Industry 4.0 and the digital service economy. Both challenges exert effects that are ex ante expected to be intertwined with many driving forces, most notably related to the structural changes associated with the COVID-19 restrictions, and the presently ongoing Russia-Ukraine conflict. Thus, the well-entangled nature of these challenges makes it hard to separate out their net impacts at the local level.

The aim of this paper is to simulate the net effects of technological transformations and global value chains, and isolate their local effects on GDP growth, thanks to a regional macro-econometric forecasting model, called *MAcroeconometric, Social, Sectoral, Territorial model*, in its fifth version (*MASST5*) (Capello et al., 2024). Results are presented against the backdrop of a reference scenario, modeling both the long-run trends characterizing the EU economy over the past decade, as well as the long-lasting consequences of both COVID-19 restrictions, and the presently ongoing Russia–Ukraine conflict.

To achieve this goal, we simulate the reference -scenario first presented in Capello and Caragliu (2023) with a full-fledged set of assumptions, aiming at capturing all relevant challenges. Next, we run alternative simulations whereby the assumptions related to GVCs and technological transformations are muted. Thus, we will be able to isolate the net impact of each of these two relevant challenges on future regional GDP growth rates. Results will in particular focus on (i) the spatial distribution of GDP growth differences, and (ii) the impact of these two simulation exercises on the future development of regional income inequalities. Results of these exercise document a remarkable spatial heterogeneity of the impacts of these challenges, both in absolute terms, as well as in terms of regional disparities.

The paper proceeds as follows. Section 2 briefly summarizes the recent geopolitical challenges whose role in driving regional growth patterns is empirically assessed in this paper. In particular we deal with the Russia-Ukraine conflict (Sect. 2.1); GVCs (Sect. 2.2); and Technological transformations (Sect. 2.3). Next, Sect. 3 briefly discusses the structure and the way to proceed of the MASST5 model. Section 4 presents the first set of empirical results, first briefly introducing the reference scenario, and then focusing on the spatial distribution of the regional impacts of technological transformations and Global Value Chains for the European case. Section 5 comments on the spatial disparities caused by these two challenges. Lastly, Sect. 6 concludes and sets out a future research agenda.

2 Geopolitical Issues

2.1 The Russia–Ukraine Conflict

As this paper is being written, the Russia-Ukraine conflict has been raging for more than a year. On February 24, 2022 Russian troops crossed the borders with Ukraine with the final goal to capture the capital city of Kiyv and replace the government with people closer to Russian preferences (Britannica, 2022). Early attempts at replacing the government were rebuffed, and in fact in the summer of 2022 the Ukrainian forces regained a substantial portion of the ground lost to the Russian invaders.

While the final outcome of the conflict still appears rather uncertain, one result that cannot be ignored is its effect on global geopolitical equilibria. Russia had hitherto thrived on its capacity to supply western Countries, mostly in Europe, with cheap energy sources feeding rapid economic development, at the expense of geopolitical uncertainty and indebtedness (Anderson, 2008). As a reaction to Russia's invasion of Ukraine, though, the European Union found new internal cohesion in the decision to levy (to date) fourteen different packages of sanctions.[1] The extent of the package and the enduring tension between Russia and its allies on the one hand, and the western bloc (including the European Union, the United States, the UK, and Japan and Korea) makes it highly unlikely that things will revert to the pre-conflict equilibrium any time soon (Chepeliev et al., 2022). For the sake of this paper, one aspect that deserves specific attention is related to how the uncertainty engendered by the conflict will eventually end.

In the absence of a clear foresight into how the conflict will eventually be solved, a reference scenario was built (Capello & Caragliu, 2022; Capello et al., 2024) which assumes that the short and medium run consequences of this conflict will remain, and, thus, international equilibria will likely suffer from a prolonged state of uncertainty and geopolitical polarization.

[1] These include "*Freezing the assets of 207 entities (including key banks) and 1473 individuals (primarily Russian officials and elites), to whom travel bans also apply. Imposing debt and equity restrictions on certain banks and companies. Restricting transactions with Russia's central bank and blocking access to its reserve holdings. Banning transactions with certain Russian state-owned military-industrial enterprises. Disconnecting 10 leading Russian financial institutions—including Sberbank, Russia's largest bank—from SWIFT (the world's dominant international financial messaging system). Broadening export controls on dual-use goods and technologies. Banning certain exports in the aviation, maritime, and technology sectors (e.g., semiconductors) and the export of drone engines and luxury goods to Russia*" (US Congress, 2023).

While this state will likely affect multiple economic outcomes, in this paper we will focus on the effects of such a prolonged state of uncertainty on GVCs and technological transformation processes, and, ultimately, on regional GDP growth.

2.2 Global Value Chains

GVCs are a relatively recent phenomenon made possible by the technological progress, allowing to control overstretched production stages with a central control function coordinating far away production sites. Chronologically, this phenomenon is tightly connected with the so called second wave of globalization. This process has been suggested to be affecting countless firms that "*now organize production on a global scale and choose to offshore parts, components, or services to producers in foreign and often distant countries*" (Antràs, 2020, p. 551).

While before the 2007/2008 financial crisis international trade linkages were mostly seen as a univocally positive phenomenon, the fast diffusion of the financial trigger to the crisis through international trade channels, coupled with growing concerns about the global dependence on China's productive plants, caused a partial reversal of the process of offshoring production towards the EU, the US, and, partially, India (Fan & Liu, 2021). This early process of GVCs upgrading was also motivated by an attempt to "move up the value chain", i.e., to gain segments of the production chain associated with higher profit rates (De Marchi & Alford, 2022).

Recently, the geopolitical tensions caused by the Russia-Ukraine conflict, triggered in the first place by Russia's attack on Ukraine, then further strengthened by Russia's retaliations for the western bloc's support of Ukraine's war effort (in the form of military supplies and training, and financial relief), prompted a second wave of policies aiming at enhancing reshoring and near-shoring processes.

From a European perspective, sanctions implemented in the immediate aftermath of Russia's invasion of Ukraine were targeting several channels of international trade, and cause as much economic damage as possible, with the ultimate goal to nudge Russia into retreating. Among these measures, the ban of the Russian Federation from the SWIFT financial messaging system, and a plan to reduce the EU's dependence on Russian energy sources to zero in the medium to long run (Estrada & Koutronas, 2022; Mellor, 2022). However, any attempt at steering the composition of spatial extent of GVCs through policies may be jeopardized by the sheer complexity of such global structures (Gereffi et al., 2021).

For the aims of the present paper, how intense the effects of these policies is will likely depend on how intense participation in GVCs is, and which industries cause this dependence, in the European regions.

2.3 Technological Transformations

A second conceptual bloc of interest for our simulations is related to the growing importance and the pervasive diffusion of technological transformation. This paper interprets as the latter as comprising the diffusion of the Industry 4.0 paradigm for manufacturing activities, and the digital service economy for tertiary ones. While for both these technological paradigm shifts this paper does not provide a novel interpretation, it is here worth briefly mentioning what is being meant.

The term "*Industry 4.0*" has been first used at the Hanover Fair in 2011, and has been subsequently adopted by policy documents by the German Federal Ministry of Education and Research and the German Federal Ministry of Economic Affairs and Energy (Drath & Horch, 2014). Industry 4.0 refers to a complex set of technologies comprising "*modular and efficient manufacturing systems and characterizes scenarios in which products control their own manufacturing process. This is supposed to realize the manufacturing of individual products in a batch size of one while maintaining the economic conditions of mass production*" (Lasi et al., 2014, p. 239).

The "Digital service economy" refers instead to a "*multifaceted phenomenon made of a sprawling range of businesses based on digital platforms and redesigning the boundaries of manufacturing towards services*" (Capello et al., 2023, p. 637). The evolution of the digital service economy is not disconnected from advanced manufacturing, in that by means of digital technologies firms are allowed to sell final products coupled with services with the aim of both better satisfying consumer preferences, while at the same time collecting real time data about their consumption behavior (Porter & Heppelmann, 2014).

These two sets of technologies are at the basis of a profound transformation in the way people live, work, entertain themselves and do business. In fact, new business opportunities arise for those firms and activities able to grasp such a transformation. The way in which local actors will be able to take advantage from this technological transformation will shape the local competitiveness of regions.

Worryingly, at the regional level Europe presents a remarkable degree of heterogeneity in the diffusion of these two sets of technologies and the technological transformations they generate. In fact, their spatial diffusion presents rather orthogonal patterns, with Industry 4.0 technologies mostly concentrating in advanced manufacturing areas, while digital service economy industries tend to be more concentrated in major urban areas (Capello & Lenzi, 2021). This means that, once again, as in the case of GVCs, the spatial exposure to policies aiming at steering the diffusion and effectiveness of these industries will be inevitably linked to the initial diffusion of these industries, thereby allowing to identify space-specific impacts.

3 A Methodology for Assessing the Role of Technological Transformations and Global Value Chains in European Regional Growth

As anticipated in Sect. 1, the effects of these mega-trends on regional growth patterns are difficult to isolate—each coming in a well-entangled bowl of feedbacks and loops. However, a macroeconometric regional growth model is exactly the type of tool allowing this exercise. To this aim, we employ the fifth and latest version of the MAcroeconometric, Social, Sectoral, Territorial model (MASST).

The MASST model is a macroeconometric regional growth model built to simulate regional growth in the medium and long-run. The acronym contains the different dimensions—Macroeconomic, Sectoral, Social and Territorial—on which the model is built. While the first version of the model is presented in detail in Capello (2007), the reader is referred to Capello and Caragliu (2021a) for a discussion of the historical evolutions of various versions of the MASST model; to Capello et al. (2024) for a technical description of the latest version of the model; and, lastly, to Capello and Caragliu (2021b) for a recent application of the MASST model to ex-ante simulate the regional costs of COVID-19 closures.[2]

In the MASST model, regional growth is explained by a combination of national (macroeconomic) and regional (micro-territorial) factors. While the former capture, through a set of Keynesian quasi-identities, the main components of aggregate demand (Consumption, Investment, Public Expenditure, Exports, and Imports), the latter explain regional competitiveness, i.e., the supply side of the economy. In particular, the sectoral, social and territorial aspects taken into consideration to characterize the region are:

- quantified tangible and intangible elements: different assets of territorial capital, especially those with an intangible nature, linked to actors' perceptions, relational elements, and cooperation attitudes;
- territorial complexity: the set of context specificities and synergies that characterize regional growth.

Empirically, the model runs across two stages:

- in the estimation stage, structural relations between explanatory and dependent variables in various national and regional equations are estimated over a long run time span through a set of equations included in the model;
- in the simulation stage, estimated coefficients are employed for simulating likely future growth patterns (usually, over a 15–20 years' horizon), and given an internally coherent sets of assumptions forming regional growth scenarios.

The model merges national and regional growth-enhancing factors by explaining regional growth (ΔY_r) as a decomposition between a national growth rate (ΔY_N)

[2] These simulations are also employed at NUTS3 level for simulating the costs of border closures due to COVID-19 restrictions in Capello et al. (2022).

and a regional differential shift (s) (Capello, 2007) (Eq. 1):

$$\Delta Y_r = \Delta Y_N + s; \;\; r \in N \tag{1}$$

Figure 1 shows the logical structure of the model. In Fig. 1, all grey-shaded figures represent an estimated equation. MASST5 is based on a panel data set covering the period 1995–2020 for the national sub-model (left-hand side of Fig. 1), and a four periods panel data set for the periods 2004–2008; 2008–2012; 2012–2016; 2016–2019 for the regional sub-model (right-hand side of Fig. 1). Within each grey shape, two types of variables are indicated: rounded-angle shapes represent variables endogenous to the model, while octagon ones represent variables treated as exogenous. The latter are bound to approach, or reach, a given quantitative target, set by the modeler within an array of conditions that shape a scenario. Scenarios are defined as combinations of internally and logically coherent conditions that allow the modeler to depict a future combination of events, that are not necessarily more likely to take place; rather, they represent possible bifurcations that help identifying the effects of such extreme events.

Exogenous variables are thus treated as levers. Defining a generic target variable x, indexed t for the time period when it is calculated, Eq. (2) shows that a variable approaches its long-run target with a speed proportional to its distance from the target value itself:

$$x_t = x_{t-1} + s(T - x_{t-1}) \tag{2}$$

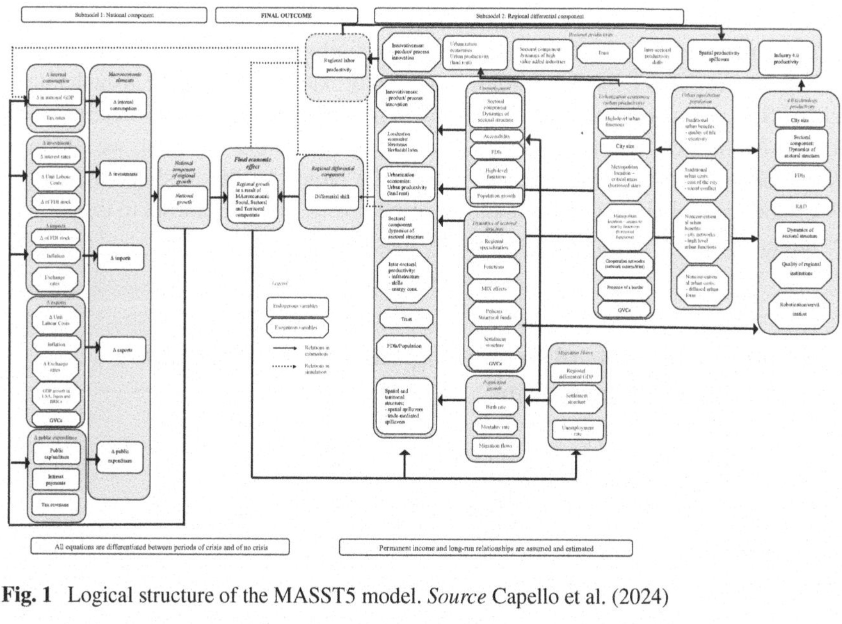

Fig. 1 Logical structure of the MASST5 model. *Source* Capello et al. (2024)

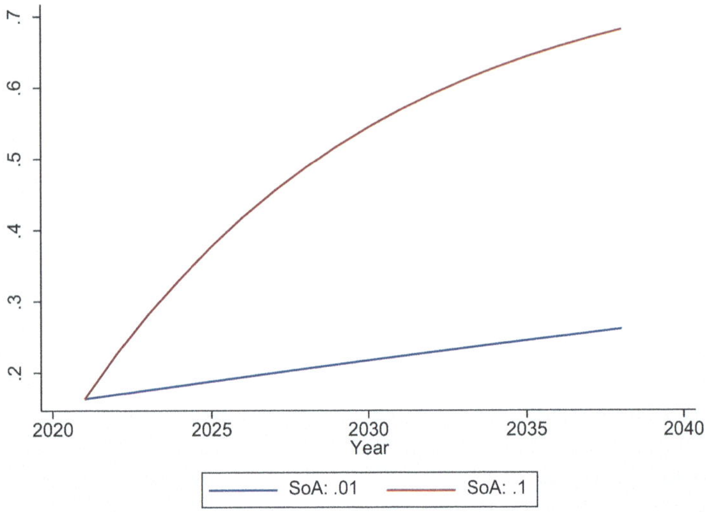

Fig. 2 Example of the target mechanism for the trust vector. *Source* Authors' elaboration

Graphically, Fig. 2 shows an example of this mechanism for the Greek NUTS2 region of North Aegean, related to the regional trust vector. The initial value of this variable for the region is equal to 16.875%. The target for this variable for 2038 is set to 78%; the blue line is drawn by setting a speed of adjustment equal to 1%, while the red line indicates a speed of adjustment equal to 10%.

In the next section, the MASST5 model is employed to empirically assess the relative impact of GVCs and technological transformations on regional growth rates. In MASST5, average annual real GDP growth is simulated for all NUTS2 regions in the EU27 plus the UK for the period 2021–2038. To achieve this goal, we run two simulations of the model, in each switching the targets of the modules modeling GVCs and technological transformations, respectively, off. This allows to isolate the *net* impact of each conceptual block of the model.

4 Regional Impacts of Technological Transformations and Global Value Chains

4.1 The Reference Scenario

As mentioned in the introductory chapter, the aim of the paper is to see how the trends in two specific challenges, namely GVCs reorientation and technological transformations, play a role in a trend scenario where two other main challenges threaten the future of Europe, namely the COVID-19 pandemic and the Ukraine-Russia conflicts.

The aim is achieved in two steps. We first build a reference scenario, an exercise already presented in previous works (Capello & Caragliu, 2023; Capello et al., 2024) and only briefly summarized here, and then we impose that the trends of the two challenges of interest, technological change and GVCs, remain as in the past. The results of these two simulations, representing the originality of the present work, are presented in next two sub-sections.

The reference scenario presents a profoundly transformed Europe, suffering from new threats concerning borders for Europe generated by terroristic attacks, pandemic, war. Europe has to set new goals for the European budget in health and security, even if it has gained more cohesion and trust among European countries that discovered the strength of solidarity among them in facing the pandemic. This leads to Common European policies, like common asylum systems for migration, the strengthening of the digital common market to overcome the strong digital divide among regions and countries in Europe, assuming therefore a more spatially widespread trend in technological transformations will occur than it is today the case. A reorganization of GVCs towards African countries, especially in the field of energy, after the Ukraine-Russia conflict that generated a drastic increase of energy prices, leading to high inflation. The geographical reorientation of GVCs is assumed to be accompanied by the capacity of Europe to upgrade its position in GVCs, as back-shoring processes take place. High interest rates reflect the uncertainty generated by the conflict on the financial markets.

The assumptions on the technological changes are therefore:

- an increase in the relative regional specialization in high-tech industries, capturing the technology producing sectors;
- an increase in the regional sectoral specialization in technology, carrier, and induced sectors, representing three types of adopting sectors;
- an increase in the intensity of regional robotization in manufacturing sectors, representing the adoption rate of automation;
- an increase in the intensity of regional online sales in service sectors, representing the digitalization of the regions.

For what concerns GVCs, we mainly assume in the reference scenario:

- a decreasing reliance on foreign final demand from extra-EU countries;
- a decreasing trend in backward participation, capturing the capacity of EU countries to position themselves in the GVCs.

These assumptions are included at both national and regional level, the last one with the possibility to select specific sectors (in particular: manufacturing industries; professional, scientific and administrative activities; financial and professional services; and the construction sector).

4.2 *Impacts of Technological Transformations on Regional Growth in Europe*

A first simulation shows the results of freezing the assumption on a more spatially widespread trend in technological transformations w.r.t. today. In operational terms, this means to keep the same trends of the past on the levers of the technological transformations. In particular, no changes are therefore assumed in:

- the relative regional specialization in high-tech industries, capturing the technology producing sectors;
- the regional sectoral specialization in technology, carrier, and induced sectors, representing three types of adopting sectors;
- the intensity of regional robotization in manufacturing sectors, representing the adoption rate of automation;
- the intensity of regional online sales in service sectors, representing the digitalization of the regions.

Figure 3 shows the result of simulating the reference scenario without the above mentioned assumptions. In Fig. 3, blue color pales indicate negative differences w.r.t. the standard reference scenario; for these regions, the lack of assumptions on a strengthening of the digital common market to overcome the strong digital divide among regions in Europe penalizes its GDP growth. Red colors indicate instead a situation where a digital common market penalizes the region in terms of GDP growth.

As Fig. 3 documents, regions penalized by a widespread digitalization are typically high-income ones, which tend to gain from a strong position in the automation and

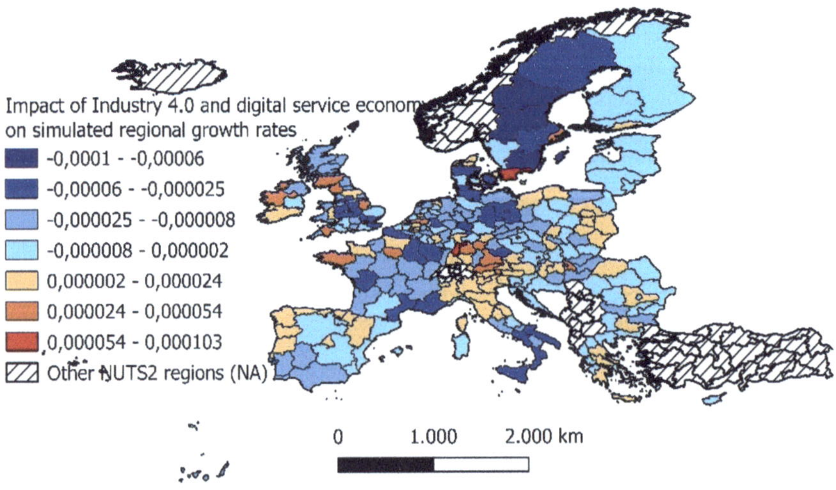

Fig. 3 Impacts of technological transformation on regional growth rates. *Source* Authors' elaborations

digitalization technologies. These are mostly areas located in the North of Italy, the North of France, in Southern Germany and in Austria. Many urban areas would suffer from a widespread digitalization. This is the case of metro areas as Paris, Madrid, Milan, Munich, Stockholm, and Helsinki.

Regions penalized by not overcoming the digital divide among regions are several; mostly, they are located in remote areas, in both Western and Eastern countries. In other words, the decision not to develop a digital common market would penalize many remote regions in all European countries, both in the West and in the East of Europe. This result suggests the great relevance of a digital common market strategy for decreasing interregional disparities.

4.3 Impacts of Global Value Chains on Regional Growth in Europe

Figure 4 provides a conceptually similar picture for the simulation freezing the assumptions on the GVCs. For this specific case, the reorganization of GVCs to nearby countries and the capacity of Europe to upgrade its position in GVCs characterizing the reference scenario have been left as they are today.

As in the case of technological transformation, blue colors represent regions that are penalized by the freezing the assumption on decreasing GVCs participation and by the ensuing repositioning, while red regions are those gaining from the absence of these assumptions. Unsurprisingly, the latter are located in Central and Eastern European countries, as they would lose their manufacturing hotspot position of Europe;

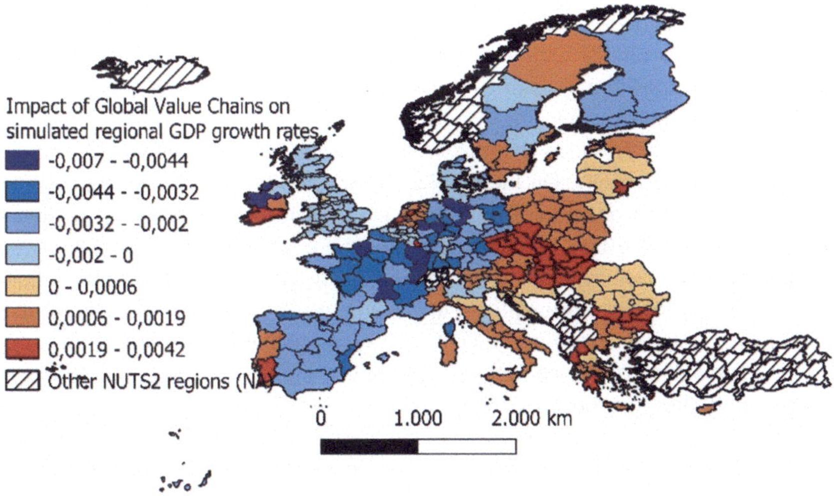

Fig. 4 Impacts of Global Value Chains on regional growth rates. *Source* Authors' elaborations

Ireland, and the Netherlands, that are characterized by a high concentration of financial services; and Swedish regions, where high-tech manufacturing is concentrated. Most Western regions (blue ones in the map) are those that would be penalized by the lack of assumptions on decreasing GVCs participation and by the repositioning. Most these areas are possible destination areas for back-shoring and nearshoring activities, because of their traditional manufacturing specialization, like German and Northern Italian regions (Lombardy and Veneto), and Spanish regions (Catalunia).

In both Figs. 3 and 4, a picture of spatial heterogeneity emerges. To address this point, Sect. 5 will present an additional analysis, by looking at the marginal impact of these two simulations on regional disparities.

5 Impacts of the Two Challenges on Regional Disparities

Figure 5 (Panels a–c) show results of calculating the Theil index (Fig. 5a) and its decomposition into Between Countries (Fig. 5b) and Within Countries (Fig. 5c) Theil indices

The Theil index can be interpreted as "*the expected information content of the indirect message which transforms the population shares as prior probabilities into the income shares as posterior probabilities*" (Theil, 1967, pp. 125–126).

Empirically, the Theil index is calculated as (Eq. 3):

$$Theil = \frac{1}{N}\sum\nolimits_{i=1}^{N}\frac{y_i}{\overline{y}}ln\left(\frac{y_i}{\overline{y}}\right) \tag{3}$$

where N is the number of spatial units (NUTS2 regions in our case), y_i is the variable of interest in the ith region (in this case, regional GDP) and $\overline{y}$ is the average regional GDP calculated for all 281 regions in our sample. The index is also amenable to an interesting decomposition, breaking it down into its between Countries component and the within Countries one.

Interestingly, Fig. 5a shows that the two simulations discussed in Sect. 4 present two rather opposite effects. On the one hand, the absence of a decreasing participation and upgrading position of regions in GVCs leads to a decrease in regional disparities. In fact, the lack of such assumptions are in favor of poorer countries, typically, the manufacturing belt of Europe, and at detriment of rich countries, that gain from back-shoring and functional upgrading of GVCs. This is reflected in the fact that without the assumptions on GVCs the between country disparities increase (Fig. 5b). Instead, as functional upgrading is led by high-productivity metro areas, within country disparities decrease (Fig. 5c).

A completely different story is presented for the case of the technological transformation. In this case, the lack of policies assuring the widespread diffusion of digitalization and automation generates an increase in total regional disparities (Fig. 5a), as it goes at detriment of poor countries. Between country disparities increase (Fig. 5b), while a less clear pattern emerges for within country disparities (Fig. 5c), that

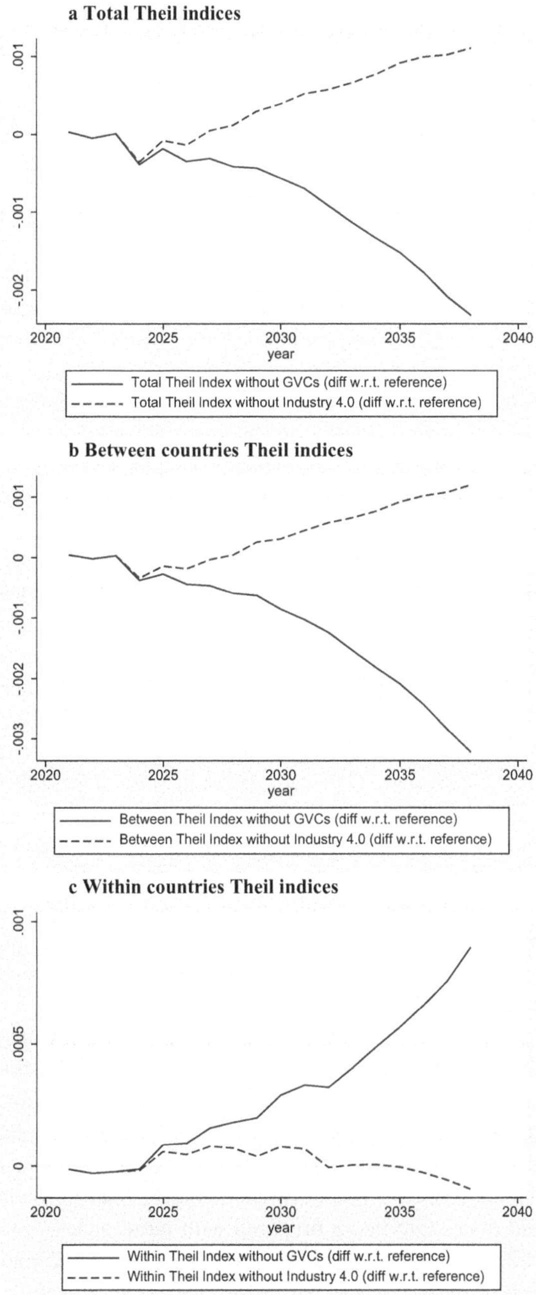

Fig. 5 Total, between countries, and within countries Theil indices switching off GVCs and industry 4.0 and digital service economy equations in MASST5. **a** Total Theil indices. **b** Between countries Theil indices. **c** Within countries Theil indices. *Source* Authors' elaborations on the basis of MASST5 model simulations

tend over the long period to decrease since regions that tend to be penalized by a widespread digitalization are the strong ones, i.e., those that at present gain from being the pioneers of technological transformations.

6 Conclusions and Ways Forward

This paper employed the MAcroeconometric, Social, Sectoral, Territorial model 5 (MASST5) model to isolate the effects two of the main challenges that Europe is facing and will likely be forced to tackle over the future decades, viz the restructuring of GVCs and the pervasive diffusion of technological transformations (in the form of Industry 4.0 and digital service economy). Results have been obtained by running two alternative simulations against the backdrop of a reference scenario modeling both the long-run trends characterizing the EU economy over the past decade, as well as the long-lasting consequences of both COVID-19 restrictions, and the presently ongoing Russia-Ukraine conflict.

The novelty of this exercise lies in allowing isolating the net impact of the effects of these two challenges that would otherwise be entangled in a complex net of feedbacks and loops that would make it hard to assess their final effect. Doing so provides useful food for thought for drafting educated guesses on the likely consequences of changes in the extent and spatial distribution of these two mechanisms in case the presently ongoing Russia-Ukraine conflict remains unsolved in the medium run.

Policy implications are numerous; here, a couple of them are worth mentioning.

On the front of GVCs, the presently ongoing conflict between Russia and Ukraine, along with the growing trade tensions between two major global players such as USA and China, has already triggered policies aiming at rerouting trade flows towards politically closer trade partners (e.g., Algeria for gas; Matalucci, 2022). While the complexity of GVCs makes it hard to assess the net effect of rerouting trade flows (Gereffi et al., 2021), MASST5 simulations make it possible to look at the aggregate impacts on regional GDP growth, highlighting substantial spatial heterogeneity in their impacts.

On the front of technological transformations, a major effort is needed to assess the spatial distribution of policies aiming at governing the diffusion of digital technologies that are expected to change the world of work for good (Acemoglu & Restrepo, 2020) For instance, recently ChatGPT, the popular chatbot coded by OpenAI broke all previous records in terms of the speed of diffusion and the growth of its users base (Hu, 2023). Anecdotal evidence suggests that a growing number of academic papers and essays are being prepared with more or less intense use of chatbots (Marche, 2022). How this will impact the future of work, and whether the spatial distribution of these impacts will also be affected, will in its turn require sound empirical assessments.

As a future line of research, MASST5 could also be employed to quantify the regional impacts of alternative scenarios, to be compared to the benchmark assumptions modeled for producing the reference scenario, but capturing the overall impacts of multiple assumptions simultaneously taking placing in the European economies. If anything, the past decade taught us that history is proceeding at an accelerated pace, and tools offering results to feed evidence-based policies may help in steering the discussion, and addressing complex challenges in a less blind manner.

References

Acemoglu, D., & Restrepo, P. (2020). *New tasks, good automation and bad automation: Implications for the future of work*. UCL Gorman Lectures, Lecture, 2.

Anderson, R. J. (2008). "*Europe's Dependence on Russian Natural Gas: Perspectives and Recommendations for a Long-term Strategy*". Retrieved July 18, 2023, from https://www.marshallcenter.org/en/publications/occasional-papers/europes-dependence-russian-natural-gas-perspectives-and-recommendations-long-term-strategy-0.

Antràs, P. (2020). Conceptual aspects of global value chains. *The World Bank Economic Review, 34*(3), 551–574.

Britannica (2022). "*Russian invasion of Ukraine*". Retrieved July 18, 2023, from https://www.britannica.com/event/2022-Russian-invasion-of-Ukraine.

Capello, R. (2007). A forecasting territorial model of regional growth: The MASST model. *The Annals of Regional Science, 41*, 753–787.

Capello, R., & Caragliu, A. (2021a). Modelling and forecasting regional growth: The MASST model. In S. Colombo (Ed.), *Spatial economics volume II: Applications* (pp. 63–88). Springer.

Capello, R., & Caragliu, A. (2021b). Regional growth and disparities in a post-COVID Europe: A new normality scenario. *Journal of Regional Science, 61*(4), 710–727.

Capello, R., & Caragliu, A. (2023). *Present challenges and possible future growth trajectories for Europe and its territory*. Unpublished manuscript.

Capello, R., Caragliu, A., & Panzera, E. (2022). Economic costs of COVID-19 for cross-border regions. *Regional Science Policy & Practice*. https://doi.org/10.1111/rsp3.12590

Capello, R., Caragliu, A., & Dellisanti, R. (2024). Integrating digital and global transformations in forecasting regional growth: The MASST5 model. *Spatial Economic Analysis, 19*(2), 133–160.

Capello, R., Lenzi, C., & Panzera, E. (2023). The rise of the digital service economy in European regions *30*(6), 637–663.

Capello, R., & Lenzi, C. (2021). *The regional economics of technological transformations: Industry 4.0 and servitisation in European regions*. Routledge.

Chepeliev, M., Hertel, T., van der Mensbrugghe, D. (2022). *Cutting Russia's fossil fuel exports: Short-term pain for long-term gain*. VoxEU.org, 9 March.

De Marchi, V., & Alford, M. (2022). State policies and upgrading in global value chains: A systematic literature review. *Journal of International Business Policy, 5*(1), 88–111.

Drath, R., & Horch, A. (2014). Industrie 4.0: Hit or hype? *IEEE Industrial Electronics Magazine, 8*(2), 56–58.

Estrada, M. A. R., & Koutronas, E. (2022). The impact of the Russian Aggression against Ukraine on the Russia-EU Trade. *Journal of Policy Modeling, 44*(3), 599–616.

Fan, X. M., & Liu, H. G. (2021). Global supply chain shifting: A macro sense of production relocation based on multi-regional input-output table. *Economic Modelling, 94*, 672–680.

Gereffi, G., Lim, H. C., & Lee, J. (2021). Trade policies, firm strategies, and adaptive reconfigurations of global value chains. *Journal of International Business Policy, 4*, 506–522.

Hu, K. (2023). *ChatGPT sets record for fastest-growing user base*. Retrieved July 19, 2023, from https://www.reuters.com/technology/chatgpt-sets-record-fastest-growing-user-base-analyst-note-2023-02-01/.

Lasi, H., Fettke, P., Kemper, H. G., Feld, T., & Hoffmann, M. (2014). Industry 4.0. *Business & Information Systems Engineering, 6*, 239–242.

Marche, S. (2022). The college essay is dead. *The Atlantic*.
Matalucci, S. (2022). *Can Algeria contribute to the EU's energy security?*. Retrieved July 19, 2023, from https://www.dw.com/en/can-algeria-contribute-to-the-eus-energy-security/a-61680466.
Mellor, S. (2022). Europe's proposed ban on Russian oil could leave Moscow scrapping for $70 a barrel on a good day. *Fortune*, May 4, 2022. Retrieved July 18, 2023, from https://fortune.com/2022/05/04/europe-eu-proposed-ban-russian-oil-moscow-scrapping-70-barrel-india/.
Porter, M. E., & Heppelmann, J. E. How smart, connected products are transforming competition. *Harvard Business Review*, *92*(11), 64–88.
Theil, H. (1967). *Economics and information theory*. Rand McNally.
US Congress (2023). *Russia's War Against Ukraine: European Union Responses and U.S.-EU Relations*. Retrieved July 18, 2023, from https://crsreports.congress.gov/product/pdf/IN/IN11897.

Debunking Common Misconceptions About Smart Cities

Chiara F. Del Bo

Abstract Smart Cities have been the object intense scrutiny by both practitioners and scholars, as the number and size of Smart city initiatives in urban areas around the world is increasing. Notwithstanding the significant amount of work around this concept, there are still however many open issues and questions. Is the SC model living up to our great expectations for it? Are cities that have invested in SC policies and programmes experiencing relatively higher positive effects? In order to provide an answer to these questions, we have to be clear about what a SC actually is, what it can achieve and its limits. Unfortunately, misconceptions around this concept abound, among practitioners and researchers alike. My aim with the present paper is to clear some of these misconceptions, lay down what serious research allows us to say about the SC model and what we still have to explore to answer the questions above. Paper submitted to the Springer Edition-Contribution to Economics.

Keywords Smart city · Urban planning · Place-based policies · Financing · Innovation · Evaluation

JEL Codes D004 · H7 · Q55 · R51 · R58

1 Introduction

Smart Cities have been the object intense scrutiny by both practitioners and scholars, as the number and size of Smart city initiatives in urban areas around the world is increasing. According to Bloomberg, the value of the global smart city market was, in 2019, more than one billion USD and the expected growth suggests that it will be

---

Paper submitted to the Springer Edition-Contribution to Economics.

C. F. Del Bo (✉)
Università degli Studi di Milano, Milan, Italy
e-mail: chiara.delbo@unimi.it

M. Mavri et al. (eds.), *Digital Economy and Green Growth*, Contributions to Economics, https://doi.org/10.1007/978-3-031-66669-8_9

worth approximately seven billion USD in 2030.[1] Notwithstanding the significant amount of work around this concept, there are still however many open issues and questions.

Is the SC model living up to our great expectations for it? Are cities that have invested in SC policies and programmes experiencing relatively higher positive effects? In order to provide an answer to these questions, we have to be clear about what a SC actually is, what it can achieve and its limits.

Unfortunately, misconceptions around this concept abound, among practitioners and researchers alike. My aim with the present paper is to clear some of these misconceptions, lay down what serious research allows us to say about the SC model and what we still have to explore to answer the questions above.

Before debunking the most common misconceptions about the concept, it is useful to understand more in detail what the SC paradigm promises at the urban level. In a nutshell, investing in SC characteristics through appropriate urban policies should help achieve successful, knowledge-creating, sustainable, livable cities. Since the SC concept has been around for quite some time, and several implementations are now in a mature phase, we are in the position of asking whether or not we can conclude that they are achieving what they promise. The answer to this question, as will be discussed below, is still not clear and requires more research. The aim of the following sections is to provide some guidance as to what we know and what we still don't know about SC and their impact, suggesting avenues for further research that can help shed light on this issue.

Analyzing the misconceptions about SC is useful in our quest of understanding what a SC truly is and what, potentially, it can achieve, given that there is at least some truth in them, they are not simply false statements. The more we understand, the more we study and the more we work on common ground, the higher the chances that we can truly reap the potential benefits of SC.

The rest of the paper is organized as follows. In Sect. 2 a discussion of the most common misconceptions around SC is presented, with specific attention to unearthing the red flags that may arise from their analysis. Section 3 proposes instead avenues for future research, while Sect. 4 summarizes and concludes.

2 Misconceptions

2.1 Lack of a Definition

The first and most frequent misconception is the following.

Misconception 1: There is no proper definition of a SC, it's only a buzz-word, an empty box.

[1] https://www.bloomberg.com/press-releases/2022-12-14/smart-cities-market-to-be-worth-6-965-02-billion-by-2030-million-insights, accessed on July 12, 2023.

While this is a very common claim, with which several academic papers introduce their work (to cite but a few recent examples, see Han & Kim, 2021; Direshan & van Zoonen, 2022; Osowska, 2023; Sobey, 2023), the current state of the art regarding our understanding of the SC concepts suggests that its foundations are weak.

It is indeed true that there are several definitions but the literature has crystallized on a consensus regarding our understanding of the concept. A useful categorization is provided by Mora et al., (2019) who suggest dividing the existing definitions along five different paths:

1. Experimental Path: urban testbeds for experimenting IoT infrastructures and service applications
2. Ubiquitous Path: cities whereby digital services are provided everywhere and anytime and their development is driven by corporate suppliers' financial interests, market perspectives and economic impacts rather than public good
3. Corporate Path: urban areas become smart when they are equipped with a platform of digital solutions provided by ICT consultancies
4. European Path: highly efficient urban systems in which digital technologies are used to tackling environmental degradation and fighting climate change
5. Holistic Path: digital technologies are assembled to meet local development needs and their development process is grounded in collective intelligence, bottom-up approach, participatory governance, open and user-driven innovation and community-led urban development.

While it is not possible to select a "winner" among these paths by examining the literature, several researchers (e.g. among several others: Camero & Alba, 2019; Komninos et al., 2020; Zhao et al., 2021) have been advocating embracing the holistic definition, which presents several advantages. These include the fact that it can reflect more clearly the planner's perspective, thus encompassing explicitly a social welfare maximizing approach and it is amenable to empirical validation.

The lesson learned from examining this first misconception is thus to consider a comprehensive, holistic definition, that reflects the main building blocks of a SC from a social welfare maximizing perspective. To conclude, a holistic definition that complies with the desired characteristics and can be the basis of further analysis on the impact of the SC model is the one presented in Caragliu et al. (2011): *cities are identified as smart when "investments in human and social capital and traditional (transport) and modern (ICT) communication infrastructure fuel sustainable economic growth and a high quality of life, with a wise management of natural resources, through participatory governance.*

2.2 Business-Driven Concept

The second misconception we focus on is related to the role of private companies, often multinational corporations in the ICT sector, providing the technical infrastructure and solutions for the implementation of the SC model.

Misconception 2: *Smart Cities are just a corporate construct, with private actors maximizing profits, with no consideration of social welfare.*

Private actors have been involved from the start and are relevant to this day (McNeil, 2015; Wiig, 2015; Kummitha, 2019, to name a few). Given the nature of SC projects, significant investment in cutting edge technology is needed to put in place both the infrastructure and the software to manage and run the operations. Typically, municipalities do not have, in house, the necessary expertise and facilities, making the outsourcing or partnership with private firms a necessity. However, the objective of a Smart City is/should be social welfare maximization, and this can be achieved if public actors remain in charge of setting policy goals with the aim of remedying societal problems. The main risk is related to the role that private corporations, whose objective is profit maximization, may take in setting the policy agenda, at the expenses of the public bodies who should be in charge, with social welfare maximization as the goal. The role of private firms should be limited by the goal and objective setting by the public actors, and should be confined to providing the necessary solutions to the local problems and needs identified by the social planner. Their role can be more proactive, in terms of suggesting solutions and products, but always in cooperation with the public sector, which is hierarchically superior in the decision making process. Their role should thus be carefully and explicitly regulated by the planner to avoid risks (Söderström et al. 2014; McNeil, 2015; Mouton & Burns, 2021; Hollands, 2008, among others).

The main lesson learned from examining this misconception is that well designed policies, both at the local/urban and higher government tiers (such as the EU) are crucial to avoid having Smart Cities as private-driven projects. Goal setting, policy design, specific project implementation should be firmly retained in public hands, with private firms considered as providers of services and goods that the municipalities cannot provide in-house. Issues of data management, property and privacy should also be at the forefront of the discussion and should be managed by the public planner with citizens' welfare in mind.

2.3 Governance

Related to what discussed in the previous sub-section, the next misconception is about governance.

Misconception 3: *There is no real autonomy for local municipalities in setting their Smart City programs, as they are now a represented by a top-down, common blueprint promoting neo-liberal urbanism.*

The SC model, at least the one stemming from the more holistic and Western-based definition, is thought to be, at least in part, a bottom-up approach, in the sense of explicitly involving the various stakeholders, both private and public. SC projects often include, or are originated from, citizen-led initiatives, and include the cooperation of various actors in the design and/or implementation of the initiatives (Leite,

2022). Thus, SC governance includes issues related to actors and their responsibilities, goal and priorities setting, organization, community and private sector involvement and multi-level governance. Rodriguez-Bolivar (2018) stresses how governance is more about the relation between actors in the public domain and the outcome of these interactions than about what government do in a more traditional public policy framework. Another important aspect of governance is related to how local governments define, set and implement their smart city policy agenda. Clement and Crutzen (2021) suggest that there is no overall smart city policy (on this see Sect. 2.4) and that municipalities draw from policy priorities at the local level to design and manage their smart city agenda.

There is a wide range of governance modes. It is thus the choice of governance that ensures that all actors are involved and that the bottom-up nature of the concept is retained. Appropriate governance mechanisms also can insure against the risk of neo-urban liberalism, as voiced for example by Cardullo and Kitchin (2019). The authors contend that, in the European context, the design of Smart City initiatives, while implemented at the local level, is strongly influenced by supranational institutions (such as the European Union) which reproduce a neoliberal view of citizenship and participation. If however governance is understood as stated above, in terms of relations between all stakeholders and actors of Smart City initiatives, and the design, setting of objectives and choice of policy alternatives is firmly in the hands of the public planner, whose objective is welfare maximization, these risks can be reduces. Funding autonomy and limited reliance on private and supranational funds also grants more autonomy to local policy makers.

The main lesson learned from examining this misconception is that several pitfalls, including the risk of promoting a neoliberal blueprint (Cardullo & Kitchin, 2019) can be avoided by adopting a comprehensive, holistic view of SC and by setting a clear and coherent governance structure, with clearly defined objectives and adherence to a SC model that encompasses all stakeholders' interests and goals.

2.4 *One Size Fits All*

As more SC projects and programs are being implemented, financed both with local and supranational funds, the idea that successful models can be replicated anywhere is present, which leads to the following misconception.

Misconception 4: *There is one Smart City blueprint that can be replicated and scaled anywhere.*

This view is in part related to the "best practice" approach to public policies in general (Dunn, 2015) where successful interventions in a country or region are exported to other areas, with little or no adaptation to the local context. This approach is in contrast to the "place-based" movement, which instead stresses the need to adapt public policies to the specific characteristics where they are applied, as objectives, functioning and impact may be affected (Barca et al., 2012). This is in particular true with respect to SC projects, where the impact and success of these endeavors largely depends on local characteristics, as documented e.g. by Caragliu and Del Bo (2022). They show that the impact of smartness is geographically uneven in a large sample of European cities, hinging upon the different local economic and social urban features. Similarly, Anand and Navío-Marco (2018) show how the local context and institutions influence the design and implementation of SC projects. Yigitcanlar et al. (2019) examine four applications of the Smart City model in the five continents (namely in Songdo Korea, Mssdar in the United Arab Emirates, Amsterdam in Europe, San Francisco in the United States and Brisbane in Australia) and show that the conceptualization and implementation is not the same across the globe. They also document how the goals of these projects differ, with Asian cities using SC project to boost technical innovation, while cities in Europe, North America and Oceania aim to achieve increases in the quality of living. These results corroborate the idea that the SC model, while sharing a common base, is and should be adapted to local conditions, to increase its ability to achieve its objectives and increase impact. Accounting for different interpretation, design and implementation of actual Smart City projects around the world is also important when evaluating their impact, as even processes that share common feature may display different effects due to local conditions (Burns et al., 2021).

The main lessons learned from examining this misconception are that there is a tension between worlding and provincialism (Burns et al., 2021) and that this concept is understood and implemented differently in the Global South and Global North. Concerning the former, "the concept can take on different meaning and manifestation in different political contexts" (ibidem, p. 462) and "Common processes can operate with disparate effects in different places" (ibidem, p. 462). Soe et al. (2022) for example, document the difference between SC projects in Western countries, which mainly revolve around improving specific aspects of existing cities, and those in Asian and Arabian countries, where a Smart City can in many instances be a planned, new, pop-up hi-tech city.

With respect to the latter, there are different roles for the public planner, private actors and citizens in the Global North and South (Mouton & Burns, 2021 for the Global South and Charnock et al. 2021 for the Global North) and there is a different weight given to the bottom-up or top-down nature of SC initiatives (Shelton & Lodato, 2019).

2.5 SC Exacerbate or Create Inequalities

A serious critique to the SC model is related to its alleged role in exacerbating or creating inequalities along several dimensions among urban dwellers.

Misconception 5: Smart Cities create new or exacerbate existing urban inequalities.

SC projects rely heavily on ICTs and the services and benefits they can offer require that users and citizens have the skills and tools to use them appropriately. This is exactly the premise on which critical concerns around the SC model are built.

SC technologies are criticized because they might exacerbate income inequalities. Four factors in particular may explain this phenomenon:

1. the uneven diffusion of information and communication technologies (ICTs);
2. that these ICTs cannot be afforded by low-income citizens;
3. that smart cities could further human capital divides;
4. and the involvement of private actors in the implementation of projects.

While from a conceptual standpoint these concerns are genuine and have grounding, they are not backed by serious empirical verification. Most of these critiques (e.g. Kharas & Remes, 2018) are in fact purely theoretical or anecdotal at best, making it difficult to verify their validity and propose solutions to account for these issues when implementing SC projects, if needed.

Among the few papers analyzing these claims, Caragliu and Del Bo (2022), test whether smart urban characteristics are associated with increases in urban income inequalities, using data on urban smartness and urban income inequality for 106 European cities. Their results, robust to a number or consistency checks and the use of causality identification techniques, show that smart cities are associated with lower levels of urban income inequality.

Along the same lines, Caragliu and Del Bo (forthcoming), focus on the role of urban smartness in driving the (within-city) digital divide. The empirical test of this hypothesis is conducted by exploiting a large data base of 181 European cities, with data on smart urban characteristics, along with the measures of digital divide obtained with the use of survey data carried out at the EU level. Empirical results, which again are robust to a number of consistency checks and to an instrumentation strategy, suggest that a negative association exists between the level of urban smartness and the intensity of the (within-city) digital divide.

The lesson learned from examining this misconception and taking it seriously is that, for a sample of European cities, the fear that SC may exacerbate or create income and digital inequalities is not supported by the data. Additional research should be conducted on these issues considering other areas of the world, in particular in the Global South, and considering the different possible models and implementations of the SC concept.

3 Avenues for Future Research

The analysis presented in the previous sections suggests that, while there still are several misconceptions about what SC truly are and what they can achieve in terms of urban planning and development, serious academic research is pushing forward to provide solid answers to the issues raised, sometimes debunking completely, sometimes only partially, these claims. There is still however scope for more serious and solid research on SC, both theoretical and empirical, with the aim of providing policy makers and stakeholders in general with a set of answers to common questions and suggestions to improve the application to urban planning of the SC paradigm.

While the following should not be seen as an exhaustive list of research topics, it reflects some of the gaps in the literature on topics and issues that, if properly examined, could help in our understanding of the functioning of SC projects, thus leading to the design of more impactful and effective policies.

As a starting point, research on SC programs, projects and policies should be framed within the boundaries of urban policy and planning. While other points of view and analysis stemming from other disciplines are important, it should be clear that the SC concept is an urban policy instrument, and, as such, should be evaluated and considered. Rodriguez-Bolivar et al. (2020) present an analysis of SC projects implemented by Spanish municipalities in 2019 and frame their empirical results within the view that smart projects should be integrated within the overall urban strategic planning. This would ensure greater coherence with the overall city's planning agenda and ultimately maximize impact.

An important and rather under-researched issue is related to how are these policies financed in a multi-level government setting. This aspect is likely to have an impact on goal and objective setting and, ultimately on impact of these initiatives. Along these lines, another important issue is related to the relative role and relationship between private and public actors in SC projects, with a specific focus on funds. How to strike a balance between private and public funds? How to make sure that objectives are set by the public planner, whatever the percentage of public funds, and how can the public–private relationship be managed while keeping social welfare maximization as the guiding principle? The financing of smart projects may be a significant obstacle, especially for smaller cities or for those located in lower income countries, where public finances, at the national and local level are scarce. Private funds are thus present in most SC programs, at varying degrees. The search for private investors, and their interaction with public funds and the related relationship between private and public actors is thus a key aspect in the design and management of SC initiatives. Blanck and Ribeiro (2021) analyze the different financing modes in the European context, highlighting the role for EU funds, PPPs, project financing from various sources and tailor-made bonds. Such a variety of funding sources requires adequate public planning and governance to ensure the achievement of the policy's objectives, and should be the object of further theoretical and empirical investigations.

Another aspect that has not been thoroughly explored is how much local conditionalities matter both at the planning and implementation phase (see e.g. Khurana & Dutta, 2023). Results on these aspects could inform policy makers on designing policies and programs best aligned with local characteristics, positively impacting on the effectiveness and alignment with policy objectives.

SC programs should, to stay true to their objectives and goals, involve explicitly and at different stages of the process all stakeholders, from the public planner, to private firms, to citizens. A focus on the latter is especially important as one of the characteristics of this planning paradigm is related to its bottom-up nature, with an important role played by citizen-led (or participated) initiatives. While some authors have explored this aspect (for a recent example, see Przeybilovicz et al., 2022) still more research is needed on the role of citizens as active stakeholders in SC programs and policies. Desdemoustier et al. (2019) for example show how local actors" appropriation of the Smart City, seen as an instrument of territorial construction, is not homogenous nor easily classifiable in categories, suggesting that more work is needed to understand the role and engagement of local actors and stakeholders in SC projects.

Finally, but arguably very relevant, it is now time to perform serious and rigorous policy evaluation on SC projects in order to answer the question presented in the introduction: are SC living up to their promises? As recently surveyed by Caragliu et al. (Forthcoming), the highest and most significant impact is to be expected in relation to economic outcomes, including innovative activity (Caragliu & Del Bo, 2019).

4 Conclusions

SC projects are increasingly being funded and implemented around the world and are the object of an impressive amount of scholarly and policy literature. However, as documented in the sections above, the concept is still plagued by several misconceptions and several aspects would benefit from further academic research. What is clear is that this policy framework is being adopted by countless cities around the world as an urban planning model and this alone should spur more research to help design more effective and impactful policies.

While our understanding of what constitutes a Smart City is now relatively clear, the policy design and implementation phase still needs additional research, given the novelty of this concept as a policy tool and the sensitivity of the technological aspects inherent to the model. The positioning of this specific policy tool within the overall urban planning pipeline, and the role of institutional arrangements are crucial aspects to be examined. Financing of these initiatives, which present a unique blend of local, national and supranational public funds along with private investment of mainly high tech, ICT companies, should also be scrutinized and policy recommendations should be distilled. Finally, time is now ripe to provide robust impact evaluations of the countless smart initiatives around the world, accounting for local specificities and moderator characteristics, in order to ensure that citizens around the world can reap the benefits that should accrue from this innovative urban planning model.

Acknowledgements The author wishes to thank Mania Mavri, Persefoni Polychronidou, Yannis Psycahris and participants at the 2023 EBEEC for the opportunity and the insightful discussions.

References

Anand, P. B., & Navío-Marco, J. (2018). Governance and economics of smart cities: Opportunities and challenges. *Telecommunications Policy, 42*(10), 795–799.

Barca, F., McCann, P., & Rodríguez-Pose, A. (2012). The case for regional development intervention: Place-based versus place-neutral approaches. *Journal of Regional Science, 52*(1), 134–152.

Blanck, M., & Ribeiro, J. L. D. (2021). Smart cities financing system: An empirical modelling from the European context. *Cities, 116*, 103268.

Burns, R., Fast, V., Levenda, A., & Miller, B. (2021). Smart cities: Between worlding and provincialising. *Urban Studies, 58*(3), 461–470.

Camero, A., & Alba, E. (2019). Smart city and information technology: A review. *Cities, 93*, 84–94.

Caragliu, A., & Del Bo, C.F. (Forthcoming). Smart cities and urban digital divide. *Npj Urban Sustainability*.

Caragliu, A., & Del Bo, C. F. (2022). Smart cities and urban inequality. *Regional Studies, 56*(7), 1097–1112.

Caragliu, A., & Del Bo, C. F. (2019). Smart innovative cities: The impact of smart city policies on urban innovation. *Technological Forecasting and Social Change, 142*, 373–383.

Caragliu, A., & Del Bo, C. F. (2012). Smartness and European urban performance: Assessing the local impacts of smart urban attributes. *Innovation: The European Journal of Social Science Research, 25*(2), 97–113.

Caragliu, A., Del Bo, C. F., & Nijkamp, P. (Forthcoming). Smart cities in Europe revisited. *Journal of Urban Technology*.

Caragliu, A., Del Bo, C. F., & Nijkamp, P. (2011). Smart cities in Europe. *Journal of Urban Technology, 18*(2), 65–82.

Cardullo, P., & Kitchin, R. (2019). Smart urbanism and smart citizenship: The neoliberal logic of 'citizen-focused'smart cities in Europe. *Environment and Planning c: Politics and Space, 37*(5), 813–830.

Charnock, G., March, H., & Ribera-Fumaz, R. (2021). From smart to rebel city? Worlding, provincialising and the Barcelona Model. *Urban Studies, 58*(3), 581–600.

Clement, J., & Crutzen, N. (2021). How local policy priorities set the smart city agenda. *Technological Forecasting and Social Change, 171*, 120985.

Desdemoustier, J., Crutzen, N., Cools, M., & Teller, J. (2019). Smart city appropriation by local actors: An instrument in the making. *Cities, 92*, 175–186.

Dirsehan, T., & van Zoonen, L. (2022). Smart city technologies from the perspective of technology acceptance. *IET Smart Cities, 4*(3), 197–210.

Dunn, W. N. (2015). *Public policy analysis*. Routledge.

Han, M. J. N., & Kim, M. J. (2021). A critical review of the smart city in relation to citizen adoption towards sustainable smart living. *Habitat International, 108*, 102312.

Hollands, R. G. (2008). Will the real smart city please stand up? Intelligent, progressive or entrepreneurial? *City, 12*(3), 303–320.

Kharas, H., & Remes, J. (2018). "Can smart cities be equitable?" Brookings Institution Op-Ed, June 11, 2018. Retrieved March 5, 2020, from https://www.brookings.edu/opinions/can-smart-cities-be-equitable/

Khurana, I., & Dutta, D. K. (2023). From place to space: The emergence and evolution of sustainable entrepreneurial ecosystems in smart cities. *Small Business Economics*, 1–29.

Komninos, N., Panori, A., & Kakderi, C. (2020). The smart city ontology 2.0. URENIO Research Discussion Papers. https://www.urenio.org/2020/12/24/smart-city-ontology-2-0

Kummitha, R. K. R. (2019). Smart cities and entrepreneurship: An agenda for future research. *Technological Forecasting and Social Change, 149*, 119763.

Leite, E. (2022). Innovation networks for social impact: An empirical study on multi-actor collaboration in projects for smart cities. *Journal of Business Research, 139*, 325–337.

McNeill, D. (2015). Global firms and smart technologies: IBM and the reduction of cities. *Transactions of the Institute of British Geographers, 40*(4), 562–574.

Mora, L., Deakin, M., & Reid, A. (2019). Combining co-citation clustering and text-based analysis to reveal the main development paths of smart cities. *Technological Forecasting and Social Change, 142*, 56–69.

Mouton, M., & Burns, R. (2021). (Digital) neo-colonialism in the smart city. *Regional Studies, 55*(12), 1890–1901.

Osowska, M. M. (2023). Smartphone, startup, laboratory-What ambitions and visions do local government officials express by their smart city stories? Case study of polish cities. *Cities, 140*, 104438.

Przeybilovicz, E., Cunha, M. A., Geertman, S., Leleux, C., Michels, A., Tomor, Z., Meijer, A., et al. (2022). Citizen participation in the smart city: Findings from an international comparative study. *Local Government Studies, 48*(1), 23–47.

Rodriguez-Bolivar, M. P. (2018). Governance models and outcomes to foster public value creation in smart cities. *Scienze Regionali, 17*(1), 57–80.

Rodriguez-Bolivar, M. P., Alcaide-Muñoz, C., & Alcaide-Muñoz, L. (2020). Characterising smart initiatives' planning in Smart Cities: An empirical analysis in Spanish Smart Cities. In *Proceedings of the 13th international conference on theory and practice of electronic governance* (pp. 585–595).

Shelton, T., & Lodato, T. (2019). Actually existing smart citizens: Expertise and (non) participation in the making of the smart city. *City, 23*(1), 35–52.

Sobey, A. (2023). Obliged smart freedom: The Singaporean experience of advanced neoliberal-developmental governance. *Urban Studies*, 00420980231169206.

Söderström, O., Paasche, T., & Klauser, F. (2014). Smart cities as corporate storytelling. *City, 18*(3), 307–320.

Soe, R. M., Schuch de Azambuja, L., Toiskallio, K., Nieminen, M., & Batty, M. (2022). Institutionalising smart city research and innovation: From fuzzy definitions to real-life experiments. *Urban Research & Practice, 15*(1), 112–154.

Wiig, A. (2015). IBM's smart city as techno-utopian policy mobility. *City, 19*(2–3), 258–273.

Yigitcanlar, T., Han, H., Kamruzzaman, M., Ioppolo, G., & Sabatini-Marques, J. (2019). The making of smart cities: Are Songdo, Masdar, Amsterdam, San Francisco and Brisbane the best we could build? *Land Use Policy, 88*, 104187.

Zhao, F., Fashola, O. I., Olarewaju, T. I., & Onwumere, I. (2021). Smart city research: A holistic and state-of-the-art literature review. *Cities, 119*, 103406.

Generation Y, Generation Z and Their Perception of Work Life

Simge Dindar Tıraş and Ayça Güzel Özbek

Abstract On the basis of the assumptions in the literature on Generation Y and Generation Z, in this article, we tried to find for both Generation Y and Generation Z, what "working" means, why they work and what they expect from work life, work place, leaders and leadership. Because that for generation Y and Z perception of work and expectations from work differs, we wanted to compare both generations. These two generations will constitute the majority of employees in organizations in the near future. And we also wanted to clarify whether all of the assumptions about Generation Y and Generation Z are valid for our culture as well. For these purposes, five people from generation Y and five people from generation Z were interviewed. Semi-structured interviews were carried out. In these interviews, individuals were asked questions about their perceptions of business life, expectations from business life and leaders, and leadership needs. Descriptive and inductive analysis were used in the analyses. In our research, it was observed that the satisfaction of low-level needs still ranked first for both generations. However, it was also observed that the need for achievement retains its importance in work life. It was concluded that there are different views between the two generations on issues such as workplace relationships and socialization, belonging, autonomy and freedom. The results showed that while some of the assumptions about generations are valid, some of them are not found in our culture.

Keywords Generation Y · Generation Z · Work life · Leadership · Perception of work life · Leadership need

1 Introduction

Now, in most organizations, employees from at least three different generations—Baby Boomers (1945–1965), Generation X (1966–1979), and Generation Y or Millennials (1980–1995)—work together. In addition to these three generations,

S. Dindar Tıraş (✉) · A. Güzel Özbek
Anadolu University, Eskişehir, Türkiye
e-mail: simgedindar@anadolu.edu.tr

M. Mavri et al. (eds.), *Digital Economy and Green Growth*, Contributions to Economics, https://doi.org/10.1007/978-3-031-66669-8_10

the Z generation has also started to take part in business life. Therefore, academics believe that organizations are faced with problems they have never faced before, as employees of four different generations are active in the labor market these days.

The perception and belief that the attitudes and values of generations differs, are kept on the agenda especially by a certain group of researchers, educators, and management consultants. According to this belief, which has become quite common, the basic values, attitudes towards work and organization of each generation in working life differ. These differences cause significant conflicts and difficulties in the working environment.

It is not surprising that employees who have lived and are living in different time periods have different worldviews, values and expectations. For this reason, the expectations of the generations for business life also differ. In this study we wanted to focus on Generation Y and Generation Z.

While Generation Y consists of people born between 1980 and 1995, Generation Z refers to people born in 1996 and later. However, the generational classification in the publications is largely inspired by the North American (USA) business and social context. For this reason, the validity of this classification in other countries and contexts is a subject worth questioning and researching.

When the literature is analyzed, the common points regarding the assumptions regarding working life about Generation X and Generation Y are tried to be explained below.

Millennials want the organization they work for to encourage creativity, to receive positive/negative feedback in every situation, to support not only professional development but also personal development, and to reward their achievements immediately and in a personalized way (Dereli & Toruntay, 2015).

Generation Y expects their managers to have high self-confidence, be confident and be a leader who gives feedback (Adıgüzel et al., 2014).

It is important for Generation Y that their superiors know their names and are aware of their achievements, and that they value each employee for what they do individually. They tend to perform better in work environments where the leader is strong and where guidance and communication work smoothly (Gursoy et al., 2013).

It can be said that Generation Y employees care that the company they will work for has values close to their own values (Lulla, 2019) and that they care about making a difference both in society and in their workplaces (Taylor, 2020).

Generation Zers demand a colorful work life where diversity is celebrated and embraced, and less hierarchy (Taş et al., 2017).

Generation Z's expectations from the business world can be summarized as flexibility in workplace and working time, establishing work-life balance, organic organization, both vertical and horizontal career progression, tasks that are far from monotonous, innovative and integrate technology. They want their success to be evaluated not according to the hours they work, but according to the work they do and create. Opportunities and returns that provide spiritual as well as material satisfaction are considered important to them. They prefer individual offices more because they prefer to work individually rather than in a team spirit. The allocation of technological tools (computers, internet, etc.) is an important issue for them (Arar, 2016).

Among the observable characteristics of Generation Z are their fondness for worldly pleasures, being hedonistic, doing their work quickly, meticulously and electronically based, learning technology quickly and adapting to changes easily. Their attachment to portable technological devices is another known fact (Williams, 2010).

Experts recommend creating an environment that is more fun and open to risk-taking in order for the expectations of Generation Z to reflect positively on business life. Many industry executives state that with the increase of Zs in the business world, there will be more screens in business environments, paper and procedures will be reduced, flexible working hours and models will intensify, many new tasks will emerge, environments similar to movie sets will turn into environments similar to movie sets, departments will be replaced by project groups, temporary teams, international team members, colorful people with different cultures, genders and beliefs will start working at an acceleration towards gender equality (Taş et al., 2017).

As Dadinidou (2021) points out in his study, providing future generations with the necessary resources to meet their needs is inevitable for countries aiming for development. The needs of each new generation in the workplace and the workplace opportunities offered to them (promotion, equipment, social security, etc.) will contribute not only to the employee but also to the organization (and at the macro level to the national economy). Therefore, this study is a pilot study that is expected to contribute to the studies for the future of work life in Turkey.

In light of this information, in this study we tried to find for both Generation Y and Generation Z, what "working" means, why they work and what they expect from work life, work place, leaders and leadership.

For these purposes, five people from generation Y and five people from generation Z were interviewed. Semi-structured interviews were carried out. In these interviews, individuals were asked questions about their perceptions of business life, expectations from business life and leaders, and leadership needs.

2 Participants

Interviews were conducted with 10 people whose information is given in the Table 1.

To summarize, five of the participants are from Generation Y and five are from Generation Z. There are different views in the literature regarding the start and end years of generations. However, as justified by Dimock (2019), the beginning of Generation Z is accepted as 1996 in this study. Four of the participants are civil servants working in the public sector, while the remaining three work in the private sector (One of them from Generation Z). All of the participants from Generation Y have a job. While two of the participants from Generation Z are working, three of them are not yet involved in business life.

Table 1 Participants

Participant number	Year of birth	Gender	Working/not	Sector
Participant 1	1996	Female	Working	Public sector
Participant 2	1999	Female	Not working	–
Participant 3	1992	Female	Working	Private sector
Participant 4	1991	Female	Working	Public sector
Participant 5	1982	Male	Working	Private sector
Participant 6	1997	Female	Not working	–
Participant 7	1998	Male	Working	Public sector
Participant 8	1991	Female	Working	Public sector
Participant 9	1994	Male	Working	Private sector
Participant 10	2000	Male	Not working	–

A heterogeneous sample was formed by paying attention to the fact that the participants were from different professions, different sectors, different cities and graduated from different fields.

In social sciences research, when using qualitative methods, the adequacy of the number of participants can be calculated with some formulas. In addition, it can be said that the number of participants is sufficient at the point where the responses received from the participants reach a saturation point (when the same responses are received from new participants as the old ones). Although the situation of reaching saturation in the number of participants is unique for each research; Hennink and Kaiser (2022) stated that this number generally varies between 9 and 17 in social sciences. From this point of view, 10 participants can be considered sufficient for a pilot study.

3 Analyzes

By conducting qualitative research, researchers can organize and interpret the data without losing the individuality and rich background of the responses (Stuckey, 2013). In this study, instead of making generalizations about the perceptions and attitudes of Generation Y and Generation Z about work, we chose to question the validity of existing generalizations in our country. Therefore, we used qualitative research methods.

We read the data thoroughly and we focused on the common words that each participant emphasize. Then we open encoded the data and then we constructed the categories. Descriptive and inductive analysis were used. Inductive analysis is to reveal the concepts underlying the data and the relationships between concepts through coding. First, data is collected through long term studies, then it is synthesized by induction to make generalization. The main objective is to reach concepts and relationships that can explain the data collected. In descriptive analysis, direct quotations are often used to reflect the views of the interviewed or observed individuals in a remarkable way. The aim of this type of analysis is to present the findings to the reader in an organized and interpreted form. Creswell, 2013; Glesne, 2013; Creswell, 2014; Miles & Huberman, 2016).

We say we used descriptive analysis because we tried to formulate our questions in line with the assumptions in the field. We used inductive analysis because our aim was to find out whether the assumptions were valid in our culture. Therefore, themes were created during the analysis process.

This pilot study is planned to pave the way for a more comprehensive generational study in the future. With the keywords and codes to be created with the responses from this study, it will be possible to create memos and themes with the data of new participants in the MaxQDA program. Thus, this study will pave the way for the analysis of qualitative data with statistical programs.

4 Results

4.1 Leadership

In the findings related to leadership, the most important characteristic that both generations look for in a leader is equality. All of them stated that the leader should treat all the employees equally.

Participant 1: "A leader must have the ability to keep the community together. At the very least, I expect him to be able to **treat everyone equally** and not to create the expectation that he takes sides."

Participant 2: "A leader must **listen to everyone's voice**."

Participant 8: He or she should **treat everyone equally**. His/her behavior should be **equal to everyone**.

It is thought that nepotism may be one of the reasons why all participants from different generations emphasized equality so much. Nepotism is a concept that takes into degree of closeness and the relationship in hiring and job placement managerially within the organization. This concept is often applied for organizational purposes (Akar, 2020). Researches have shown that Turkey continues to move forward on the basis of a public personnel regime based on the legacy of the Ottoman Empire (Yıldırım, 2013). Because of nepotism in organizations, employees can be assigned to high-level jobs regardless of their merit status, and other employees who are not favored are negatively affected by this situation (Akar, 2020). It is stated that nepotism is mostly observed in the public sector and family-owned businesses. However, it would not be wrong to say that this is a general situation observed in all working life. Today, in the context of merit, Turkey has taken a serious path but it is still a long way from the point that it desires; yet, Turkey wants to reach the targets in the context of European Union criteria. We need to put into practice the meritocracy principles that are only on paper (Özler & Gümüştekin, 2007; Yıldırım, 2013).

Another reason for this situation is thought to be the clan culture, which is also seen intensively in the public sector but is observed in all business life. Small groups where face-to-face communication is at the forefront are called clans. In clans, there is a distinction between in-groups and out-groups. Clans spread information by sharing it within the in-group. In this way, they establish superiority over out-groups (Sargut, 2001). We think that all participants are aware of this situation and they usually are facing these kinds of problems. Because of that, the equality is one of the most important things that employees and our participants are looking for.

The second category about leadership is proficiency. All participants think that a leader should be good at his/her job.

Participant 1: "What else do I expect? Well, I expect **competence/proficiency** in the field."

Participant 5: "First of all, he has to be **very good at his job**. In other words, he must be a person **who knows exactly what he is doing**, who knows what he is doing, and he must be able to explain this well to his employees."

As explained above, this situation is thought to be related to the lack of a merit system. In terms of legislation, it has been determined that the system of favoritism has never been respected in Turkey and that there are provisions in the legislation that command the merit system will be implemented. However, legislation and practice do not coincide. In a country, various rules and institutions can be established to ensure merit in the public personnel system. However, first of all, there must be an "intention" to implement the system and this intention must be implemented with determination. What needs to be done is that the only criterion for both recruitment and promotion within the service should be the candidate's knowledge, ability and skills, and these should be measured objectively through an examination system. Everyone should be able to participate in these exams under equal conditions and opportunities, and the exams should be organized openly and fairly (Özkal Sayan, 2017). In Turkey, in organizations, employees can be assigned to high-level jobs regardless of their merit status, and other employees who are not favored are negatively affected by this situation (Akar, 2020). In sum, due to the problems related to merit in our country, it can be observed that managers are appointed without considering their knowledge, skills and competencies. For this reason, it is thought that all participants, regardless of their generation, look for competence in leaders.

The last finding on leadership is related to Generation Z. Generation Zers wants the leader to respect differences and be integrative in this regard.

Participant 1: As I said, he/she needs to have that **unifying, gathering power**. I think it is also necessary for people to have confidence in him/her.

Participant 6: He/she should definitely **respect the differences**. I think this is the most important point. Because **differences are richness**. In order to ensure this richness, he/she has to respect this. And he/she has to provide an environment where differences and minorities can be heard.

Studies have shown that Generation Zers is highly creative, seeks its rights to the end, and can establish good relations with different cultural and sociological structures (Çetin Aydın and ve Başol, 2014). Generation Zers demand a colorful work life where diversity is celebrated and embraced, and less hierarchy (Taş et al., 2017). They see themselves as part of the global village and they are accepting a diverse population (Gupta & Gulati, 2014). Therefore, our findings in this regard are expected and in line with the literature.

4.2 Working Life

Our first finding regarding the expectations of generations towards working life is related to success. When both Generation Y and Generation Z participants were asked which needs (success, relationships, self-efficacy, belonging (a component of being related), autonomy) they expect work to fulfill, both generations put the need for success in first rows. In fact, research suggests that achievement orientation and being idealistic are more characteristic of Generation X (Senbir, 2004). But besides that, it is also stated that Generation Y also want a constant flow of feedback and are in a hurry to succeed. They have been working on their resumes almost since they were toddlers. They are used to overachieving academically and if employers keep them engaged, and they will be happy to overachieve (Meister & Willyerd, 2010). According to our findings, this situation continues to be valid for Generation Z.

In this regard, we believe that there is one more thing should be said, especially regarding our country. Since unemployment rate, especially youth unemployment in our country is very high, it is likely that employees fear that they will be unemployed if they don't succeed. We think this makes satisfying the need for success more important.

When it comes to belonging, Generation Y thinks that for an employee it is important to feel belong to company/organization.

Participant 3: "First of all, **there has to be a sense of belonging**. There definitely needs to be a heart bond/bonds of communion."

Participant 4: "I would say **belonging is also very important**. Doing the job you love, the job you want, in the organization you feel you belong to is important for job satisfaction."

Participant 5: "…I always think that an employee should have a high level of organizational belonging, no matter what. No matter what."

Participant 9: "In order to add something to yourself, you need to feel a sense of belonging to the place where you work. **You can't learn anything in a place where you don't belong**."

Generation theory characterizes Generation X as a generation that is contented and loyal (Senbir, 2004). And studies often (but not all) show that organizational commitment declines as generations change. For example, Smola and Sutton (2002) reported that Generation X is less loyal to their organizations and more self-centered than the previous generation. In a study conducted by Lub et al. (2012) on 359 hotel employees in the Netherlands, it was found that Generation Y had lower levels of commitment compared to Generation X. As a result of the meta-analysis conducted by Costanza et al. (2012), it was found that older generations had higher job satisfaction and organizational commitment compared to younger generations. According to a study conducted in Turkey, it is understood that the Baby Boomers (1945–1965) has a higher level of emotional commitment to the organizations they work for compared to the following generations X (1966–1979) and Y (1980–1995). Similarly, Generation X is a group with higher emotional commitment than Generation Y. However, it is also noted that these differences are very small (Gürbüz, 2015).

We think that when participants talk about sense of belonging, underneath it is also related with organizational commitment. So, we can say that employees from Generation Y have higher levels of organizational commitment and thus sense of belonging than employees from Generation Z. Because only two of five participants from Generation Z mentioned sense of belonging but it should be emphasized that it was conditional. For Generation Z individuals who say that a sense of belonging is important, the conditions for having this feeling are quite detailed. In order for this to happen, they put forward many conditions such as the organization not restricting their freedom, respecting their ideas and making them feel valued. Generation Y employees, on the other hand, did not put forward a condition when talking about sense belonging and stated that it absolutely had to happen, otherwise they would not be happy and would not have job satisfaction.

Because sense of belonging is about relatedness, we think we should also talk about our culture. The concept of self is defined and understood differently in different cultures. In environments where human relations are emphasized, the self is understood as relational, whereas in American and Western psychology, the self is defined as self-sufficient and separate from others (Kağıtçıbaşı, 2017). In the dichotomy of individualism and collectivism, Turkey is classified as a collectivist society (Hofstede, 2001 as cited in İmamoğlu, 2003, p. 369). So, we can say that in Turkey, people have relational selves. The Turkish socio-cultural structure is associated with close ties with relatives, neighbors and *all social groups* in general (İmamoğlu et al., 1993). However, in better educated people and those in the upper strata of society, there is a tendency towards individualization that does not seem to lead to a decrease in relatedness (İmamoğlu, 1987, 2002; Karadayı, 1998 as cited in İmamoğlu, 2003). Thus, the reason why Generation Y mentions so much about the sense of belonging and why two of the participants from Generation Z said that the sense of belonging is important despite being told that they have low commitment (Taş et al., 2017) could be related to culture.

We also mention that in Turkey, there are more small and medium-sized enterprises (SMEs) than corporate companies in working life. And SMEs function like family-owned businesses. So, there is always the emphasis that "we are a family". This may have caused our perceptions to evolve in this direction and the sense of belonging to be so important.

The findings show that While Generation Y continue to believe in hierarchy to some extent, Generation Z does not want hierarchy and authority.

Participant 8 (Generation Y): "**I don't think it's right to be friends with top managers**. … Professionalism at work can be lost."

Participant 9 (Generation Y): "I think there should not be a completely friendship environment at work. At certain points, **it needs to preserve the subordinate-superior relationship**. … If it becomes all about friendship, discipline breaks down."

Participant 1(Generation Z): "I **don't want a leader to be authoritarian**."

Participant 2 (Generation Z): "**If the workplace is an authoritarian place, I probably wouldn't feel comfortable**. I would feel more comfortable with what we call democratic leadership."

Participant 10 (Generation Z): "If the workplace is **authoritarian** and there is a **strict hierarchy**, I don't want to work there."

Generation Y expects their managers to have high self-confidence, be confident (Adıgüzel et al., 2014). They tend to perform better in work environments where the leader is strong and where guidance and communication work smoothly (Gursoy et al. 2013). These may probably be the reason why they still believe in hierarchy and authority to some extent.

But Generation Zers demand less hierarchy (Taş et al., 2017). They also want an organic organization rather than a hierarchical structure (Arar, 2016). This finding is consistent with the literature.

Another finding is that Generation Y want work to be meaningful.

Participant 4: We contribute something to our students, and then they continue to add new things to themselves in high school. And then if we hear that they have gotten into a good university, we can say that **we are preparing them for life**. … We become one of the **contributors** or **guides** in that process.

Participant 8: I always wanted a work environment where I could work and **produce**. … For example, when I go to class, if I can **contribute something to the students**, if the students can understand something, I am very happy.

Participant 9: "I want the workplace to contribute to me. But **I also want to contribute something to my workplace and society**."

Employees from Generation Y care that the company they will work for has values close to their own values (Lulla, 2019) and that they care about making a difference both in society and in their workplaces (Taylor, 2020). According to a study conducted by Meister and Willyerd (2010), Generation Y thinks that work is a key part of their lives. They want work to connect them to a larger purpose and that sense of purpose is a key factor in their job satisfaction. We can say that this finding is also consistent with the literature. When it comes to Generation Z, only one of the five participants mentioned that work is supposed to be meaningful.

All of the participant from Generation Z emphasized the use and importance of technology. They all want technology to be involved in their work or they want to work in technology-related jobs. Generation Yers didn't mentioned about the technology when they talked about the job they wanted or the job would make them happy.

Participant 6: "Whatever job I do, I definitely want it to be something **related to technology**. … I want to be **constantly interacting with technology**."

Participant 7: "…to be able to work on computers with today's current technology. This will be enough for myself, at least for now." (He works at public sector; he is a civil servant and he is not happy with the working conditions that his job provides him. He thinks that his organization is outdated in terms of technology.)

The internet plays a significant role in the lives of Generation Z (Turner, 2015). Technology, especially the rapid evolution of how people interact and communicate, is one of the factors shaping the generation. The Baby Boomers grew up at a time when television was dramatically expanding, fundamentally changing their lifestyles and their connection to the world. Generation X grew up during the computer revolution, and Generation Y came of age during the internet boom. In this progression, what's unique about Generation Z is that all of the above has been part of their lives from the beginning (Dimock, 2019).

Generation Y met technology at a young age but at later eras in their life. Generation Z was born into technology. Therefore, for them this is a must. This already exists. The absence of technology is the same for Generation Z as the absence of electricity is for Generation X. They cannot imagine otherwise.

All Generation Z participants mentioned that the workplace should embrace diversity and listen to different voices. In addition, they also mentioned that meeting different people was important for them and they also stated that they would like to work in a multicultural and international company.

Participant 6: At the same time, I would also like to have **LGBTi or friends with other different backgrounds** at work. I would like to work in such a multicultural area.

As we mentioned above studies have shown that Generation Zers can establish good relations with different cultural and sociological structures (Çetin Aydın & ve Başol, 2014). Generation Zers demand a colorful work life where diversity is celebrated and embraced (Taş et al., 2017). They see themselves as part of the global village and they are accepting a diverse population (Gupta & Gulati, 2014). So, we can say that this finding is expected.

Generation Z wants to work autonomously and in a free environment. While Generation Z puts so much emphasis on autonomy and freedom, working autonomously and in a free environment is not a priority for Generation Y.

Participant 1: "I expect a more independent and autonomous environment. ... Working with friends who match my mind, being able to write and draw what I want **more freely** at work... Being **able to speak more freely**...".

Participant 6: "Being **independent** is important to me."

Compared to other generations, Gen Zers were raised by older and more protective parents and grew up with limited responsibility (Schroth, 2019). However, the results of the study show that this does not prevent them from seeking autonomy and responsibility at work. This can be considered as a result of the fact that Generation Z does not like excessive supervision and rigid rules.

In addition, Generation Y, which is known to give importance to work-life balance and prioritize flexible working (Waworuntu et al., 2022 and Bayramov et al., 2021), gave different answers from the literature in this study. This may be due to the fact that our sample is coincidentally composed of Generation Y individuals who love to work to the degree of workaholism or who do not find it difficult to work for long periods of time because they have few responsibilities within the family (Kalliath &

Brough, 2008). In the later stages of the study, their direct opinions can be obtained by adding a question on this topic while structuring the interviews.

Many Generation Z participants see work as exploitation.

Participant 1: "... that it has a very unique mechanism of **exploitation**. I thought it would be more comfortable to work without imposing this mechanism of exploitation.

Participant 6: "I want to be exploited as little as possible, as I think I **will be exploited** in any way under the current conditions."

A survey conducted in France by BNP Paribas and The Boson Project (group.bnpparibas) among 3,200 French youth between the ages of 15 and 20 shows that Generation Z has a very different perspective on working life and the corporate environment. Although this study was conducted only with French youth, it gives a good idea about the youth of the world, which has been brought closer together by globalization and new technologies. The results of this survey show that when young people talk about the company and working life in the company, the perceptions of 'too difficult', 'too complicated', 'boring', 'ruthless', 'wild jungle' are at the forefront and 36 out of 100 young people say that the company means 'stress' (group.bnpparibas/communique-de-presse/bnp-paribas-boson-projectpublient-premiere-etude-generation-grande-invazion). We think these findings can also explain why Generation Zers in Turkey thinks that why they view work life as a mechanism of exploitation.

Generation Y does not believe that it is necessary to be friends with colleagues outside of work. Generation Y focuses on only professional relationships when talking about relationships in business life. Only one of five participants of Generation Y said that she sees her colleagues outside of the work.

Generation Z does not make such a distinction. They also include friendship relationships. Socialization is important for them in business life.

Participant 3: "Since I am a person who likes formality and distance in all relationships... I prefer to **leave my relationship with my colleague at work**. Seeing my colleague at work and going out and having tea in a cafe at the same time, **this doesn't feel very good** to me. I think it also **harms professionalism**."

Participant 5: "I am **not in much contact with the people in the group I am currently working with**. In other words, I am not in much communication outside of work life, outside the workplace."

Participant 9: "I think the workplace environment **should not be a completely friendship environment**. At certain points, the **subordinate-superior relationship must be maintained**. If it turns into friendship, **discipline starts to break down**. When I think in terms of employees in an equal position with myself, perhaps friendship relations can be established with them. But this may also create some problems. For example, when someone from that group is promoted, there **are problems regarding authority**."

We think that these findings can also be related with Generation Y continue to believe in hierarchy to some extent.

But many research findings show the opposite. For example, Anne Marie McEwan (2009) mentioned that Gen Y are socially conscious, strongly relationship-focused and collaborative (Islam et al., 2011). Blogs and popular press articles about Generation Y states that they freely and openly express that they prioritize close personal relationships over career ("Cara" 2009; Raines 2002 as cited in Myers & Sadaghiani, 2010).

We think that other reason of this finding can be related to trust problems. When we look at recent international surveys, it is seen that Turkey has unfortunately received a poor rating in terms of social trust. When Turkish people asked the question that if they would say that most people can be trusted or that they need to be very careful in dealing with people, only 14 percent of them answered positively. 84 percent of them agreed that they need to be very careful in dealing with people (World Values Survey Wave 7, 2017–2022). In addition, in a survey conducted by Areda Survey, the rate of those who trust their friends in Turkey was 51.8, while this rate was 64.5 per cent in a survey conducted in August last year. When the participants were asked "Which of the following do you agree with in terms of trust in your friends?", 51.8 per cent of the participants said that they trust them in all matters, 15.0 per cent said that they neither trust nor distrust them and 33.2 per cent said that they do not trust them. When the same question was asked in 2021, 64.5 per cent of the respondents answered that they trust in all matters, 20.4 per cent answered that they neither trust nor distrust, and 26.0 per cent answered that they do not trust (ntv.com.tr).

Generation Z does not want to be physically at the workplace all the time. They prefer hybrid or remote working. Generation Y does not mention this issue at all. Being physically at work is not a problem for them. For Generation Z, work should not be the main purpose of life. The emphasis on leisure time is more apparent.

Participant 1: "We are **expected to come to school all the time**, we are expected to be here. I am **dissatisfied with the fact that we are constantly expected to be here** like civil servants."

Participant 2: "I actually like to go to the office for a day or two and **work hybrid**, which has become widespread recently. I would like to work in such an environment."

Participant 6: "Nowadays, most jobs are actually capable of doing this. In fact, we have seen during the Covid process, a lot of work can be done remotely. …to be in the dark environment of the workplace and to be under constant surveillance, to have cameras watching you… it's very uncomfortable for me."

Flexible working is expected to be an important variable for Generations Y and Z, both of whom are fond of freedom. In this study, it was observed that Generation Y did not mention this issue at all, but Generation Z participants prioritized flexible/hybrid working. Generation Z participants stated that they do not consider it necessary to be physically present at the workplace and to work in the morning and return from work in the evening. This situation can be associated with the fact that Generation Z, the oldest of which is 27 years old today, has internalized flexibility practices in both education and working life due to reasons such as pandemic/earthquake in our country. In addition, it can also be thought that the interest in flexible working is a result of the strong entrepreneurial aspect of Generation Z (Taş et al., 2017).

In addition, Generation Y, which is known to give importance to work-life balance and prioritize flexible working (Waworuntu et al., 2022 and Bayramov et al., 2021), gave different answers from the literature in this study.

Both Generation Y and Generation Z participants were given a list of words (job security, wages, working conditions, relations, autonomy, responsibility, success, recognition) related to business life and asked to rank these words from important to less important. We have observed that the need for lower/basic level needs such as high wages and job security still persists in Turkey.

Participant 1 (Generation Z): "I want to work with **job security**, of course. I wish not to feel threatened by the fear that I will lose my job if I say something wrong or if I say something against the manager. In this respect, I actually expect to be protected. … First of all, of course, I expected my **welfare level** to increase."

Participant 3 (Generation Y): "There must be **job security**. After that, motivation comes. Then the **wage**, I think the wage should be a satisfactory wage."

Participant 5 (Generation Y): "I think it's the **wage**. The good wage provides motivation. Secondly, I think **job security**, that is, the guarantee of your job at work, is also important."

Participant 6 (Generation Z): "I think it's the wage. The good wage provides motivation. Secondly, I think job security, that is, the guarantee of your job at work, is also important."

In a study conducted in Turkey, respondents, like many developing countries, seem to have a mindset that emphasizes the priority of making money at work. It is observed that the job security is also very important in Turkey. Respondents in Turkey seem to prefer that it is not easy to be dismissed or lose their jobs and that the labor market is not too flexible. The respondents in Turkey, together with the respondents in developing countries, emphasise the importance of high income at work (Kalaycıoğlu & Çarkoğlu, 2018). It seems that in Turkey because even the need for lower/basic level needs can't be fully satisfied, the need for these needs the demand for them remains.

Generation Y focuses on only professional relationships when talking about relationships in business life. Generation Z does not make such a distinction. They also include friendship relationships. Socialization is important for them in business life.

Participant 1: "In the work environment, I could not take many steps in socialization due to the hybrid education process. I mean, I thought that at least in academics I would meet people I could get along with better and I would be more comfortable."

Participant 8: "Since I am a social person, one-to-one communication with people will make me happier. In these communication processes, getting to know new people, discovering people, and both collaborating and exchanging ideas with them will make me happier and more peaceful."

Although Turkey exhibits a collectivist structure in cultural research, it is observed that the importance given to individualism has tended to increase in recent years. Despite it is known that each new generation exhibits less need for relatedness than the previous one (Güzel Özbek, 2022), interpersonal relationships are still important in our country. The importance that Generation Z attaches to socialization can be channeled into teamwork (Taş & Kaçar, 2019). Thus, it can be ensured that employees both satisfy these needs and work with higher performance.

Only three of participants mentioned wages but didn't mention about job security. All of these three participants work at public sector and they all are civil servants.

In our country, the private sector and the public sector represent two quite different structures. The values and organisational structures adopted by the private and public sectors are different from each other (Dindar Tıraş, 2018). It is stated that the public sector provides its employees with a non-competitive environment and job security and is therefore characterised as good work (Arbak, 2005). The private sector, on the other hand, is a sector where competition is higher and job security is much lower (Dindar Tıraş, 2018). So, we think that such conditions in the country were a factor in obtaining these findings.

Generation Z attaches great importance to gender equality in addition to equality in the workplace. 4 out of 5 Generation Z participants are women. Therefore, their awareness and concerns on this issue are higher. As women, they want to feel safe in the workplace. In the Y generation, this issue has never been mentioned. Therefore, Generation Z is much more sensitive about gender equality.

Participant 3: First of all, as a woman, I want to feel safe. I want to be away from any mobbing or harassment. Or when I experience such thing, I would like to be in an environment where there is someone I can trust.

Participant 6: I want to feel really safe at work. I don't want to experience discrimination because of my identity, because of my gender. I don't want to be subjected to any form of harassment, racism, sexism at work.

As mentioned above, compared to previous generations, Generation Z is more sensitive to differences and embraces differences more. For this reason researches say that project groups, temporary teams and international team members will replace departments; colorful people with different cultures, genders and beliefs will start to work at an acceleration towards gender equality (Taş et al., 2017).

5 Conclusion

To sum, in Turkey, for both generations it has been determined that lower-level needs continue to exist and it is important to fulfil the need for success. While it is important for Generation Y to have a meaningful job, Generation Z does not want the job to be the main purpose in their life.

Generation Y is based on professional relationships when talking about relationships with colleagues and does not find it important to establish relationships with colleagues outside of work. On the other hand, Generation Z wants to socialize in business life. This expectation of Generation Y may be related to the low level of trust in Turkey. The fact that Generation Z emphasizes socialization so much may also be due to the fact that they stay away from social relations during the pandemic (this constitutes an important part of their lives) and generally make friends mostly through social media and/or online channels.

In addition, while Generation Y does not mention autonomy in business life, it has been determined that autonomy and freedom are very important for Generation Z.

Another finding is related to belonging. It is important for Generation Y to feel belonging to the organization they work for. Since only two of the Generation Z participants mentioned belonging, this finding for Generation Z was not significant.

This study was designed as a pilot study to determine whether the expectations of generations towards working life and leadership in Turkey coincide with the assumptions in the field.

During the study, we have found that the questions related to leadership need to be further elaborated, because research indicates that the need for paternalistic leadership continues, especially in countries such as Turkey. However, we could not reach any findings that could make inferences about paternalistic leadership.

Social desirability, which is encountered in most of the studies in which face-to-face interviews were conducted with participants (Stockemer et al., 2019), can be considered as a limitation for our study. In the study, it was accepted that the participants gave sincere and truthful answers.

Due to the great earthquake in our country, the online education has created a problem especially in reaching Generation Z. So, we want to improve the study by increasing the number of participants and questions in future studies. Future studies with an increased number of participants will make it easier to compare the generations in Turkey with their peers in the world.

References

Adıgüzel, O., Batur, Z., & Ekşili, Z. (2014). Kuşakların değişen yüzü ve Y kuşağı ile ortaya çıkan yeni çalışma tarzı: Mobil yakalılar. *Süleyman Demirel Üniversitesi Sosyal Bilimler Enstitüsü Dergisi, 9*, 165–182.

Akar, S. (2020). Örgüt kültüründe bir iş ahlakı problemi olarak nepotizm. *Uluslararası Yönetim Akademisi Dergisi, 3*(1), 241–251.

Arar, T. (2016). Z kuşağında kariyer geliştirmede yetenek yönetimi. *Yüksek Lisans Tezi*, 104–105.

Arbak, Y. (2005). Dominant values of Turkish organizations: A contradictory phenomenon. *Review of Social, Economic & Business Studies, 5*(6), 69–88.

Bayramov, S., Geylan, A., & Benligiray, S. (2021). X, Y ve Z Kuşak Çalışanlarının Esnek Çalışmaya Yönelik Tutumlarının Karşılaştırılması. *Anadolu Akademi Sosyal Bilimler Dergisi, 3*(1), 122–139. https://dergipark.org.tr/en/pub/anadoluakademi/issue/60142/871012

Çetin Aydın, G., & ve Başol, O. (2014). X ve Y kuşağı: Çalışmanın anlamında bir değişme var mı? *Electronic Journal of Vocational Colleges, 4*(4), 1–15.

Costanza, D. P., Badger, J. M., Fraser, R. L., Severt, J. B., & Gade, P. A. (2012). Generational differences in work-related attitudes: A meta-analysis. *Journal of Business and Psychology, 27*, 375–394.

Creswell, J. W. (2013). *Qualitative inquiry & research design: Choosing among five approaches.* Sage.

Creswell, J. W. (2014). *Research design: Qualitative, quantitative, and mixed methods approaches.* Sage.

Dadinidou, S. (2021). Development policies through the European programs: The case of the "Eastern Macedonia & Thrace" region. In *13th International EBEEC conference proceedings book* (p. 107).

Dereli, B. Ve Toruntay, H. (2015). *Örgütlerde kuşakların iş değerleri, motivasyon ve mentorluk kavramlarına dayalı yönetimi.* İstanbul Ticaret Üniversitesi Dış Ticaret Enstitüsü Tartışma Metinleri, WPS No/03/2015-05.

Dimock, M. (2019). Defining generations: Where millennials end and generation Z begins. *Pew Research Center, 17*(1), 1–7.

Dindar Tıraş, S. (2018). *Benlik kurgusu ve işe ilişkin duygusal iyilik hali arasındaki ilişki: Kamu ve özel sektörde karşılaştırmalı araştırma* [Master thesis]. Anadolu University Institute of Social Sciences.

Glesne, C. (2013). *Nitel araştırmaya giriş* (3. Edi.). In A. Ersoy, P. Yalçınoğlu (Trans. Edt.). Anı Publishing.

Gupta, O., & Gulati, G. (2014). Psycho-analysis of Mobile applications usage among Generation Z Teens. *International Journal on Global Business Management & Research, 3*(1), 80–95.

Gürbüz, S. (2015). Kuşak farklılıkları: Mit mi, gerçek mi. *İş Ve İnsan Journal, 2*(1), 39–57.

Gursoy, D., Chi, C. G. Q., & Karadag, E. (2013). Generational differences in work values and attitudes among frontline and service contact employees. *International Journal of Hospitality Management, 32*, 40–48.

Güzel Özbek, A. (2022). *İş yerinde kuşaklararası iklim ile algılanan motivasyon ikliminin ilişki yönelimli liderlik ve ilişkisellik ihtiyacı bağlamında incelenmesi* [Unpublished Doctoral Dissertation]. Anadolu University Institute of Social Sciences.

Hennink, M., & Kaiser, B. N. (2022). Sample sizes for saturation in qualitative research: A systematic review of empirical tests. *Social Science & Medicine, 292*, 114523.

İmamoğlu, E. O. (2003). Individuation and relatedness: Not opposing but distinct and complementary. *Genetic, Social, and General Psychology Monographs, 129*(4), 367–402.

Islam, M. A., Cheong, T. W., Yusuf, D. H. M., & Desa, H. (2011). A study on generation Y behaviours at workplace in Penang. *Australian Journal of Basic and Applied Sciences, 5*(11), 1802–1812.

Kağıtçıbaşı, Ç. (2017). *Benlik, aile ve insan gelişimi, kültürel psikolojide kuram ve uygulamalar* (4. Edi). Koç University Publications.

Kalaycıoğlu, E., & Çarkoğlu, A. (2018). İşe Yönelim'de Türkiye'ye karşılaştırmalı bir bakış.

Kalliath, T., & Brough, P. (2008). Work–life balance: A review of the meaning of the balance construct. *Journal of Management & Organization, 14*(3), 323–327.

Lub, X., Bijvank, M. N., Bal, P. M., Blomme, R., & Schalk, R. (2012). Different or alike? Exploring the psychological contract and commitment of different generations of hospitality workers. *International Journal of Contemporary Hospitality Management, 24*(4), 553–573.

Lulla, A. (2019). The millennial managers are here: Four ways millennials are reshaping the workplace (again). *Forbes.* https://www.forbes.com/sites/forbeshumanresourcescouncil/2019/12/03/the-millennial-managers-are-here-four-ways-millennials-are-reshaping-the-workplace-again/?shZ5dce4f46e044

Meister, J. C., & Willyerd, K. (2010). Mentoring millennials. *Harvard Business Review, 88*(5), 68–72.

Miles, M. B., & Huberman, A. M. (2016). *Genişletilmiş bir kaynak kitap: Nitel veri analizi.* In S. AkbabaAltun & A. Ersoy (Trans. Ed.). Pegem Akademi.

Myers, K. K., & Sadaghiani, K. (2010). Millennials in the workplace: A communication perspective on millennials' organizational relationships and performance. *Journal of Business and Psychology, 25*, 225–238.

Özkal Sayan, İ. (2017). Türkiye'de liyakat, performans değerlendirme ve sözleşmeli istihdam üzerine…. *Journal of Yüzüncü Yıl Üniversitesi Sosyal Bilimler Enstitüsü, 1*(4), 1–7.

Özler, H., Özler, D. E., & Gümüştekin, G. E. (2007). Aile işletmelerinde nepotizmin gelişim evreleri ve kurumsallaşma. *Selçuk Üniversitesi Sosyal Bilimler Enstitüsü Dergisi, 17*, 437–450.

Sargut, S. (2001). *Kültürler arası farklılaşma ve yönetim* (2 Basım). İmge Kitabevi.

Schroth, H. (2019). Are you ready for Gen Z in the workplace? *California Management Review, 61*(3), 5–18.

Senbir, H. (2004). *Z son insan mı?* Okuyan Us Publications.

Smola, K. W., & Sutton, C. D. (2002). Generational differences: Revisiting generational work values for the new millennium. *Journal of Organizational Behavior, 23*, 363–382.

Stockemer, D., Stockemer, G., & Glaeser, J. (2019). *Quantitative methods for the social sciences* (Vol. 50, p. 185). Springer International Publishing.

Stuckey, H. L. (2013). An overview of the rationale for qualitative research methods in social health. *Journal of Social Health and Diabetes, 1*(01), 006–008.

Taş, H. Y., & Kaçar, S. (2019). X, Y ve Z kuşağı çalışanlarının yönetim tarzları ve bir işletme örneği. *OPUS International Journal of Society Researches, 11*(18), 643–675.

Taş, H. Y., Demirdöğmez, M., & Küçükoğlu, M. (2017). Geleceğimiz olan Z kuşağının çalışma hayatına muhtemel etkileri. *Uluslararası Toplum Araştırmaları Dergisi, 7*(13), 1031–1048.

Taylor, C. (2020). The millennial managers have arrived. Korn Ferry. https://www.kornferry.com/insights/articles/the-millennial-managers-have-arrived

Turner, A. (2015). Generation Z: Technology and social interest. *The Journal of Individual Psychology, 71*(2), 103–113.

Waworuntu, E., Kainde, S., & Mandagi, D. (2022). Work-life balance, job satisfaction and performance among millennial and gen Z employees: A systematic review. *Society, 10*(2), 384–398. https://doi.org/10.33019/society.v10i2.464

Willliams, S. (2010). Welcome to generation Z. *BandT Magazine, 60*, Sayı:2731.

Yıldırım, M. (2013). Kamu yönetiminin kadim paradoksu: Nepotizm ve meritokrasi. *Celal Bayar Üniversitesi Sosyal Bilimler Dergisi, 11*(02), 353–380.

https://www.worldvaluessurvey.org/WVSDocumentationWV7.jsp

https://group.bnpparibas/communique-de-presse/bnp-paribas-boson-project-publient-premiere-etude-generation-grande-invazion

https://www.ntv.com.tr/galeri/n-life/lifestyle/arastirma-turkiyede-arkadaslara-guven-giderek-azaliyor,kwkLDpw1ika2BX5KaKFAZg/hcGwRj85h0S6e0_6_vCYfw

Current Crises and Sustainable Development Goals—A Regional Approach

Artemis Giourgali and Ioulia Poulaki

Abstract Crises are by definition unexpected, despite the warning signs that sometimes appear, like the case of climate change, that has become progressively noticeable. Crises' forms vary depending on their main cause, length, severity and extent. Each crisis has unique characteristics which upon analysis, can be developed into practical implications of either general or specific apply. Being majorly unpredictable and future uncertain, crises will continue to evolve and transform along with the evolution of society, industries, and technology. At the same time, they generate opportunities that may be beneficial for social change and economic recovery, if not growth. Heading towards full recovery from the Covid-19 pandemic crisis, new crises pose major threats to the Sustainable Development Goals (SDGs). The Russia–Ukraine ongoing war is causing immense suffering, humanitarian crisis (world's largest modern displacement crisis) and economic shock with disrupted supply chains and global trade. Meanwhile, climate emergencies, natural disasters, geopolitical rivalries and socioeconomic inequalities, make it increasingly difficult for Europe to maintain its focus on SDGs' targets and timelines. This paper aims to provide a holistic understanding of the current crises' impact on the progress of European approach of SDGs. It offers a theoretically-oriented review that reflects the context of how the European region is affected by these challenges; and how the efforts on building more effective policies and directives may act catalytically. Therefore, recently published papers and reports are analysed in relation to the effects of how these goals can contribute with appropriate management practices towards recovery.

Keywords Sustainable Development Goals · Current crises · SDGs · Sustainability

JEL Classification Codes Q01 · Q56 · O33

A. Giourgali (✉) · I. Poulaki
Department of Business Administration, University of the Aegean, Chios, Greece
e-mail: agiourgali@aegean.gr

I. Poulaki
e-mail: i.poulaki@aegean.gr

M. Mavri et al. (eds.), *Digital Economy and Green Growth*, Contributions to Economics, https://doi.org/10.1007/978-3-031-66669-8_11

1 Introduction

Our world has been beset by multiple crises that have wreaked havoc on almost every aspect of our lives, leaving us reeling and struggling to cope. The covid-19 pandemic has been particularly devastating, wiping out more than four years of progress on many of the Sustainable Development Goals (SDGs); the existential threat of climate change is causing irreversible damage to Earth's ecosystems; and adding to these woes, we are currently witnessing the largest number of violent conflicts since the end of World War II, with a quarter of the world's population living in countries affected by war and strife (UN, 2022). The recent outbreak of war in Ukraine has created particularly far-reaching consequences, causing inflation, disrupting supply chains, and throwing global financial markets into turmoil. As a result, the threat of a global food crisis looms large.

The scale and severity of these challenges require us to take sweeping action on a truly monumental scale. One crucial step towards addressing these crises is to put an end to armed conflict and pursue a path of diplomacy and reconciliation. At the same time, we must also adopt policies and practices that are designed to mitigate the impact of climate change and conserve our precious natural resources. This includes building better food systems that are more sustainable and equitable, and that can withstand the shocks and stresses of a rapidly changing world. It is through initiatives like the SDGs that we can hope to build a greener, more inclusive, fair, and sustainable future for ourselves and for generations to come. By working together to achieve these goals, we can strengthen our societies and ensure that they are more resilient and better equipped to withstand the challenges to come.

This paper's significance lies in its threefold contribution: firstly, it involves a classification of scholarly articles on how the current crises have impacted the progress of the Sustainable Development Goals (SDGs) in the European region; secondly, it entails the identification and examination of pivotal theoretical frameworks, and highlights the ways in which the SDGs can contribute to the development of appropriate management practices that can support coping and recovery efforts. Lastly, it offers insights into effective strategies for leveraging the interconnections among the SDGs, thereby fostering its successful realization. By providing an overview of the various challenges that have affected Europe, light is shed on the complex interplay between these crises and the efforts to build more effective policies to address them, resulting to a more informed and strategic approach to the ongoing efforts to achieve the SDGs.

2 Literature Review

2.1 Conceptual Placement on Crisis Management

In order to profoundly understand the crisis concept, it is important to mention the root of the word itself, coming from the Greek 'krisis', which means judgment. The word is used in terms of decision, between something fair or unfair for example. The increase in the linguistic use of the term, has brought into discussion the "crisis" phenomenon, as a critical change in important variables that endanger or destroy a system (Glaesser, 2003). There are several types of crises such as natural ones, financial, technological, social, crises of organizational misdeeds and others. As crises differ in many extents, crisis management also differs from normal management in terms of time, emergency and activities.

Although there are several definitions of the term crisis management, none of them is standard. The division of the term into two main activities, crisis prevention and crisis management, has proven to be satisfactory (Glaesser, 2003). Crisis management is a very important process, where preparation is a key factor for effectiveness, as the cost of crises can escalate when there is a lack of preparedness. As Henderson (2007) comments in his book on crisis management in 2007, the stages of crisis management can be summarized in four key opponents: reduction, readiness, response, and recovery. For an easier understanding, these phases are shown in Fig. 1. The first two concepts include protocols, guidelines and procedures to follow in cases of uncommon/disastrous events. The devising and documenting of these plans is necessary in order to prevent crises that could be general or specific. Opposed to organization, the parts of response and recovery are more practical concepts and require broader frameworks. These may be communications, community relief, professional training, redevelopment and risk management action plans. The final stage of recovery is also an opportunity for reflection and evaluation, able to lead to appropriate revisions and future readiness. Therefore, plans must be flexible enough to accommodate modifications and upgrades.

Looking at the crisis management overall process, we see a transition from prevention to actually coping with the crisis. What is certain, is that some of the causes of the crises will persist in the future, as factors such as economic instability, disease, environmental pollution, etc., remain in the spotlight. Modern society is particularly exposed to crises due to climate change, which is related to many variables and vulnerable factors, such as natural disasters, the economy, health crises, etc. The importance of studying crises in order to improve their understanding and management is paramount. Historical facts are valuable sources of information and can be the basis for theories and insights in order to avoid, or at least ameliorate past experiences.

In a knowledge management system, there can be classification of crises and disasters into different categories. The categories are shaped by the correlations that may exist in a series of crises related for example to political events (Russian–Ukrainian war, riots, terrorist threats and attacks), natural disasters (earthquakes,

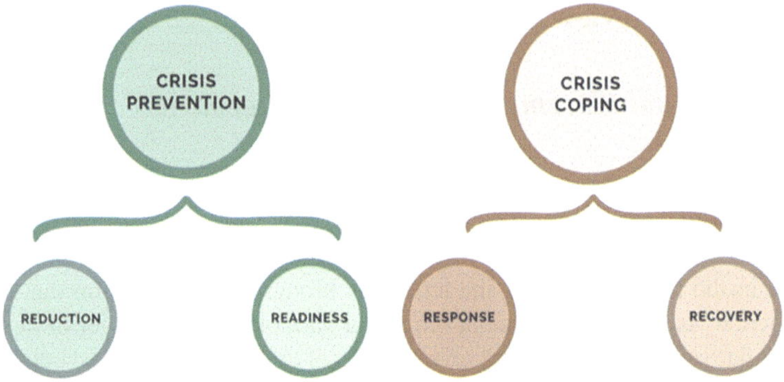

Fig. 1 Phases of crisis management. *Source* Adapted from Henderson (2007); processed by the authors

volcanic eruptions, fires, floods, extreme weather conditions), epidemics (SARS, COVID-19, avian influenza) or economic events like stock market crashes or extreme exchange rate fluctuations (Valeri et al., 2021). Each category may require a different type of information, communication and response. Each case has a different degree of weight or dimension that affects its management and the actors involved.

Today's crises such as energy, food, inflation, natural disasters, and wars; bring new challenges to address. The Sustainable Development Goals explained and analysed in this article, are a collaborative, multi-stakeholder crises management approach on a global level, towards a roadmap out of crises and preparing for future ones.

2.2 *Methodological Approach*

This research aims to investigate the effects of the ongoing crises on the SDGs, explore the various interrelations, and assess how these might affect the overall crisis management process. Initially, the authors carried out a case analysis in order to assess the various direct and indirect effects that the latest massive crises have signified for the SDGs agenda, and to determine their impact. The analysis was focused on the recent, major crises and their effects on the SDG agenda, and has helped to not only distill information from multiple sources into a concise summary, but also serves as a tool to unearth both unfavorable consequences and potential advantages. The research delves into the intricacies of the identified issues, and aims to take advantage of the interconnections among the SDGs, facilitating informed decision-making, which is of paramount importance for driving meaningful advancement.

Furthermore, the background research on the previous agendas, solutions, and crisis management as a general theory, is instrumental in embracing a multitude of perspectives, thus fostering the establishment of effective management strategies aimed at improvement. Latest secondary sources such as articles, newspapers, books and reviews related to these effects were collected and analyzed, providing the most relevant information and objectively evaluating the studies. The second stage consists of a factual analysis, in which the authors propose some recommendations for urgent interventions to save the SDGs. In addition, the authors explain how these goals can also act as catalysts, for the exit from the crises but also as drivers of indispensable advancements for the people and the planet.

2.2.1 SDGs, Agenda 2030 and Crises Effects

The SDGs were formulated in 2015 by the United Nations General Assembly, as part of the Post-2015 Development Agenda (UNSD, 2023). Putting sustainability at the heart of development, these goals emphasize the interrelated environmental, social and economic aspects of a more sustainable future. As formally formulated and adopted with the 2030 Agenda, each goal has specific targets and provides indicators to measure progress. Most targets are to be met by 2030, although some do not have an end date (UNSD, 2023). The SDGs are monitored by the United Nations High-Level Political Forum on Sustainable Development (HLPF), responsible for the organization's policy on sustainable development, which adopts negotiating declarations; reviews commitment and progress on the 2030 Agenda (UNSD, 2023). The Covid-19 pandemic and other current crises have had serious negative impacts on all 17 SDGs, with the result of the world being far from track to implement the SDGs by 2030 (Biermann et al., 2022).

The Sustainable Development Goals (SDGs) are composed of 17 interrelated goals, designed to act as a "shared blueprint for peace and prosperity for people and the planet, now and in the future" (UNESC, 2020). A quick introduction to these goals and a rapid update on their progress is analyzed below:

1. *No Poverty:* The SDG 1 aims to "End poverty in all its forms everywhere" (Ritchie et al., 2018). The covid-19 pandemic has reversed the progress of the goal, with increasing the number of people in extreme poverty, for the first time in a generation (UN, 2022). At the same time, this fact has revealed the fragility of the progress. People living just above the extreme poverty line who have fallen below it because of the disease, were obviously vulnerable despite not being officially poor (BMGF, 2020). The rising inflation in 2022 and the impacts of the Russian-Ukrainian war are expected to furtherly affect this goal. Despite continued progress in the past 20 years, 10 percent of the world's population (especially in low-income countries affected by conflict and political unrest) lives in poverty and struggles to meet basic needs such as health, education, and access to water and sanitation (UNDESA, 2023). There is a need for major changes in social policy to prevent further growth.
2. *Zero Hunger:* SDG 2 is to "end hunger, achieve food security, improve nutrition and promote sustainable agriculture" (Ritchie et al., 2018). The world is bordering on a global food crisis, with a rising number of people experiencing

hunger and food insecurity (UN, 2022). Globally, 1 in 9 people are undernourished, the vast majority of whom live in developing countries. Undernutrition causes wasting (low weight for height, a manifestation of chronic malnutrition) and nearly half of the deaths in children under five years of age (UNICEF, 2018). Food supply systems such as local food markets, consumers, and small-scale farmers were all affected due to the covid-19 crisis, on top of growing conflicts, climate-related shocks, and widening inequalities, which threatened livelihoods (BMGF, 2020). The outbreak of the Russian-Ukrainian war adds an additional threat to food insecurity, hunger and malnutrition, especially among the most vulnerable (UN, 2022).

3. *Good Health and Well-Being:* SDG 3 aims to "ensure healthy lives and promote well-being for all, at all ages" (Ritchie et al., 2018). Significant evolution has been made in increasing life expectancy; immunization and treatment of communicable diseases, and reducing common causes of child and maternal mortality (UNICEF, 2018). Despite that progress, the covid-19 crisis posed important challenges to people's health and well-being globally, and is impeding progress in meeting the goal's targets. The pandemic has infected more than 500 million people worldwide and the deaths attributable to it have been extreme (UN, 2022). Apart from the deaths, the pandemic has increased anxiety; triggered depression; disrupted essential health services; lowered global life expectancy; and derailed progress in immunization coverage for the first time in the last decade (UN, 2022). There is an urgent need of action to set the SDG3 back on track.
4. *Quality Education:* The SDG 4 aims to "ensure inclusive and quality education for all and promote lifelong learning" (Ritchie et al., 2018). Major progress has been made in the last decade, in providing access to education, specifically at the primary school level. The covid-19 pandemic has caused severe disruptions in education systems worldwide. School closures had important consequences on children's learning, particularly for children with disabilities, rural dwellers, and ethnic minorities (UN, 2022). The focus must be turned to the implementation of ambitious programs to recover the learning losses. Distance learning can help in some of the cases, but remote learning opportunities are also beyond the reach of many students, especially in developing countries. While the exact number of students accessing technology is unknown, less than one-third of the population across Africa has access to broadband education. Thus, the need of a greater focus on helping build and rebuild basic skills like literacy and numeracy is highlighted (BMGF, 2020).
5. *Gender Equality:* SDG 5 aims to "achieve gender equality and empower all women and girls" (Ritchie et al., 2018). Efforts are being made in order to grant women equal rights; opportunities to live free without any type of discrimination, or any violence. Women have now better access to decision-making positions and in 2020, women's representation in parliament roles increased slightly by 3% compared with 2015 (UNESC, 2020). At the same time, female genital mutilation is becoming less common, although UNICEF estimated that 200 million women in 30 countries (Indonesia, Iraq, Yemen, and 27 African

countries), had been subjected to one or more types of female genital mutilation (UNICEF, 2018). Despite the above, the world is not on track to achieve gender equality by 2030. Decision-making regarding sexual and reproductive health; violence against women; unpaid labor and gender-responsive budgeting are aspects that are falling behind (UN, 2022). During the covid-19 pandemic, women did nearly three times more unpaid care and domestic work than men (BMGF, 2020).

6. *Clean Water and Sanitation:* SDG 6 is to "ensure access to water and sanitation for all" (Ritchie et al., 2018). Demand for water is rising due to rapid population growth, urbanization, and increasing pressure from agriculture, industry, and the energy sector (UN, 2022). Studies reported that in 2017, 4.5 billion people did not have safe sanitation, and only 71% of the global population used safely managed drinking water (UNICEF, 2018). The covid-19 pandemic has forced people to pay closer attention to hygiene in order to reduce its spreading, as sanitation and hygiene services are vital to human health. Safe sanitation would help, but there is a challenge in tracking sanitation progress. The world is currently standing in decades of misuse, poor management, over-extraction and contamination of fresh water and ground water supplies. SDG 6 established a new, "safely managed" sanitation goal, but the world is behind schedule in tracking data according to this new framework. (BMGF, 2020).
7. *Affordable and Clean Energy:* SDG 7 aims to "ensure access to affordable, reliable, sustainable and modern energy for all" (Ritchie et al., 2018). Progress in expanding access to electricity has been made in several countries, with the global population without access to electricity being decreased to about 840 million in 2017 from 1.2 billion in 2010 (IEA et al., 2019). Renewable energy accounted for 17.5% of global total energy consumption in 2016, with the fastest being renewable electricity (IEA et al., 2019). In 2022, the UN report showed that the world continues to advance towards sustainable energy targets but with an insufficient pace. Improvements in energy efficiency have to accelerate to reach the climate goal of reducing greenhouse gas emissions (UN, 2022). Meanwhile, the covid-19 crisis and the related lockdown measures resulted in an improvement of energy use and greenhouse gas emissions. Restrictions on many social and economic activities affected severely the transport sector, which is a key source of GHG emissions. (Eurostat, 2022). On the other hand, the rise of energy and shipping prices have increased the cost of producing and transporting solar photovoltaics, wind turbines and biofuels worldwide, adding uncertainty to a development trajectory that is already far below the SDG7 ambitions (UN, 2022). Between 2023 and 2030 and in order to achieve the goal's targets, the annual average investment will need to increase significantly on a systematic scale, to expand energy access and improve energy efficiency.
8. *Decent Work and Economic Growth:* SDG8 is about "promoting inclusive and sustainable economic growth, employment, and decent work for all" (Ritchie et al., 2018). Over the past five years, economic growth in developing countries has been increasing. Addressing youth employment; skills development and training; decent and productive working positions are important aspects of this

goal. In 2019, about 22% of the world's young population was unemployed, and was not in education or some type of training. This figure has hardly changed since 2005 (UNSD, 2023). The covid-19 pandemic reversed the progress of the goal, as it precipitated the worst economic crisis in decades. Although the global economy was starting to rebound in terms of improvement in unemployment the progress remained fragile (UN, 2022). Many small firms and particularly those in lower-middle-income countries, have limited capacity to remain viable. In 2021 the goal was hampered by major supply-chain disruptions, pandemic infections, market challenges and uncertainties (UN, 2022).

9. *Industry, Innovation and Infrastructure:* SDG 9 aims to "build resilient infrastructure, promote sustainable industrialization and foster innovation" (Ritchie et al., 2018). Since the beginning of the century, a very small percentage of the working population is employed in manufacturing activities. The share differs, with the lowest percentage being in the African continent and the highest in Eastern and South-Eastern Asia (UNESC, 2020). While nowadays nearly the entire world population lives in mobile network-covered areas, it is estimated that 47% of it is unable to access the internet due to cost, coverage, and other reasons. As more of the world becomes digital, it is crucial that everyone gets the opportunity to get online (WWWF, 2022). The importance of industrialization, technological innovation and development of infrastructures is undeniable, especially during the covid-19 pandemic, where economies with a resilient industrial sector and strong infrastructures such as transport, online connections and utility services, faced faster recovery (UN, 2022).
10. *Reduced Inequalities:* SDG10 targets to "reduce income inequality within and among countries" (Ritchie et al., 2018). This goal's indicators, measure the average annual growth rate of incomes or consumption, of the bottom 40% incomes of a given country. The target aims to reduce inequalities and progressively sustain income growth of that percentage, at a rate higher than the national average (Ritchie et al., 2018). Women, people with disabilities and immigrants, are more likely to experience discrimination. From 2014 to 2019 and with data recorded from 31 countries, almost 20% of people had personally experienced discrimination on at least one of the grounds established by international human rights law (UN, 2022). The main causes for discrimination can be religion, ethnicity, disability, sex, and race, pointing to the urgent need for tackling measures (UN, 2022). Most regions still have work to do establishing adequate migration policies, as only 54% of the 111 countries with available data have measures to facilitate orderly, safe, regular and responsible migration (UN, 2022). The covid-19 pandemic appeared discouraging signs on the numbers of indicators, as it intensified structural and systemic discrimination. People with relatively low incomes are at risk of falling behind (UN, 2022). Meanwhile, the Russian-Ukraine war is creating one of the largest latest refugee crises, on top of already disappointing numbers of worldwide refugees and migrants' deaths (UN, 2022).
11. *Sustainable Cities and Communities:* SDG 11 aims to "make cities inclusive, safe, resilient, and sustainable" (Ritchie et al., 2018). Globally, 3.9 half of the

world's population currently lives in cities, and it is projected that this will increase by 28% by 2030 (Kaviti et al., 2020). Even though cities across the world occupy just 3% of the Earth's land, they account for 60 to 80% of the world's energy consumption and 75% of the carbon emissions (Kaviti et al., 2020). In 2018, 24% of the world's urban population was slum dwellers, with half of them not having convenient access to public transport (UNESC, 2020). Basic requirements such as access to food, water, sanitation, mobility, energy, and education, are globally unmet, a fact that causes serious challenges for the viability and safety of cities to meet increased future demands. In the SDGs report of the UN in 2020, studies showed that 90% of the population living in urban areas worldwide, are breathing air that does not meet the World Health Organization air quality guidelines. During the covid-19 pandemic, over 90% of the cases were occurring in urban areas, where it hit the most vulnerable the hardest, including the residents of the world's densely populated slum dwellers. The global progress of SDG11 has been reversed by the pandemic, although there are several lessons taken from the resilience and adaptability of urban communities in adjusting to new norms. Whether cities can be prepared and rapidly adapted to future crises, will depend on how fast data-driven inclusive and sustainable urban development can advance.

12. *Responsible Consumption and Production Patterns:* SDG 12 is about "ensuring sustainable consumption and production" (Ritchie et al., 2018). Its implementation will assist in achieving overall development plans, reducing economic, environmental and social costs; strengthening economic competitiveness and reducing poverty (UN, 2022). Targets such as renewable energy, reducing global carbon dioxide emissions and changes such as decreasing waste and increasing the circularity of the economy are basic steps of this goal. Countries develop national policies to promote sustainable consumption and production patterns, but the unsustainable use of natural resources that includes gigantic amounts of waste and unsafely managed waste, weakens the health of the planet causing climate change crises, biodiversity loss and pollution (UN, 2022).
13. *Climate Action:* SDG 13 purpose is to "take urgent action to combat climate change and its impacts" (Ritchie et al., 2018). Accelerating progress towards reducing climate risks and addressing sustainable development priorities, involves different stakeholders' adeptness to processes that improve the health and well-being of people and the planet. The year 2019 was the second warmest on record, and the end of the warmest decade (UN, 2022). The planet has faced massive wildfires, hurricanes, droughts, floods and other climate disasters across continents (UN, 2022). Global temperatures are expected to rise as much as 3.2 °C by the end of the century and the window to forestall is closing rapidly. Currently, climate change is affecting the global community in every nation across the world, not only in terms of economy, but also in livelihoods, places, animals and communities (UN, 2020). SDG 13 and SDG 7 are closely related and complementary (IEA et al., 2019). The main targeted outcome is to lower the planet's temperature by 1.5–2 °C (Paris Agreement) and it's checked on a

five-year cycle. Countries need to focus on greenhouse gas savings, switching fuels to renewable energy and enhancing end-use energy efficiency (UN, 2022).

14. *Life Below Water:* SDG 14 aims to "conserve and sustainably use the oceans, seas and marine resources for sustainable development" (Ritchie et al., 2018). Oceans combined with the fishing industries, support the global population's economic, social, and environmental needs. They are the source of life in the planet, home to nearly a million known species, and they contain 97% of the planet's water (UNESC, 2020). Ocean temperatures and pollution are directly related to climate change, oxygen loss, and ocean acidification. There is an urgent need to protect oceans, marine ecosystems and small-scale fishers, as regional and food stability are at risk (Laffoley et al., 2017). Overfishing, caused by illegal fishing; not only threatens the above, but also causes major human rights violations, and even organized crime. Furthermore, oceans provide a valuable service to human societies as not they absorb a high percentage of carbon dioxide emission; and while this uptake is moderating the severity of climate change, it comes at a cost for the oceans (Laffoley et al., 2017). During the covid-19 pandemic, there was a drastic reduction in human activity, which brought a chance for oceans to recuperate. With this opportunity, it is now the time to chart a sustainable recovery path that will ensure livelihoods in harmony with the natural environment, for the decades to come (UN, 2022).
15. *Life on Land:* The SDG 15 is to "protect, restore and promote sustainable use of terrestrial ecosystems, sustainably manage forests, combat desertification, and halt and reverse land degradation and halt biodiversity loss" (UN, 2022). Humans depend deeply on earth and oceans, as our diet is primarily composed of plant life, forests are the habitats for millions of species, clean air and water, as well as being crucial for combating climate change. Meanwhile, the terrestrial ecosystem's conservation is currently not sustainable. Forest areas are still declining at alarming rates, protected areas with biological diversity are not respected, and species remain threatened with extinction (UN, 2022). The surging wildlife crime, deforestation for agriculture, and species extinction; lead to spreading poverty and the degradation of cropland to drylands (UNDESA, 2023).
16. *Peace, Justice, and Strong Institutions:* SDG 16 aims to "promote peaceful and inclusive societies for sustainable development, provide access to justice for all and build effective, accountable and inclusive institutions at all levels" (UN, 2022). In 2019, the number of people fleeing war, persecution and conflict exceeded 79.5 million (UN, 2022). With the new Russian-Ukrainian war, that number is much higher, the highest recorded since the beginning of these goals. As of May 2022, a record number of 100 million people had been forcibly displaced worldwide (UN, 2022). Furthermore, civilians are daily killed in armed conflicts, despite protections under international law every day (UN, 2022). There is certainly more to be done to prevent, reduce and resolve ongoing conflicts; economically empower refugees; build resilient and sustainable food systems; and put in place renewable energy transition methods (Bin-Nashwan et al., 2022).

17. *Partnerships for the Goals:* SDG 17 is about "strengthening the means of implementation and revitalizing the global partnership for sustainable development" (UN, 2022). SDG17's main purpose is to assure that countries and organizations cooperate towards the overall success of the SDGs instead of competing. International cooperation and investments in data and statistics must be increased significantly, in order to find lasting solutions and to stay ahead of crises (UN, 2020). There are many persistent challenges for implementing the SDGs, as financial resources remain scarce, trade tensions have been increasing, and crucial data are still lacking (UN, 2022). The recent covid-19 pandemic has threatened past achievements with the decline of investments, although it appeared to be accelerating the use of technology.

2.2.2 Current Crises and Correlations of SDGs

The SDGs 2022 report, highlighted the gravity and immensity of the current world crises, having severe impacts on the environment, food and nutrition, health, education, peace and security. Ongoing challenges put in danger all the developments and highlight the need for continued and improved efforts. The current crises impact on SDGs are exposed in Table 1. They extensively impacted all SDGs, although neither preventive nor readjusting measures have been taken to address them (Birch & Rosengren, 2023).

The SDGs are highly interdependent and require a holistic approach to achieve meaningful progress. The interdependent nature of the SDGs is widely considered to be axiomatic, despite the fact that the linkages between the individual goals are not uniform (Toth et al., 2022). Figure 2 visually presents a selection of instances demonstrating the inherent interconnectedness that defines the Sustainable Development Goals (SDGs), as depicted by the authors. Through this representation, the authors shed light on specific instances where these goals intersect and influence one another, and serves to emphasize the multifaceted nature of sustainable development and the need for a holistic approach to address the world's challenges. While the correlation analysis of SDG interlinkages cannot fully capture the complexity of the connections between the goals, they are able to illustrate the deep interdependence of the SDGs, where achieving one goal is not feasible in isolation from the others (Pradhan et al., 2017). Certain SDGs exhibit beneficial interconnections, which are commonly known as synergies, while others display trade-offs. For instance, interactions between SDG13 (Climate Action), SDG9 (Industry, Innovation and Infrastructure) and SDG11 (Sustainable Cities and Communities) demonstrate synergistic effects. Such findings provide credence to the idea that eco-friendly infrastructure not only enhances the quality of life in cities and communities but also helps to counteract the dangers of global warming (Pradhan et al., 2017). Likewise, indications of synergies have begun to emerge between SDG5—gender equality and SDG16—peace, justice and strong institutions; between SDG14—life below water and SDG15—life on land; SDG5—gender equality and SDG10—reduced inequalities; and SDG1—no poverty and SDG2—zero hunger (Yang et al., 2020). An

Table 1 Current crises Impact on SDGs

SDG	Covid-19	Russian-Ukrainian war	Climate change	Information Source
No poverty	No of people in extreme poverty increased	Rising inflation	Extreme weather events and threats of livelihoods	United Nations Statistics Division (2023)
Zero hunger	Affected food supply systems	Global food and supply chain threats. inflation	Food and water security is under threat	International Institute for Sustainable Development, 2022
Good health and well-being	Essential health services disruption	Refugees and migrants' deaths	Extreme weather events affecting air quality and diseases	World Health Organization, 2023
Quality education	In-person education disruption	Difficult access to education for refugees. Severely traumatized children	Affected concurrently with other SDGs	United Nations Economic & Social Council, 2020
Gender equality	Affected concurrently with other SDGs	Gender equality and global peace and are inextricably linked	Affected concurrently with other SDGs	UNICEF, 2018
Clean water and sanitation	Affected concurrently with other SDGs	Affected concurrently with other SDGs	Over-extraction and contamination of water supplies	Lafortune et al. (2022)
Affordable and clean energy	Disrupted global trade	Rising in energy and shipping prices	Energy inefficiency and destroying of infrastructures	United Nations Statistics Division, 2023
Decent work and economic growth	Job losses and market uncertainties	Market challenges and uncertainties	Agriculture, fishing, and forestry unemployment	UN. Economic and Social Affairs, 2023
Industry, innovation and infrastructure	**Technological innovation**	Disrupted global trade	Affected concurrently with other SDGs	Lafortune et al. (2022)
Reduced inequalities	Unpaid care and domestic work mostly for women	Refugee crisis	Affected concurrently with other SDGs	BMGF, 2020
Sustainable cities and communities	Affected concurrently with other SDGs	Affected concurrently with other SDGs	Bad quality air breathing, biodiversity loss etc	BMGF, 2020

(continued)

Table 1 (continued)

SDG	Covid-19	Russian-Ukrainian war	Climate change	Information Source
Responsible consumption and production	Increased pollution, single-use plastics (masks, gloves, food containers)	Disrupted supply chains	Affected concurrently with other SDGs	UNICEF, 2018
Climate action	**Reduction In Greenhouse Gas Emissions**	Limited direct impact	**Primary Driver of the Need for Action**	Lafortune et al. (2022)
Life below water	Affected concurrently with other SDGs	Affected concurrently with other SDGs	Climate disasters	World Health Organization (2023)
Life on land	Affected concurrently with other SDGs	Affected concurrently with other SDGs	Climate disasters	World Health Organization (2023)
Peace, justice, and strong institutions	Affected concurrently with other SDGs	Refugee crisis	Affected concurrently with other SDGs	UNICEF (2018)
Partnerships for the goals	Disrupted global trade	Disrupted global trade	Affected concurrently with other SDGs	Lafortune et al. (2022)

Source Author's Own Elaboration

SDG correlation study made by Pradhan et al. in 2017, showed that SDG 1 (No poverty) has the most synergetic relationships with other SDGs. Essentially, this means that by prioritizing SDG1, it can set off a virtuous cycle of progress toward multiple SDGs, resulting in significant benefits beyond just addressing poverty. In relation to the three dimensions of the SDGs (environmental, social and economic), it becomes apparent that the SDG synergies are primarily observed within the social and economic dimensions, whereas trade-offs exist mainly between the environment and the rest (Yang et al., 2020). The key challenge for policymakers here, will be to effectively reconcile the inherent trade-offs arising from the interactions among the SDGs, converting them into synergy opportunities. This challenge calls for a delicate balance where policymakers must navigate the complexities of pursuing one goal without inadvertently hindering progress towards others. The transformation of these trade-offs into synergistic outcomes demands a strategic approach that not only acknowledges the interrelated nature of the SDGs but also capitalizes on their potential to reinforce each other. By doing so, policymakers can unlock innovative solutions that address multiple goals simultaneously, driving holistic and sustainable progress across various dimensions of development (Pradhan et al., 2017).

At a practical level, there is a pressing need to determine how to effectively translate the correlated SDGs and their interactions into tangible actions that contribute

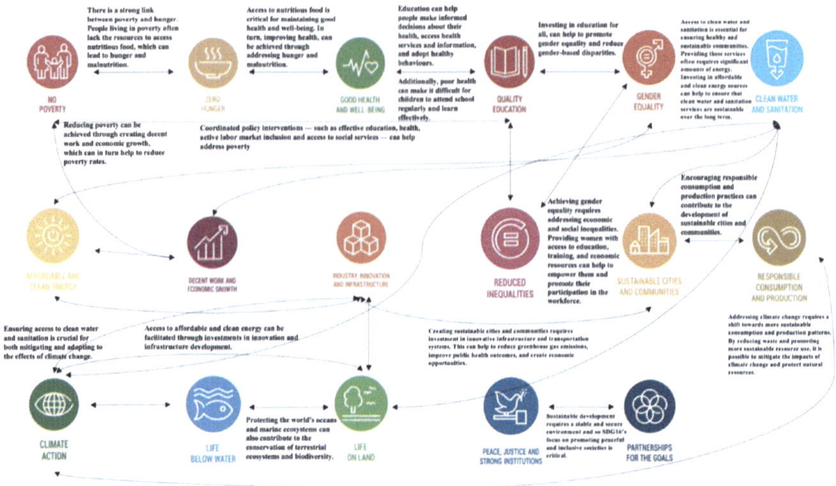

Fig. 2 Correlations among SDGs. *Source* Author's elaboration

to achieving them. Currently, most governments are struggling to effectively address the multi-sectoral, multi-scale, and multi-actor challenges posed by the indivisible nature of the SDGs and deal with them simultaneously (Toth et al., 2022). To successfully achieve the SDGs, it is essential to implement strategies at various levels, from local to global. Hence, a methodological approach to support the implementation of SDGs should not only assess the interactions between SDG targets, but also evaluate the direct influence of one's implementation actions on other targets (Toth et al., 2022). In a world where countries are highly interconnected, actions taken by one country towards sustainable development can have positive or negative impacts on other countries' ability to achieve the SDGs (Birch & Rosengren, 2023). For instance, the investing in clean energy, the strengthening of social protection systems and the improved infrastructures can address the root causes of reducing inequality (SDG5), climate change (SDG13) and economic growth (SDG8). As a result, governments must consider the potential transboundary effects of their domestic policies to avoid counteracting progress towards the SDGs (Eurostat, 2022). Vulnerability to achieving the SDGs can vary significantly between countries and regions, depending on factors such as the current state of development, political stability, economic development and environmental conditions of a country or region. Transboundary effects can either foster or hinder sustainable development efforts, and it is crucial to measure and understand international spillovers resulting from international trade. Given that all countries both import and export, it is essential to design sustainable development strategies that have positive impacts beyond domestic borders (Eurostat, 2022).

Table 2, is a summary of the performance of the region against the SDGs. Within Europe, there are major differences in SDG performance and progress across regions, countries and goals, with the Northern European countries such as Finland, Sweden and Denmark performing best (Eurostat, 2022). According to estimates, halfway into the SDGs, the EU has achieved a little over than two-thirds of the SDG targets, with Northern Europe reaching approximately at 78% of the targets, and Southern, Central and Eastern Europe with about 53% of the SDG targets achieved (Lafortune et al., 2022).

The EU has made progress in several areas, including reducing greenhouse gas emissions, increasing the share of renewable energy, and improving resource efficiency. Part of the European Green Deal focuses on the trade policy of the region and a focus on making it compatible with a more sustainable growth model. One of its objectives is to make supply chains more sustainable by addressing the impacts of the EU's consumption and trade on the rest of the world. However, several challenges still persist, such as biodiversity loss, social inequalities, and climate change adaptation (Lafortune et al., 2022). Some SDG indicators particularly impacted by crises, that may be considered more vulnerable in Europe include:

SDG1 (No Poverty) and SDG2 (Zero Hunger)—While many countries in Europe have relatively low levels of poverty compared to other regions, poverty remains

Table 2 Dashboard of SDG indicators in Europe

SDG	Achievements	Tracking
No poverty	Difficulties persist	Gradual growth
Zero hunger	Major impediments remain	No progress
Good health and well-being	Difficulties persist	Gradual growth
Quality education	Difficulties persist	Gradual growth
Gender equality	Difficulties persist	Gradual growth
Clean water and sanitation	Difficulties persist	Gradual growth
Affordable and clean energy	Difficulties persist	Gradual growth
Decent work and economic growth	Difficulties persist	Gradual growth
Industry, innovation and infrastructure	Difficulties persist	Gradual growth
Reduced inequalities	Difficulties persist	Gradual growth
Sustainable cities and communities	Difficulties persist	Meeting milestones on schedule
Responsible consumption and production	Significant impediments remain	No progress
Climate action	Major impediments remain	No progress
Life below water	Major impediments remain	No progress
Life on land	Major impediments remain	Gradual growth
Peace, justice, and strong institutions	Difficulties persist	No progress
Partnerships for the goals	Significant impediments remain	Gradual growth

Source Adapted from the "2022 SDG Dashboards by country and sub-regions"; Lafortune et al. (2022); processed by the authors a significant issue for marginalized groups such as migrants, refugees, and Roma communities in Europe. In contrast to many regions of the world grappling with hunger, the EU's primary nutritional challenge is obesity (Eurostat, 2022). This can have adverse effects on healthcare systems, government budgets, and economic growth. Maintaining sustainable and productive agricultural systems is critical for ensuring a consistent supply of nourishing food, especially in the face of climate change and population growth. These SDGs were particularly impacted by recent crises in Europe that caused disruptions in food and supply chains, as well as inflation.

SDG8 (Decent Work and Economic Growth) and SDG10 (Reduced Inequalities)—Europe is generally considered a relatively equal region, but income inequality and social exclusion issues still exist. The number of young people not in employment, education, or training (NEET) has risen in the last five years, which is a cause for concern. The recent crises, including the COVID-19 pandemic, have contributed to job losses and market uncertainties, making it even more challenging for young people to enter the labor market (Eurostat, 2022). Despite these challenges, Europe has made gradual progress towards the EU targets of these goals. The employment rate has been growing, and the long-term unemployment rate has been decreasing. These are positive developments that suggest Europe is on the right track, but there is still more work to be done to address the root causes of youth unemployment and social exclusion (Eurostat, 2022).

SDG 13 (Climate Action), SDG 14 (Life Below Water) and SDG 15 (Life on Land)—Climate change is a significant threat to Europe, with the region experiencing more frequent and intense heatwaves, floods, and other extreme weather events (Lafortune et al., 2022). Climate change is having a growing impact on the marine and coastal environment, which is of great importance to the livelihoods and well-being of Europeans who rely on the health and productivity of marine ecosystems. The region has indeed made efforts to become a prosperous and resource-efficient society in the face of challenges. These efforts include pursuing initiatives like the European Green Deal and the Paris Agreement, as well as supporting climate-related projects globally. However, while the plans are well-organized, the goals are susceptible to crises and rely heavily on the success of other SDGs. Indicators such net greenhouse gas emissions from land use and forestry, mean surface seawater acidity, and climate-related economic losses are currently moving away from the EU target (Eurostat, 2022).

3 Discussion—A Roadmap Out of Crises

For years, rising geopolitical and regional conflicts and significant social polarization have been observed across all continents. The climate and biodiversity crises are intensifying social and economic disparities, particularly in societies where livelihoods rely heavily on nature. Simply segregating human well-being from environmental sustainability and neglecting to address root causes of poverty, environmental degradation, and issues of equality, will not be devastating on the ambitious development agenda (Schleicher et al., 2018). Between the Sustainable Development Goals, the Paris Agreement and the European Green Deal, Europe needs a realistic approach in order to finance sustainable development. As the EU seeks to redefine its position in a multipolar world, it must enhance its strategic independence by creating collaborative partnerships with a wide array of allies and aligning its external policies to serve the global public interest. The more stable, peaceful and prosperous these partnerships are, the better the world and these priorities will be supported (Lafortune et al., 2022). When it comes to the fulfillment of SDGs, Europe is confronted with significant obstacles, especially with the environmental SDGs which pertain to sustainable production and consumption, climate change, and biodiversity, as well as SDGs related to industry, innovation, and infrastructure.

A crucial component for making progress, is enhancing education (SDG4) and it needs coordinated action. The pressing nature of current crises have prompted individuals for adopting an alternative approach towards leading a sustainable lifestyle (Wolff, 2020). To enhance education systems and foster skills and innovation that promote sustainable development across Europe, several priorities have been proposed. These include reinforcing education while also addressing inequalities in access and quality of education, particularly in areas that have been exacerbated by the pandemic. Additionally, it is important to prioritize promoting education for sustainable development in school curricula at all levels. There is a pressing need for substantial modifications in the education system to acknowledge economic interests and sustainability efforts as mutually supportive concepts rather than impartial and apolitical facts. Education must encourage skepticism, foster critical thinking and societal transformation, and motivate students to generate innovative visions and paradigms that contribute towards a better world (Wolff, 2020). Furthermore, increasing support for research, development, and sustainable innovation is necessary to expedite progress towards the SDGs and enhance European competitiveness in strategic sectors and technologies (Lafortune et al., 2022). Governments and institutions have the duty to undertake deliberate measures aimed at incorporating social and environmental considerations into their operational framework (Horobet et al., 2019). Growth has to be associated with responsible investing, entailing the environment into the decision-making transcending mere financial factors (Karanovic et al., 2021). Nevertheless, a considerable number of enterprises within the European Union still remain to comprehensively embed social and environmental considerations within their operations (Horobet et al., 2019).

An additional vital factor for advancing is the European Green Deal, Europe's climate and growth strategy, aiming to all sectors of the economy with the objective to turn the EU into the first carbon–neutral continent by 2050, while maintaining economic growth (European Commission, 2019). The implementation of the Green Deal is a complex undertaking, and the EU is already mired in several crises (financial, covid-19, economic recovery, energy crisis, and climate change), which hampers its ability to effectively address all of them (Lafortune et al., 2022). Although the European Green Deal has set forth ambitious proposals and goals endeavoring to promote sustainability, citizens' well-being, and attempting to mitigate catastrophic climate change; a rapid transformation could result in increased challenges, disruptions, and adjustment costs, that include job losses in industries that rely heavily on fossil fuels, changes in land use and agricultural practices, and increased costs for consumers and businesses (Filipović et al., 2022). It is important to address these potential "transformation pains" through appropriate policies and measures to ensure a just and inclusive transition towards a more sustainable future. Such measures can only be successful if they gain broad public support, with the promise to leave no one behind (Lafortune et al., 2022).

Similarly, an essential factor for progressing out of crises, is sustainable cities. Cities have the potential to be powerful drivers of growth, offering significant benefits such as job creation, innovation, higher wages, and a wide range of services and amenities. However, if not properly managed, cities can also incur agglomeration costs (OECD, 2015). Despite SDG11's focus on cities and communities, with specific targets on housing and mobility, progress towards achieving these goals is currently inadequate. Countries around the world are grappling with issues such as slums and overcrowded settlements, urban sprawl, air, noise, or water pollution, inadequate or unaffordable housing, and limited access to basic services that are either too expensive or insufficient (Lafortune et al., 2022). Ensuring active and clean urban mobility is a key factor in promoting sustainable mobility and accessibility, and achieving the SDG11. Therefore, it is crucial to establish regional public transportation networks and improve their integration with rural areas. In light of the recent covid-19 crisis and the decrease in ridership due to concerns about the virus, it is important to modify public transportation to accommodate physical distancing. These measures will not only address environmental concerns such as urban pollution; but also mitigate negative externalities of urban agglomeration such as traffic congestion and air pollution, by decreasing private car usage (Lafortune et al., 2022).

4 Conclusions and the Way Forward

It can be inferred that Europe confronts significant challenges in attaining the SDGs. Such challenges include poor performance on environmental goals, outlined in unsustainable food systems and diets, as well as domestic and imported greenhouse gas emissions and threats to biodiversity. Even the top-ranking countries (Northern Europe), perform poorly on indicators related to sustainable diets, thus there is an urgent need to shift towards healthier and more sustainable diets to fulfill the SDGs related to climate, biodiversity, and health. Another challenge relates to inequalities within countries, as there are still significant gaps in the availability and accessibility of services and opportunities among certain population groups in several EU member states. Moreover, there are persistent variations in the achievement of SDGs among European countries and challenges with the negative international spillovers. The region is putting significant effort on supporting and financing sustainability though the current numerous crises.

In relation with the spillovers, there were some limitations on the research, as current literature represents the SDG correlations in pairwise interactions rather than a network. As previously discussed, the three dimensions of the SDGs (environmental, social and economic), show significant trade-offs between the environmental and the other two dimensions of SDGs, and the formulation of implications as a network will solve this issue. Future research on this would help account for both direct and indirect interactions and their effects on the total network, distinguishing positive and negative connections. Finally, there are important SDG data gaps at the subnational level in the EU so the indicators cannot fully conclude; and a lack of readiness protocols for the SDGs against crises, rendering them even more intolerant to severe disruptions and forcing them onto a path of coping and recovery rather than prevention. A factor to consider in future studies, involves quantifying the influence of the goals on the overall accomplishment of the SDGs.

It is shown that there are numerous EU policies, both proposed and in place, are aligned with the 2030 Agenda, even if they are not explicitly articulated with SDGs. While international organizations typically support governments in achieving SDGs, they can influence national policies by financing particular aspects of development plans and their formation. This underscores the possibility of focusing on the current trade-offs of the environmental dimension, applying the mechanisms and thus improving global coordination, to ensure consistency in the roadmap to the potential synergies. Given the pressing character of current crises, the EU stakeholders have prioritized a common commitment and crucial policies for implementing these goals like education, financing, monitoring, reporting, and of course, leave no one behind. Although there is no requirement to initiate a new SDG strategy process across the EU, it is crucial to sustain a robust dedication to eliminate trade-offs, monitor progress, and disseminate information regarding the efforts and focus of these goals, in order to achieve global inclusion and support.

References

Bill & Melinda Gates Foundation (BMGF). (2020). *Covid-19 a global perspective—2020 goalkeepers report*. Goalkeepers.

Biermann, F., Hickmann, T., Sénit, C., & Grob, L. (2022). The sustainable development goals as a transformative force?: Key Insights. In F. Biermann, T. Hickmann, & C. Sénit (Eds.), The political impact of the sustainable development goals: Transforming governance through global goals? (pp. 204–226). Cambridge University Press. https://doi.org/10.1017/9781009082945.009

Bin-Nashwan, S. A., Hassan M. K., & Muneeza, A. (2022). Russia–Ukraine conflict: 2030 Agenda for SDGs hangs in the balance. *International Journal of Ethics and Systems*. Emerald Publishing Limited.

Birch, S., & Rosengren, H. (2023). World risks big misses across the Sustainable Development Goals unless measures to accelerate implementation are taken. *UN Department of Global Communications & UN Department of Economic and Social Affairs*. Press material.

European Commission. (2019). *The European green deal*. Communication from the Commission to the European Parliament, the European Council, the Council, COM (11.12.2019). European Commission.

Eurostat. (2022). Sustainable development in the European Union. In *Monitoring report on progress towards the SDGs in an EU context*. https://doi.org/10.2785/313289; KS-09-22-019-EN-N
Filipović, S., Lior, N., & Radovanović, M. (2022). The green deal—just transition and sustainable development goals Nexus. *Renewable and Sustainable Energy Reviews, 168*, 112759. https://doi.org/10.1016/j.rser.2022.112759
Glaesser, D. (2003). *Crisis management in the tourism industry*. Butterworth-Heinemann publications.
Henderson, J. C. (2007). *The management of hospitality and tourism enterprises*. Managing Tourism Crises (Vol. 10, pp. 163–179). Elsevier.
Horobet, A., Belascu, L., Polychronidou, P., & Karasavvoglou, A. (2019). Global, regional and local perspectives on the economies of Southeastern Europe. In *Proceedings of the 11th international conference on the economies of the Balkan and Eastern European Countries (EBEEC) in Bucharest, Romania*. https://doi.org/10.1007/978-3-030-57953-1
IEA, IRENA, UNSD, WB, WHO. (2019). Tracking SDG 7: The Energy Progress Report 2019 International Bank for Reconstruction and Development. Washington DC.
Karanovic, G., Polychronidou, P., Karasavvoglou, A., & Maskarin Ribaric, H. (2021). *Tourism management and sustainable development* (pp. 161–176). Springer. https://doi.org/10.1007/978-3-030-74632-2
Kaviti Musango, J., Currie, P., Smit, S., & Kovacic, Z. (2020). Urban metabolism of the informal city: Probing and measuring the 'unmeasurable' to monitor Sustainable Development Goal 11 indicators. *Ecological Indicators, 119*, 106746, Elsevier.
Lafortune, G., Fuller, G., Bermont-Diaz, L., Kloke-Lesch, A., Koundouri, P., & Riccaboni, A. (2022). *Achieving the SDGs: Europe's compass in a multipolar world*. Europe Sustainable Development Report 2022, SDSN and SDSN Europe. Paris.
Laffoley, D., Baxter, J., Turley, C., & Lagos, N. (2017). An introduction to ocean acidification: What it is, What we know, and What may happen. *International Union For Conservation of Nature*. The Latin American And Caribbean Edition.
OECD. (2015). *The metropolitan century: Understanding urbanisation and its consequences*. OECD Publishing. https://www.oecd-ilibrary.org/urban-rural-and-regional-development/the-metropolitan-century_9789264228733-en
Pradhan, P., Costa, L., Rybski, D., Lucht, W., & Kropp, J. P. (2017). A systematic study of sustainable development goal (SDG) interactions. *Earth's Future, Agu Publications, 5*, 1169–1179. https://doi.org/10.1002/2017EF000632
Ritchie, H., Roser, M., Mispy, J., & Ortiz-Ospina, E. (2018). Measuring progress towards the Sustainable Development Goals. *Our World in Data's SDG Tracker*.
Schleicher, J., Schaafsma, M., & Vira, B. (2018). Will the sustainable development goals address the links between poverty and the natural environment? *Current Opinion in Environmental Sustainability, 34*. ISSN 1877-3435, Science Direct, Elsevier.
Toth, W., Vacik, H., Pülzl, H., Carlsen H. (2022). Deepening our understanding of which policy advice to expect from prioritizing SDG targets: introducing the Analytic Network Process in a multi-method setting. *Synergies and Trade-offs between Sustainable Development Goals and Targets, Institute for Global Environmental Studies, 17*, 1473–1488. https://doi.org/10.1007/s11625-021-01009-7
UNICEF. (2018). From promise to impact: Ending malnutrition by 2030. Data and analytics section division of data, research and policy, p. 22.
United Nations Economic and Social Council (UNESC). (2020). Progress towards the Sustainable Development Goals. Report of the Secretary-General. (E/2020/57).
United Nations. (2022). The sustainable development goals report 2022. Retrieved February 10, 2023, from https://unstats.un.org/sdgs/report/2022/
United Nations. Department of Economic and Social Affairs. (2023). Sustainable Development, the 17 goals. Retrieved January 23, 2023, from https://sdgs.un.org/goals
United Nations Economic and Social Council. (2020). Progress towards the sustainable development goals. Report of the Secretary-General (E/2020/57).

United Nations Statistics Division (UNSD). (2023). SDG indicators global indicator framework for the sustainable development goals and targets of the 2030 agenda for sustainable development. Retrieved January 23, 2023, from https://unstats.un.org/sdgs/indicators/indicators-list/

Valeri, M., et al. (2021). *An overview of crisis management in hospitality enterprises: The case of operating at an international level hotel in Adiyaman*. Emerald Publishing Limited.

Wolff, L. (2020). Sustainability education in risks and crises: Lessons from Covid-19. *Sustainability, MDPI*, *12*, 5205. https://doi.org/10.3390/su12125205

Yang, S., Yanxu, L., Cherubini, F., Fu, B., & Pereira, P. (2020). Prioritizing sustainable development goals and linking them to ecosystem services: A global expert's knowledge evaluation. *Geography and Sustainability*, 12. Elsevier.

The manufacturer's authorised representative in the EU is Springer Nature Customer Service Centre GmbH, Europaplatz 3, 69115 Heidelberg, Germany. If you have any concerns regarding our products, please contact ProductSafety@springernature.com

Printed and bound by CPI Group (UK) Ltd, Croydon, CR0 4YY
30/09/2026
02225507-0007